IMAGES
of America

PLAINFIELD

On the Cover: *March of the Tin Soldiers* was the name of the play, and the participants were children from the Plainfield elementary schools. The group, ready for dress rehearsal in their matching white soldier costumes, stands in front of the John C. Reeder house at the corner of East Main and Wabash Streets. The photograph is from the early 1920s.

IMAGES
of America

PLAINFIELD

Reann Lydick Poray

ARCADIA
PUBLISHING

ISBN 978-0-7385-9448-4

Published by Arcadia Publishing
Charleston, South Carolina

Printed in the United States of America

Library of Congress Control Number: 2012939274

For all general information, please contact Arcadia Publishing:
Telephone 843-853-2070
Fax 843-853-0044
E-mail sales@arcadiapublishing.com
For customer service and orders:
Toll-Free 1-888-313-2665

Visit us on the Internet at www.arcadiapublishing.com

Dedicated to Susan Miller Carter, who inspired the love of local history to all who knew her

Contents

ACKNOWLEDGMENTS

My sincere thanks to my husband, John Poray, for great encouragement, understanding, and for being willing to act as my sounding board and consultant every time I'd say, "Hey, look at this!" Thanks also goes to Bob and Judy Lydick for their support, suggestions, and automobile dates and for looking in lots of old newspapers; Phyllis Walters for her skills as a proofreader extraordinaire; and to the many others who knowingly or unknowingly contributed to this book by providing answers to random questions about Plainfield: John and Phyllis Parsons, Beverly Smith, James Gilbert Sr., William Strafford Jr., Luann Heald, Kristy Keith, the Plainfield Old Timers Group, Tom Newlin, Tom Hilligoss, Jack Moon, Kevin Moore, Sandy (Starbuck) Norris, and Meredith Thompson. I also wish to thank Sandy Shalton at Arcadia Publishing for answering my many questions throughout this fun adventure.

Unless otherwise noted, all images appear courtesy of the Guilford Township Historical Collection, Plainfield-Guilford Township Public Library.

INTRODUCTION

In 1820, abolitionist Quakers from North Carolina settled in Plainfield, Indiana. Those early settlers provided the foundation for Plainfield's rich heritage that has evolved into a diverse blend of residents today. In 1832, Levi Jessup and Elias Hadley platted the town of Plainfield with 64 lots straddling the National Road. The first lot recorded as being sold was dated May 2, 1833, and much has happened since that day. This visual journey into Plainfield's past is designed to inspire memories from those who remember, as well as spark curiosity from those who are seeing Plainfield's past for the first time.

The town of Plainfield really did come into being because of the Society of Friends (also known as the Quakers), who settled in this area specifically to get away from the issue of slavery that was plaguing the American South. Most of the early settlers arrived from Guilford County, North Carolina; hence the name Guilford Township. The influence of the Quakers is evident all over town in everything from the Plainfield High School nickname ("the Quakers") to the Western Yearly Meeting, to Sugar Grove Meeting and Cemetery, and to even the name of the town itself. The early Quakers led a plain and simple lifestyle, and what better name to choose for your town than one reflecting that concept?

As the years passed, the diversity of the town began to develop. Residents with different religious backgrounds and lifestyles moved in. The opening of the House of Refuge, the predecessor of the Indiana Boys' School, brought another different group of residents to the area. More recently, the blend changed a little more when the Islamic Society of North America headquarters was located in Plainfield.

Time moves on, life evolves, and each day adds another element of history to a place. Plainfield has changed over the years, but the essence of community is strong and thriving.

One of the most enjoyable aspects of creating a book of photographs on Plainfield was getting to look at all the wonderful images of our town. There's a whole treasure trove of interesting photographs in the Guilford Township Historical Collection (at the Plainfield-Guilford Township Public Library), which is where most of the images in this book were found. It was difficult to select one photograph over another!

One

Early Plainfield

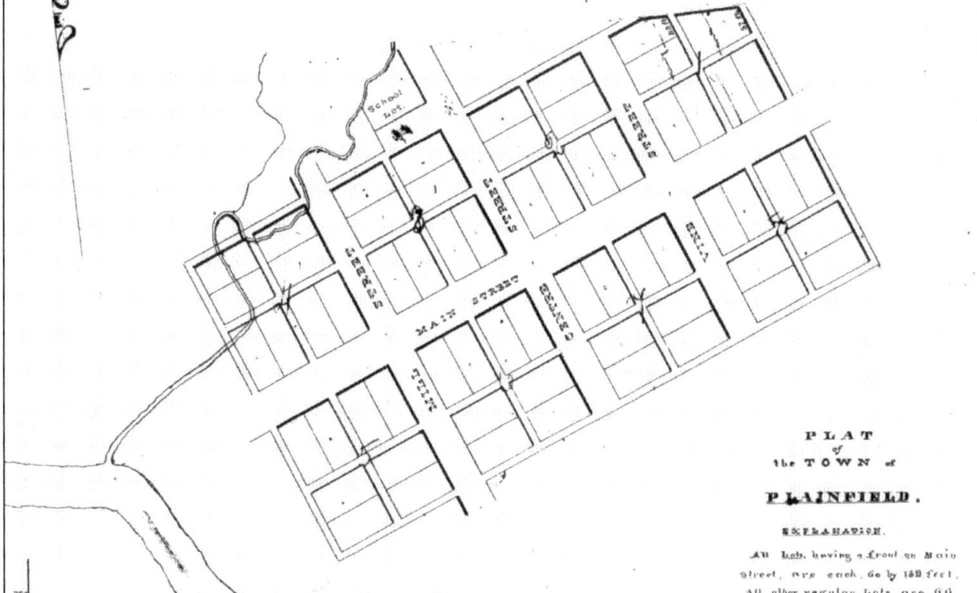

Although not the first settlers in the area, Levi Jessup and Elias Hadley, two members of the Society of Friends, platted the town of Plainfield, Indiana, in July 1832 with 64 lots straddling the National Road. The first lot sold was recorded on May 2, 1833. This original plat shows how the town was arranged, and names the three new streets, which are still here today: Mill, Center, and Vine.

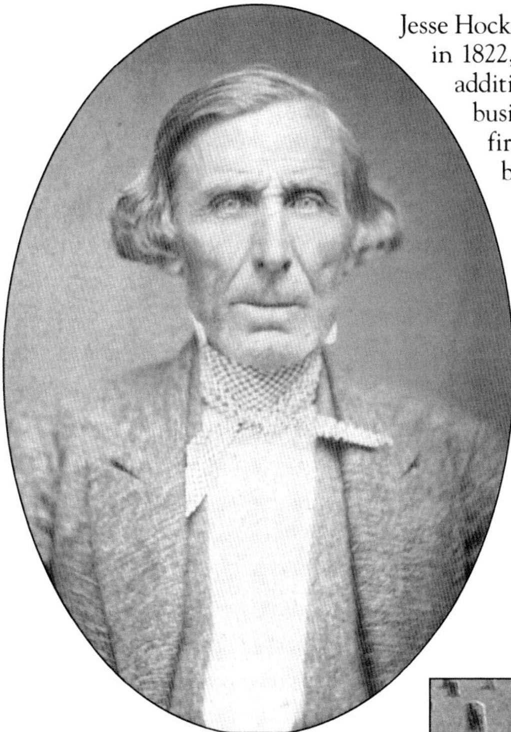

Jesse Hockett, whose family settled in Guilford Township in 1822, was one of Plainfield's first entrepreneurs. In addition to being a schoolteacher, he owned several businesses, including a dry goods store, Plainfield's first hotel, and a tavern. He eventually sold his businesses in town and purchased a large farm just outside Plainfield, where he lived until his death in 1876.

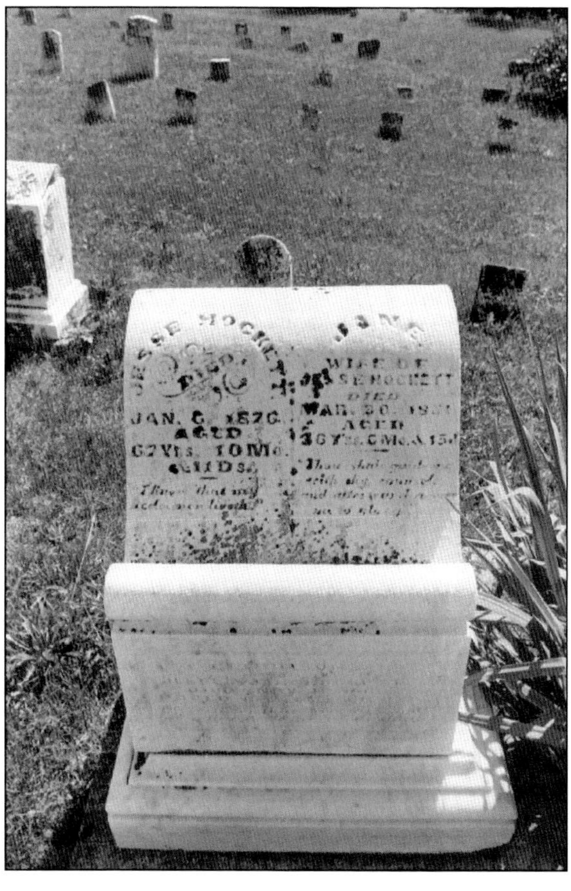

Sugar Grove Friends Cemetery, located on the south side of Plainfield, is the final resting place for many of the early Quaker settlers in the community, including Jesse Hockett and his first wife, Jane. The faded white marble tombstone pictured here notes that Jane died in 1851 and Jesse in 1876.

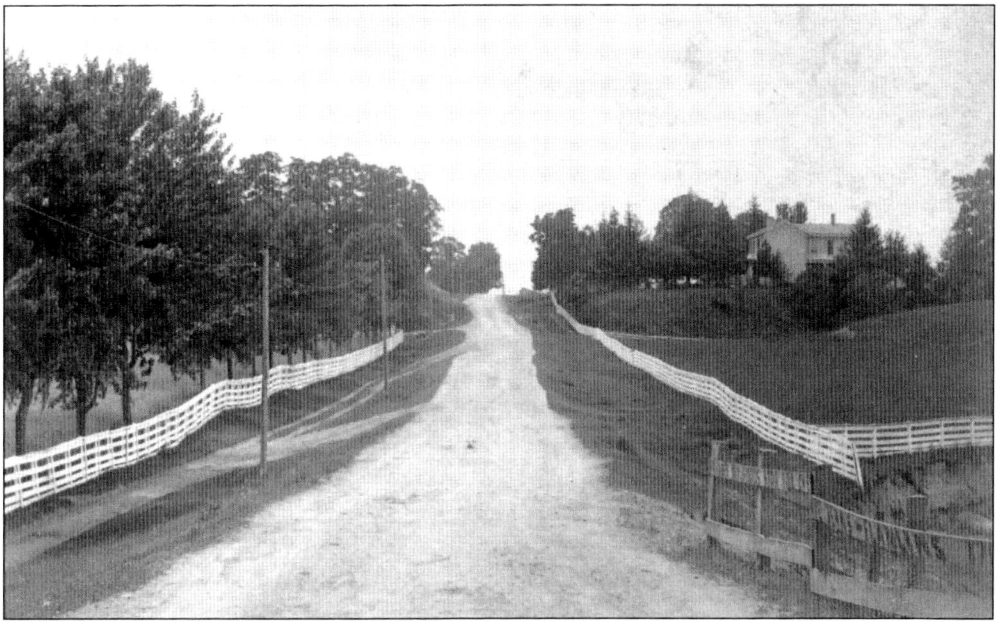

Heading west out of Plainfield looks quite different in this photograph than it does today. Seen here is the dirt National Road just across White Lick Creek. Morgan's Hill and home is visible on the right in the distance. The structure, known as the Morgan home, has been well-preserved and still stands today in the 500 block of Main Street (near Wedding Lane). John Morgan was a successful businessman in Plainfield. The white split rail fence on the left leads to the entrance of the Indiana House of Refuge.

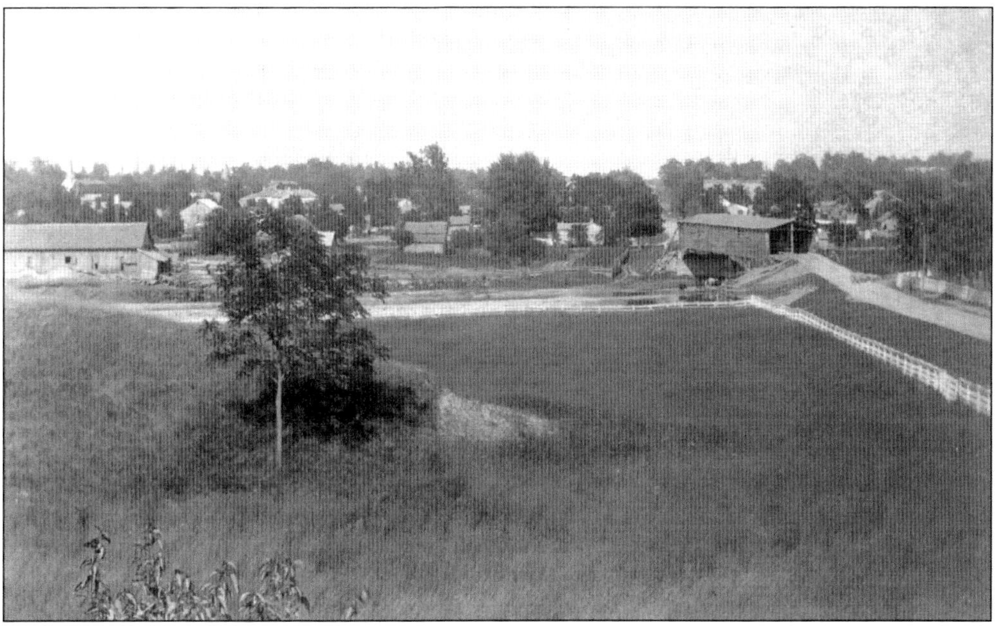

One of the earliest photographic views of Plainfield, looking east, was taken from Morgan's Hill. The National Road is visible on the right, along with the covered bridge that spanned White Lick Creek. John Morgan owned the home atop a hill west of town, across from the Indiana Boys' School entrance. Morgan's white split rail fence is visible near the road.

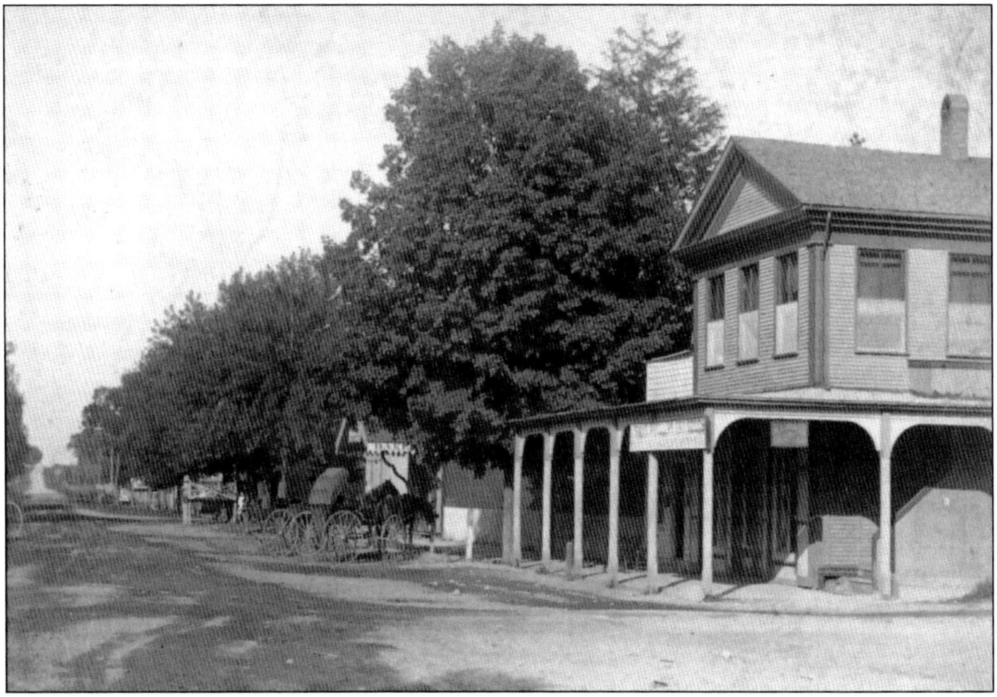

These two photographs from the early 1900s provide a glimpse of the early Plainfield downtown. Preceding the brick buildings of today, the corner of Main and Center Streets shows the buildings that comprised the south side of the National Road. The frame building on the corner in the above photograph was built in 1851 by Jesse Hockett. In the distance is the east hill, which took travelers out of town toward Indianapolis. Today, the Masonic building, the Knights of Pythias building, and the Village Theater stand here. In the photograph below, taken from Center Street, this western view of Plainfield shows the wide, tree-lined street. The covered bridge on the National Road that spanned White Lick Creek is just visible in the distance.

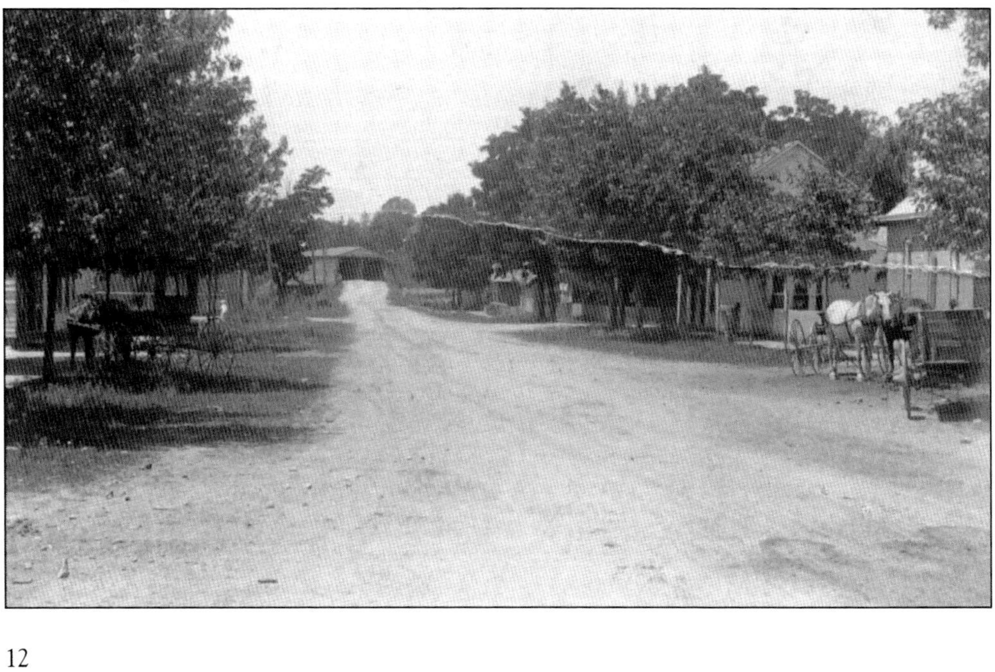

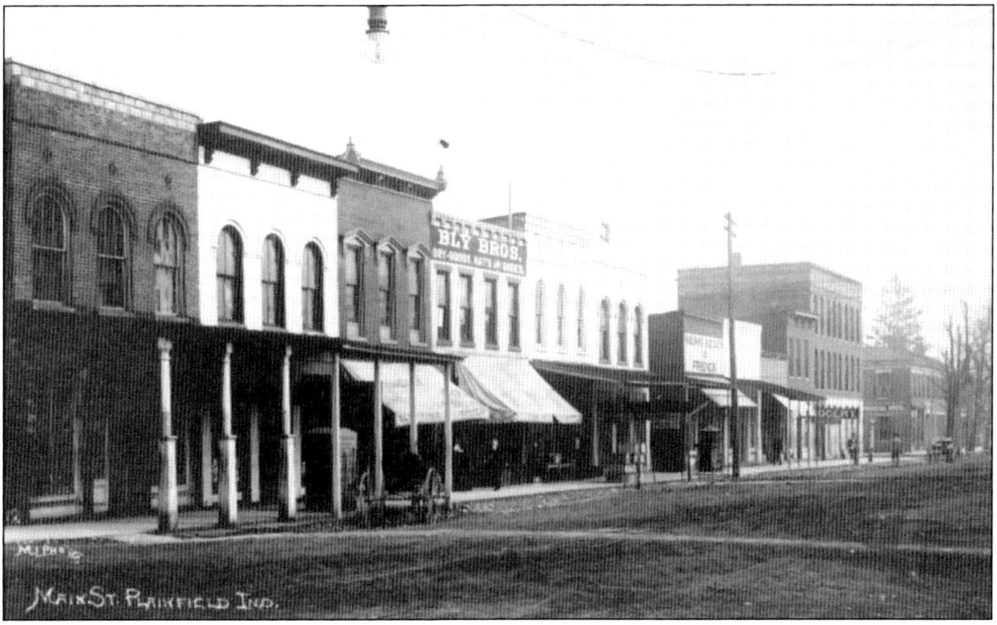

Quiet and a bit sleepy looking, the businesses on the north side of Main Street stand guard over the town. Bly Brothers Dry Goods store and the Publishing Association of Friends are clearly visible. In the distance at the corner of Main and Vine Streets is the Commercial Hotel. One small electric streetlight spans the intersection of Main and Center Streets. This photograph was taken between 1900 and 1910.

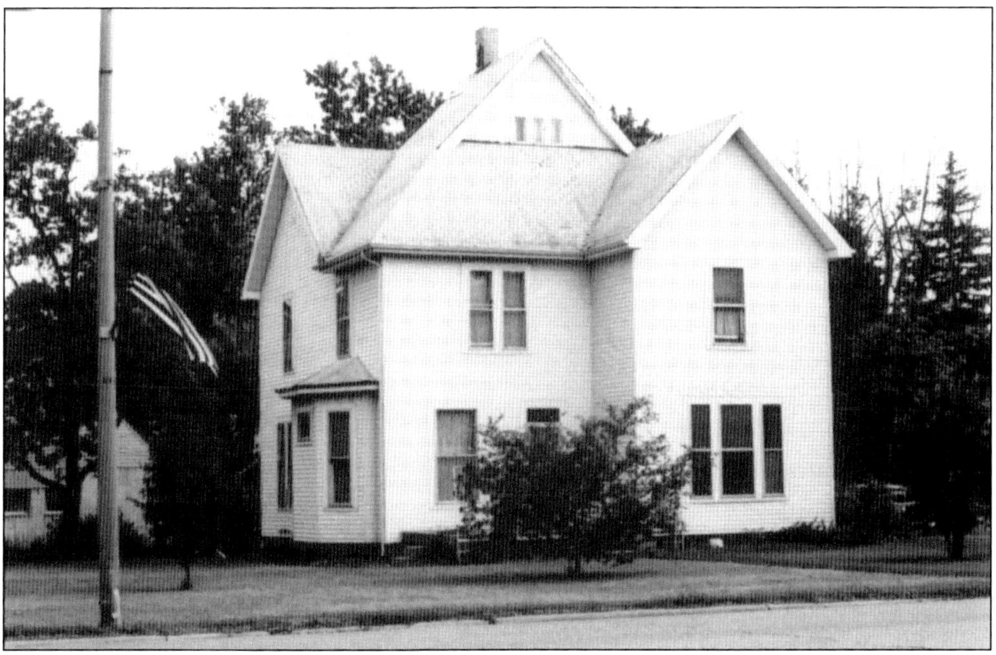

Built in 1904, the Elijah Shaw house, located at 507 East Main, fronts US 40. Shaw owned more than 30 acres and eventually divided his farm into four lots. His former home is built on two of those lots and stands just east of Shaw Street. The present Van Buren Elementary School land was also part of the Shaw farm.

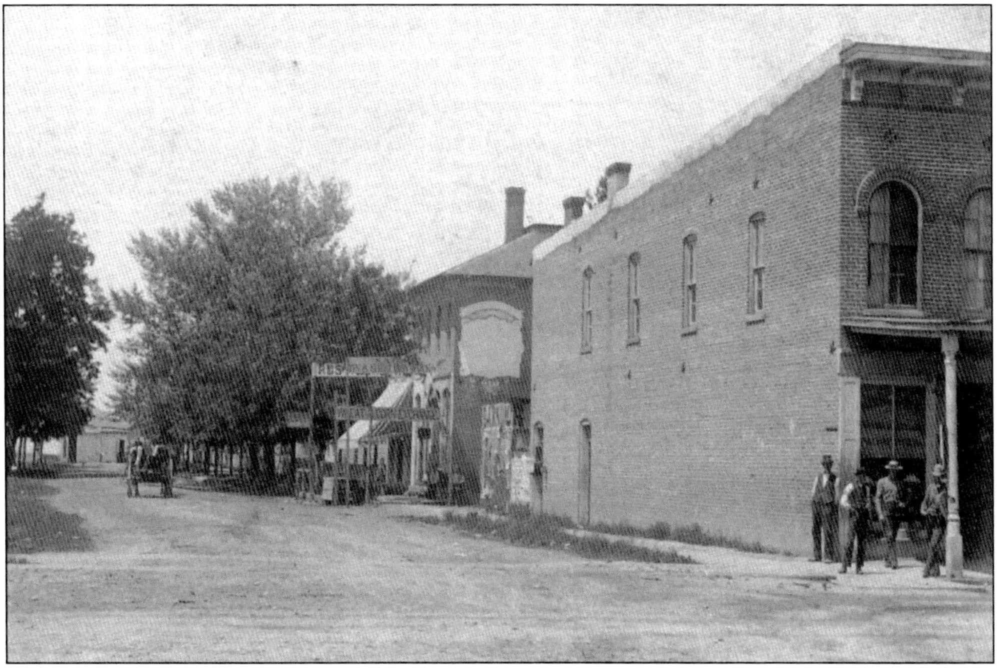

Looking north on Center Street in downtown Plainfield, the Green and Hadley Apothecary building, which operated during the 1880s and 1890s, sits on the northeast corner at Main Street. In the distance is the Fraternal Order of Eagles (FOE) building, which housed the group from 1893 to 1958. Both buildings are still standing, and currently, the Green and Hadley Apothecary building houses a bicycle shop, and the old FOE building is home to a tavern.

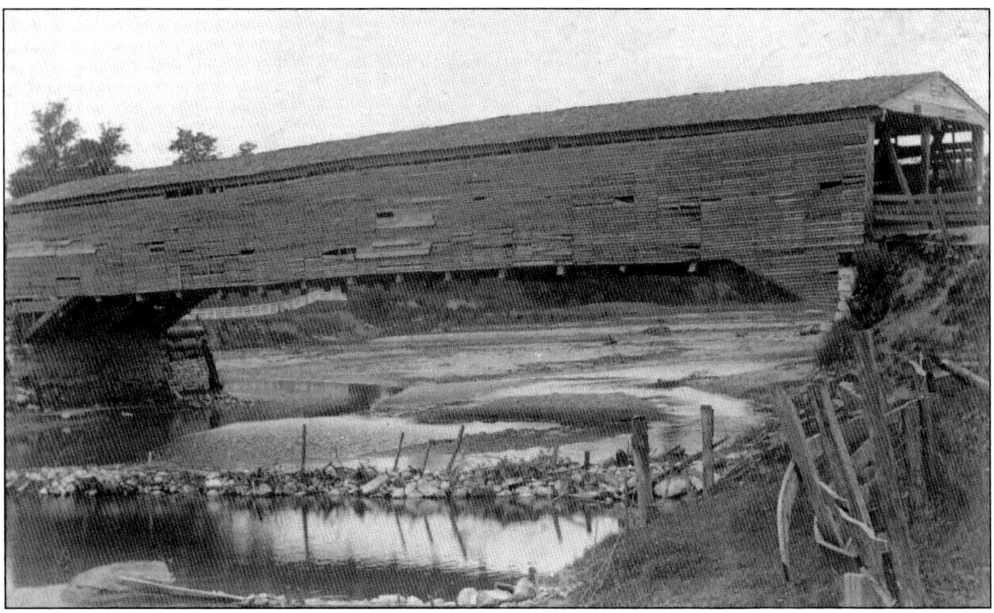

Spanning the White Lick Creek west of Plainfield, this covered bridge provided residents an easy way to travel in and out of town. Built of black walnut timbers, the covered bridge remained until 1888, when it was replaced by a new steel bridge. When the bridge was razed, the timber was sold to a furniture factory in Indianapolis.

Two

Downtown Plainfield

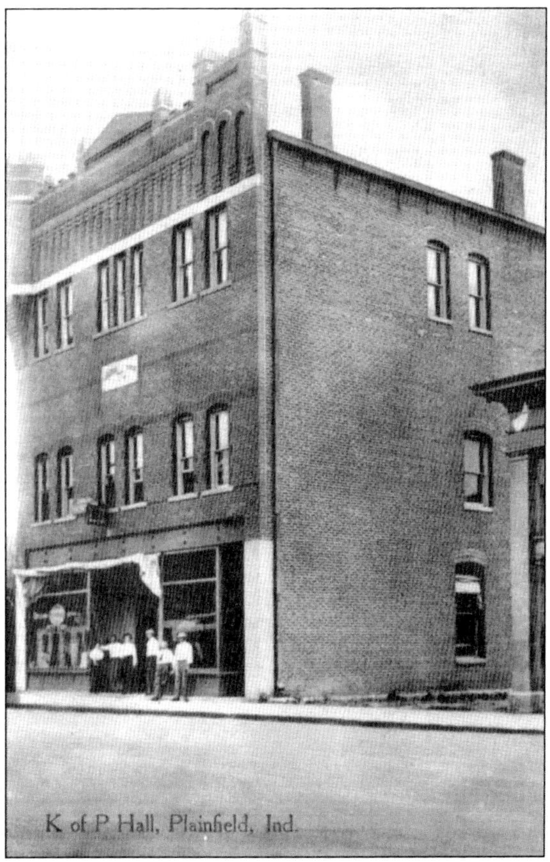

The stately Knights of Pythias building, built in 1900, stands at 115 West Main Street on the south side of the street. The lower level of the structure housed several businesses, including the Spot Cash Store, a popular dry goods merchant. Currently, the Knights of Pythias building is home to a local florist.

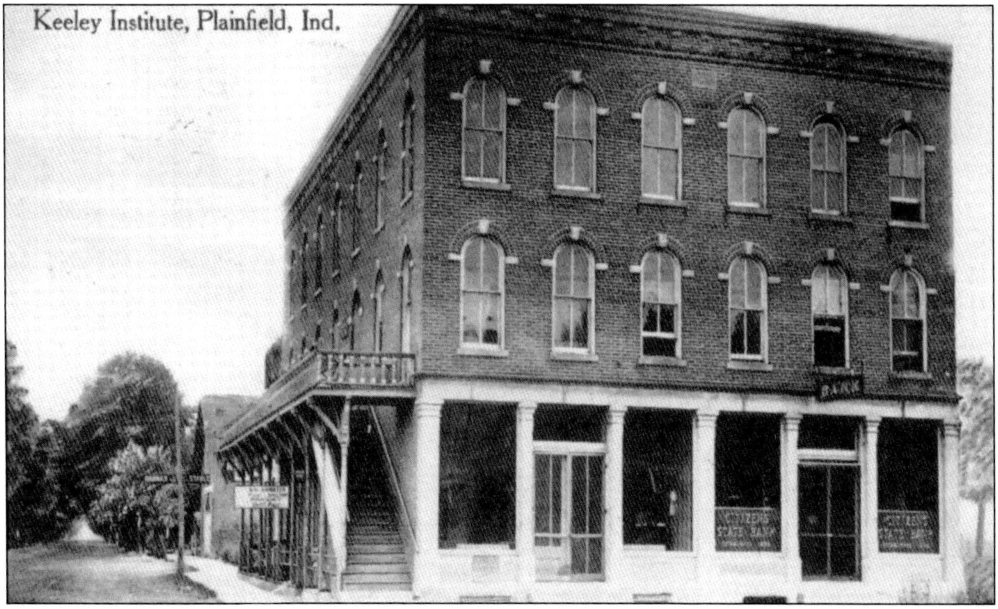

Most commonly known as the Keeley Institute, this building, located on the southwest corner of Main and Center Streets, was built in 1874. It was also known as the Hamlet House and the Mansion House. In 1891, the Keeley Institute moved in, offering residential treatment for drug and alcohol rehabilitation. This photograph shows the Citizens State Bank on the lower level. South of the building was Hanna's Livery Stable.

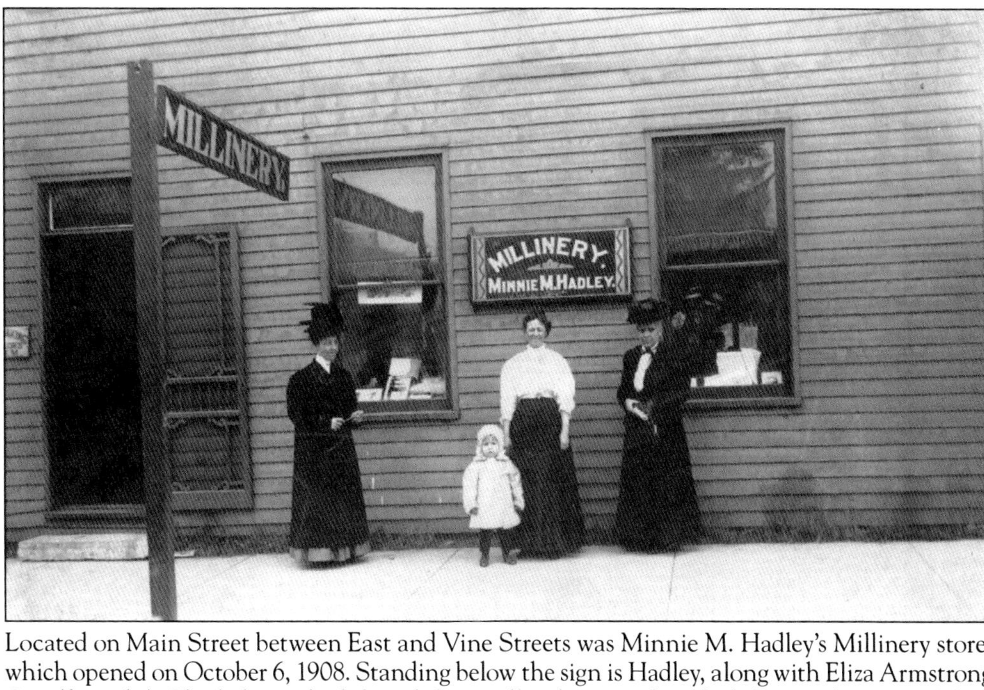

Located on Main Street between East and Vine Streets was Minnie M. Hadley's Millinery store, which opened on October 6, 1908. Standing below the sign is Hadley, along with Eliza Armstrong Cox (far right). The lady on the left and the small girl are unidentified, but surely are modeling the finest hats that Minnie had to offer.

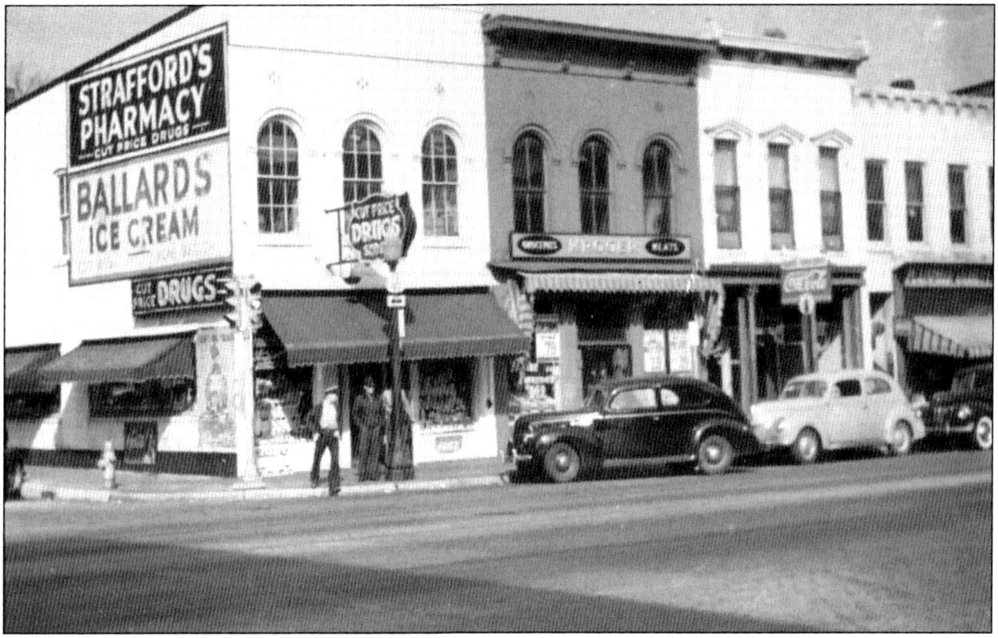

This mid-1930s photograph of downtown Plainfield shows the north side buildings at Main and Center Streets. Customers shop at Strafford's Pharmacy, Kroger Grocery store, the Gates Café, and the Plainfield Variety Store. Note that the stoplight for the intersection is located on the curb in front of Strafford's Pharmacy.

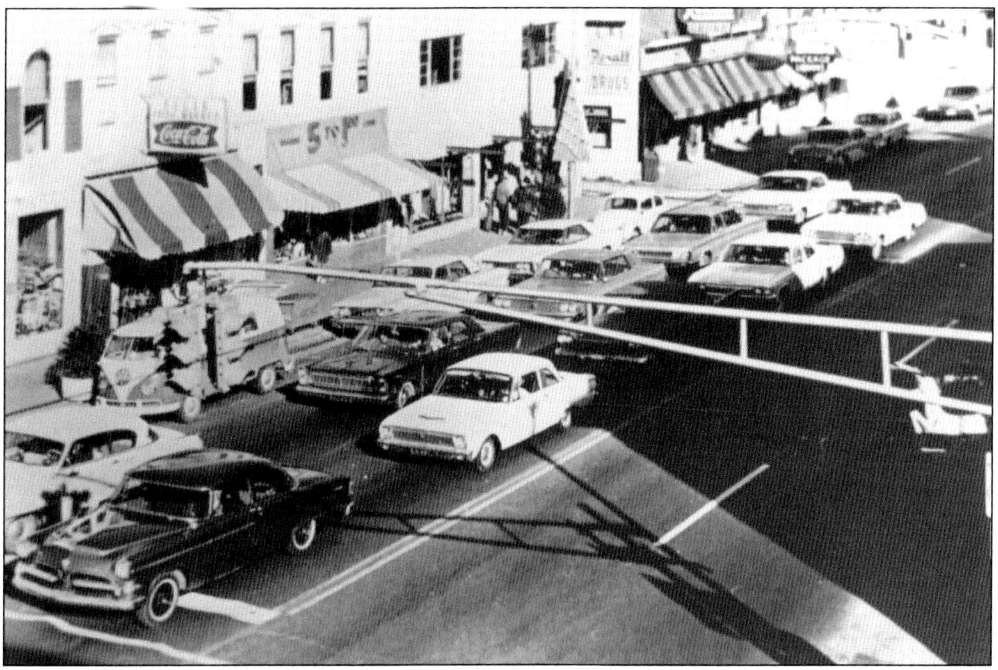

Taken around 1966, this photographs shows busy traffic headed west out of downtown Plainfield on US 40. North side businesses featured here include Ellis Market, Plainfield Variety Store, Beecham's Department Store, C & E Rexall Drugs, Package Liquors, and the Town Café. Notice the Volkswagen van parked along the curb.

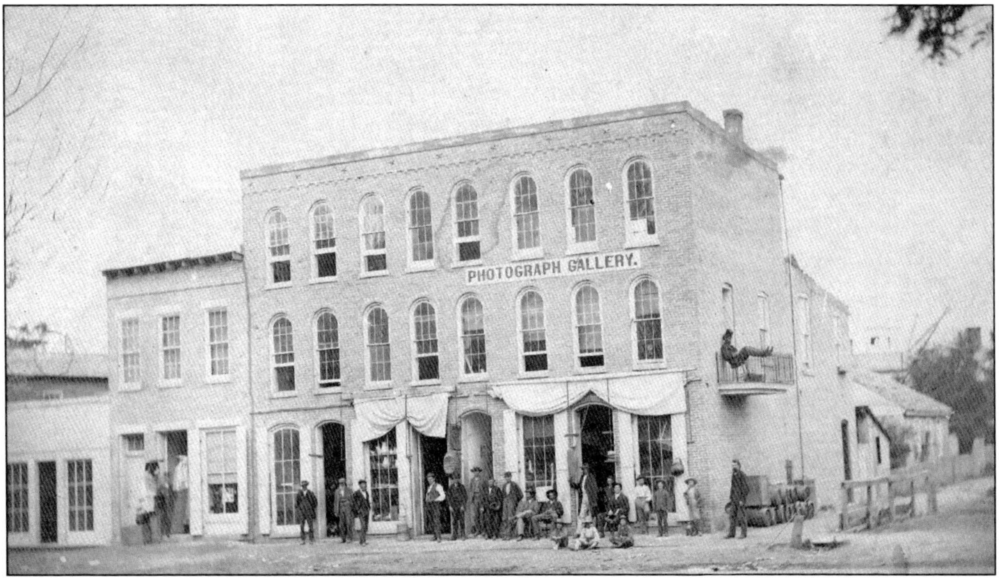

These two photographs, taken at different times, feature the same building located at 104 West Main Street. Many different businesses have occupied the structure, including Moses Tomlinson's photographer's gallery on the second floor (above photograph). Symons Hardware sold a variety of products, including paint, stoves, furniture, auto parts, and appliances. Charles Symons arrived in Plainfield in 1916 and opened his first store in the Masonic building. He then moved his hardware business to the Cope building, seen below, at the corner of North Vine Street and US 40. After his father's passing in 1935, Larue Symons took over the family business and expanded it to include radios and televisions.

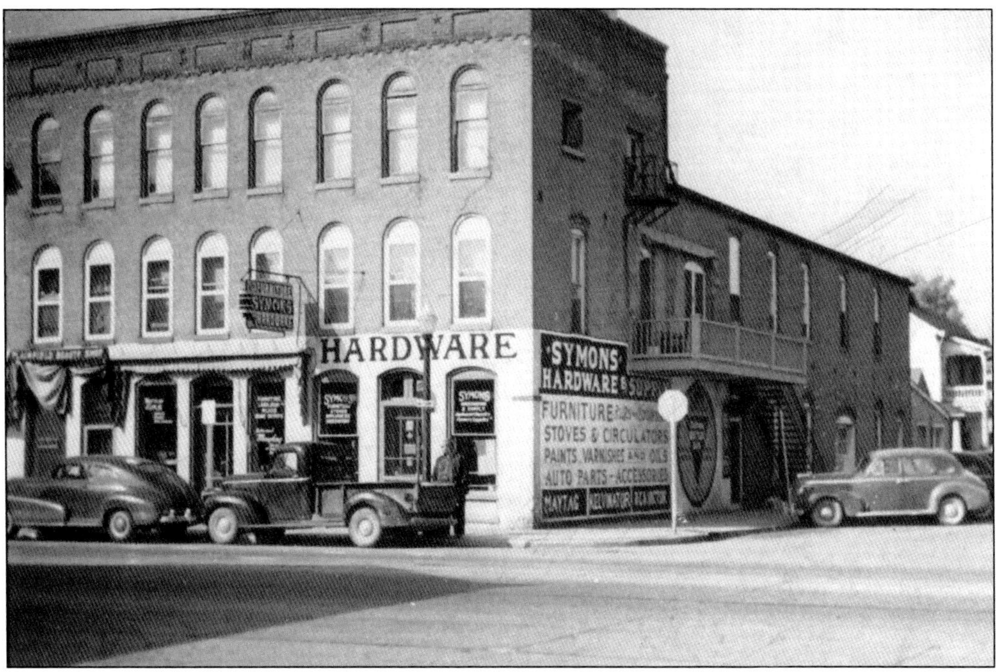

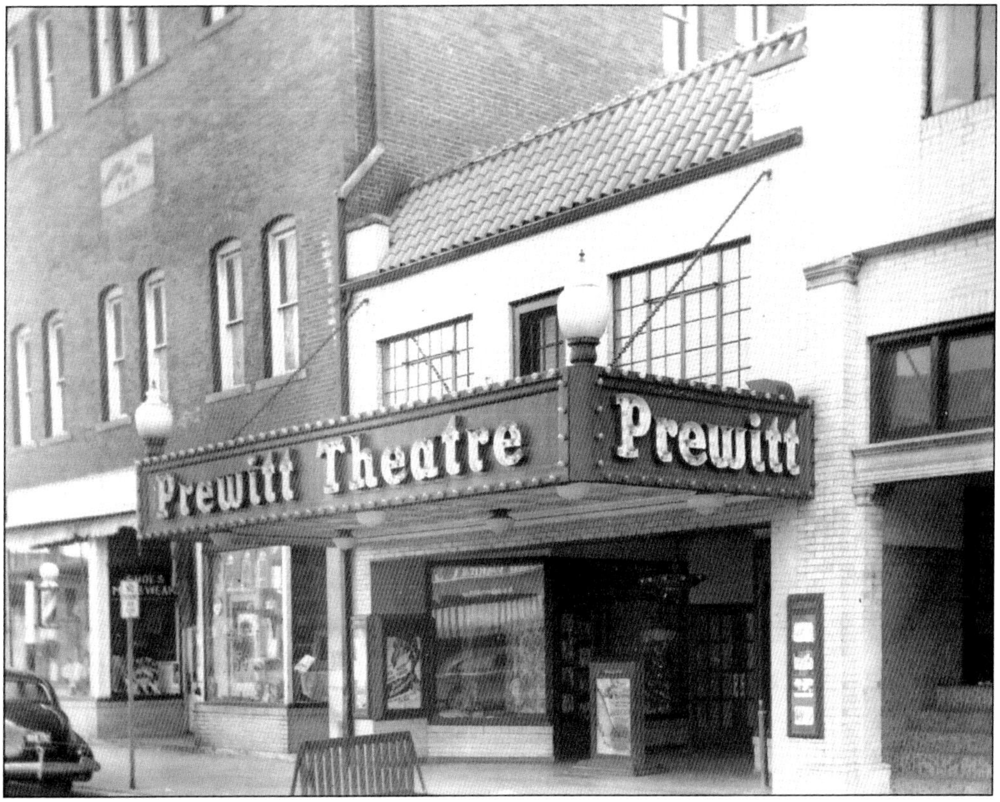

The glorious Prewitt Theatre formally opened on November 23, 1927. Owned by L.M. Prewitt, the theater, located at 119 West Main Street, offered folks a place to watch motion pictures, eat popcorn, and have fun with friends. The above photograph from 1948 shows the movie marquee posters featuring *Melody Time* and *Julia Misbehaves*. Although currently vacant, the Prewitt Theatre building is still standing and is locally known as the Village Theater. Prior to the theater, the property housed Prewitt's Motor Sales, where owner Joseph Prewitt also sold Goodrich tires. The service station was in a prime location on the National Road to assist to travelers.

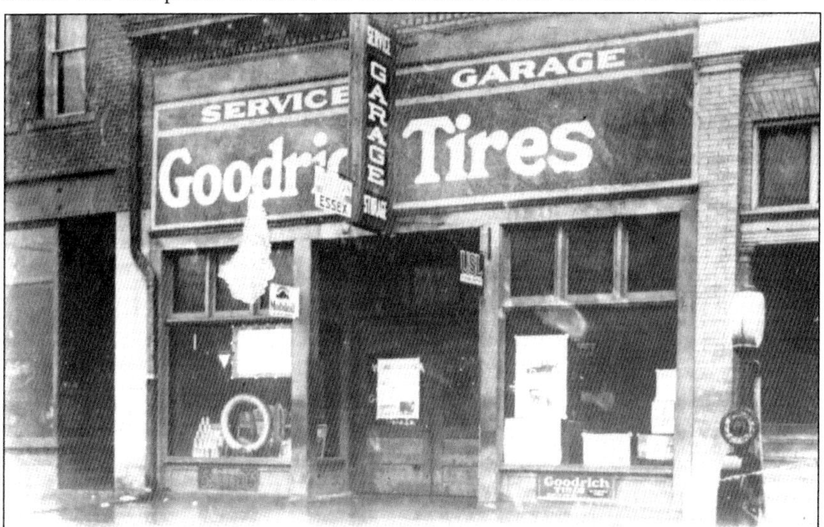

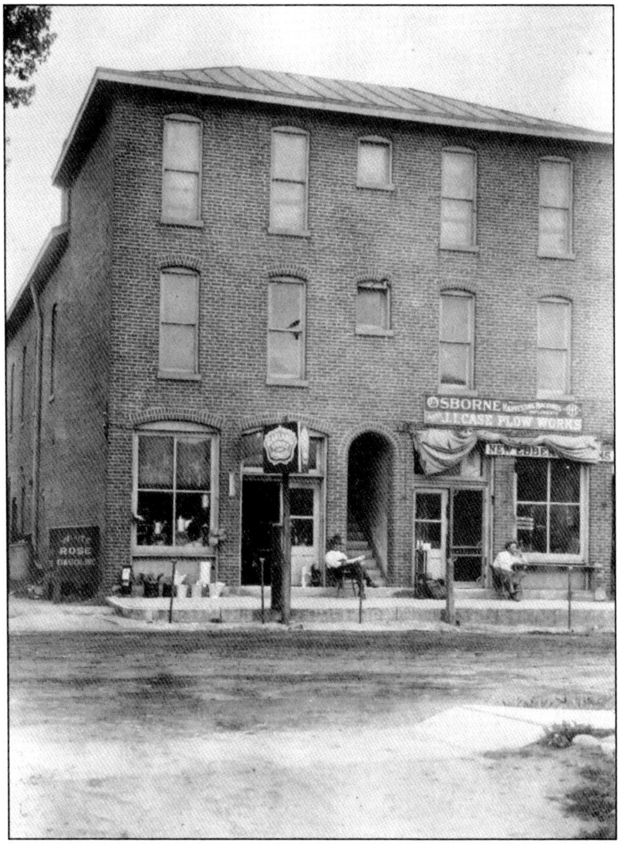

The Fraternal Order of Eagles building stood at 115 North Center Street. The FOE occupied the second story from 1893 to 1958. This photograph shows the lower level stores and storekeepers patiently waiting for customers. Some of the items sold here included stoves, ranges, and harvesting machines. Beecham's Billiard Parlor owned the building from 1958 to 1969. More recently, Timothy's Pub was the occupant.

The very recognizable corner of South Center Street and US 40 is seen here around 1940. Businesses included, starting from the white building on the far left, the Chrisman Café, First National Bank, a barber shop, the Knights of Pythias building, the Prewitt Theatre, and the Morris Café, located in the lower level of the Masonic Lodge. Notice that full chicken dinners were only 60¢.

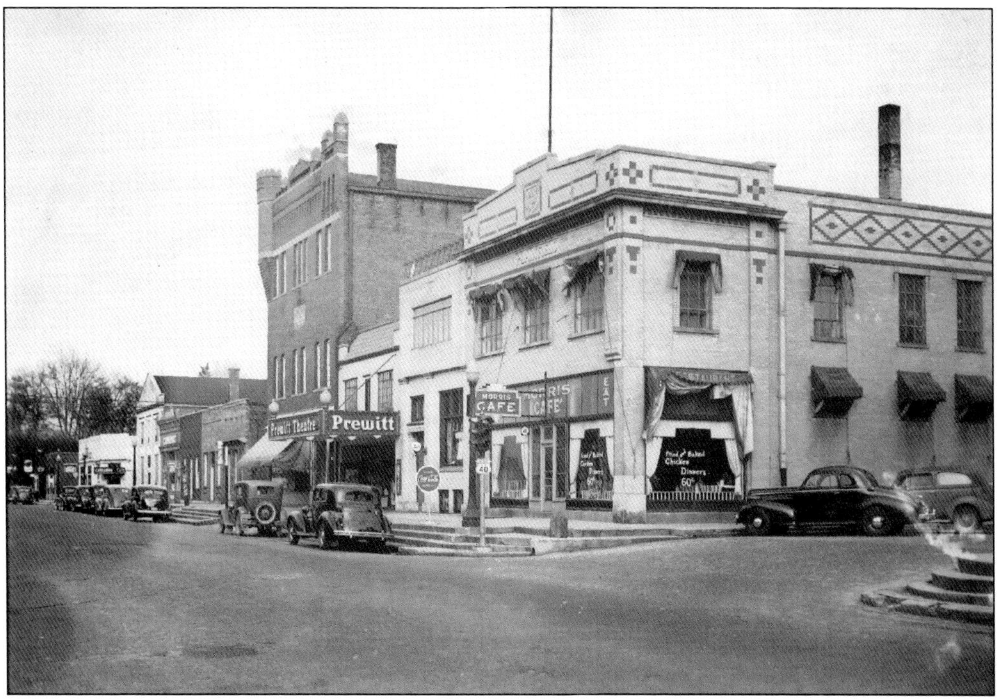

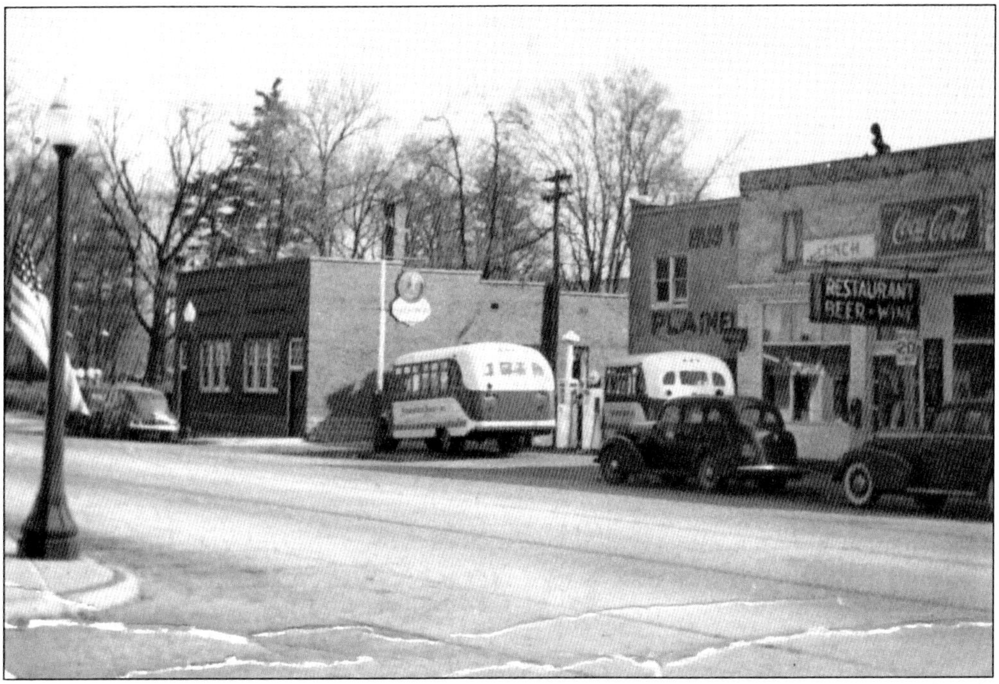

These two photographs, both taken in the fall of 1944, show the businesses along the south side of US 40 between East and Vine Streets. Two buses, providing local service to Indianapolis, await passengers at the Plainfield bus station. Deem's Restaurant, formerly the Knoll Café, at the corner of Vine and Main Streets, served lunch and dinner. V.R. Deem purchased the restaurant in September 1944 and gave the establishment its eponymous name; however, Deem's enthusiasm for his restaurant was short lived, as he quickly sold the business to J.W. Cassell in November 1944.

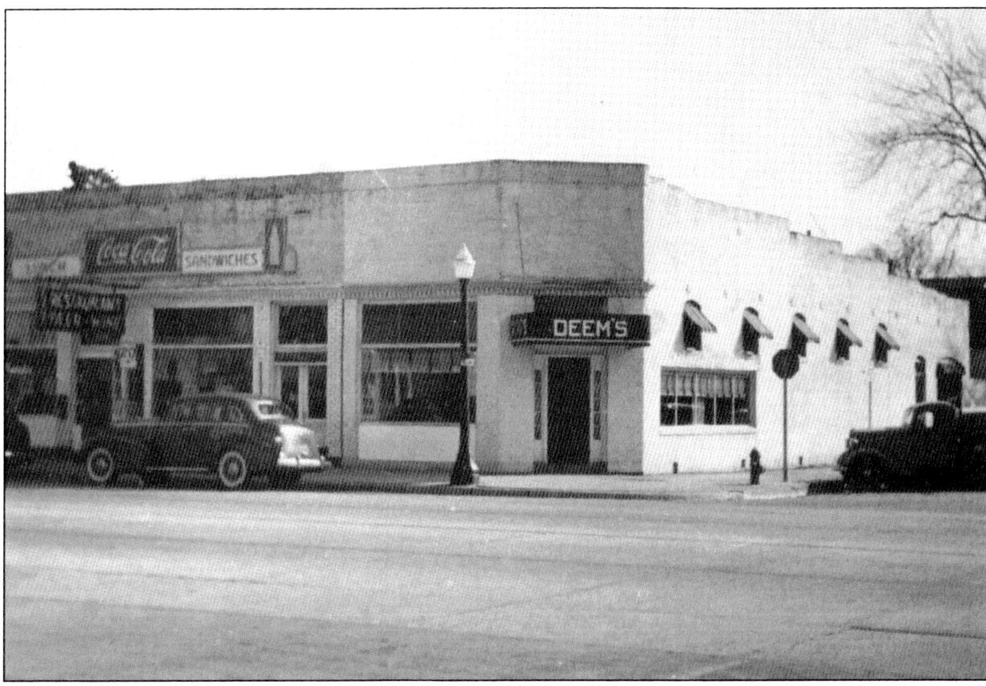

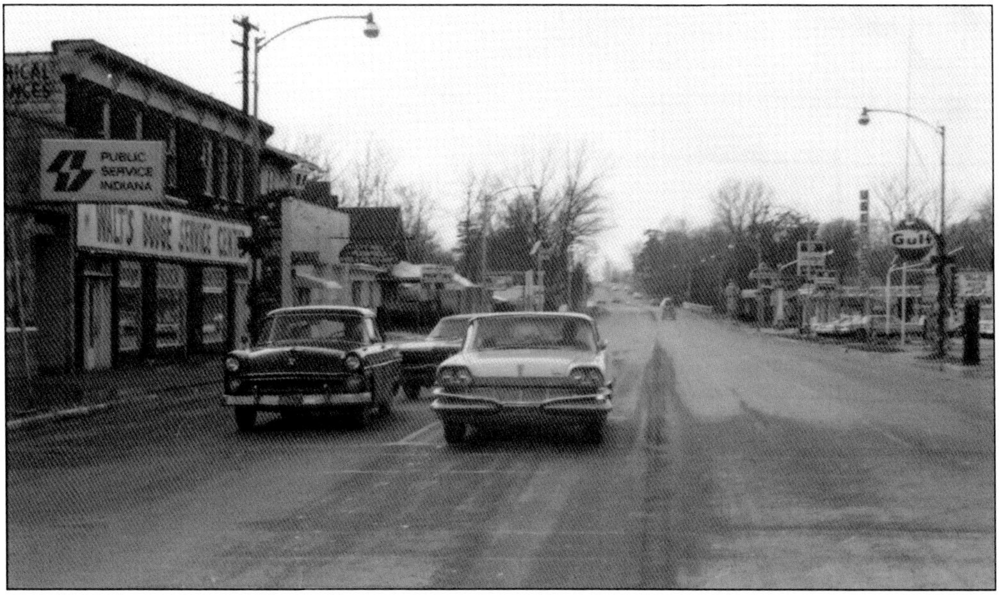

Coming into downtown Plainfield from the west, travelers on US 40 passed the Dairy Queen, Walt's Dodge dealership, Plainfield City Hall, the Plainfield police and fire station, Walt's Dodge Service Center, and the local office of Public Service Indiana. This photograph is from the late 1950s.

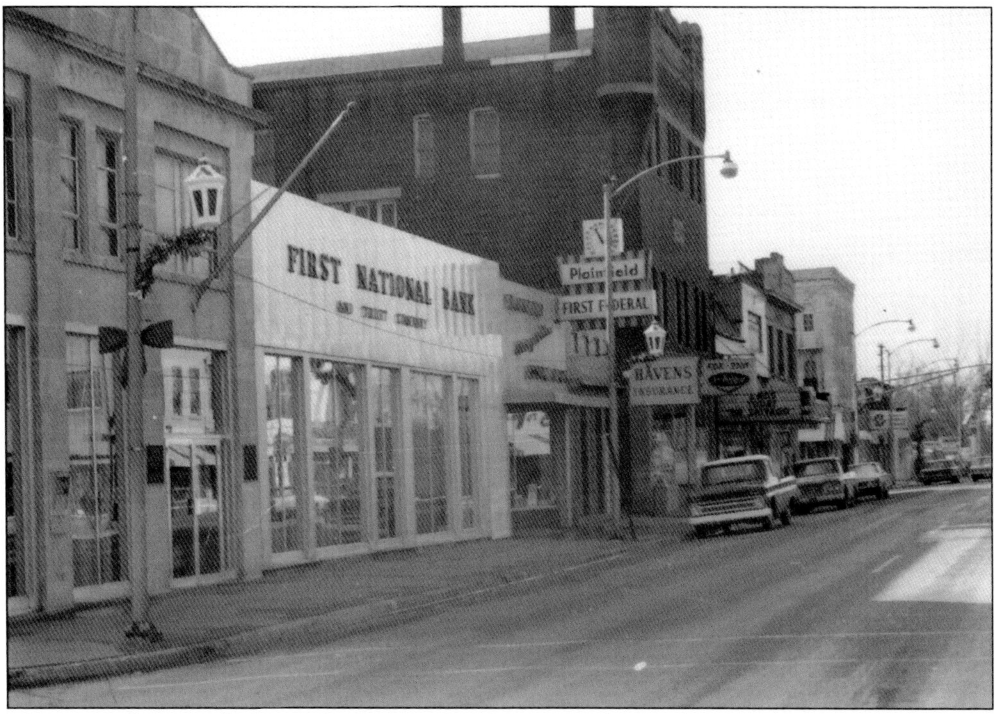

This 1965 photograph shows the business landscape on the south side of US 40 in downtown Plainfield. The merchants included First National Bank, Plainfield First Federal Bank, Fraternal Order of Eagles No. 3207 (located in the Knights of Pythias brick building), Havens Insurance, and the movie theater. The movie playing is *Dr. Zhivago.*

Three

School Time

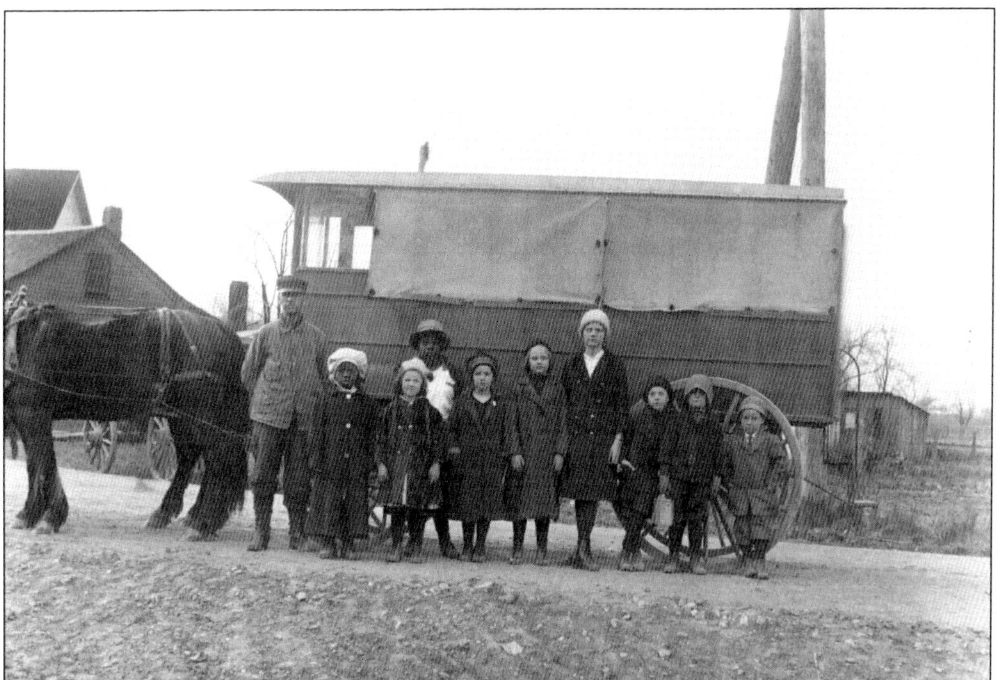

Long before motorized buses were available, students were driven to school in school hacks or wagons. Here, wagon driver Ernest Louis (left) transports nine young children to their school. Louis was a very active resident of Guilford Township and died at the age of 89 in 1974.

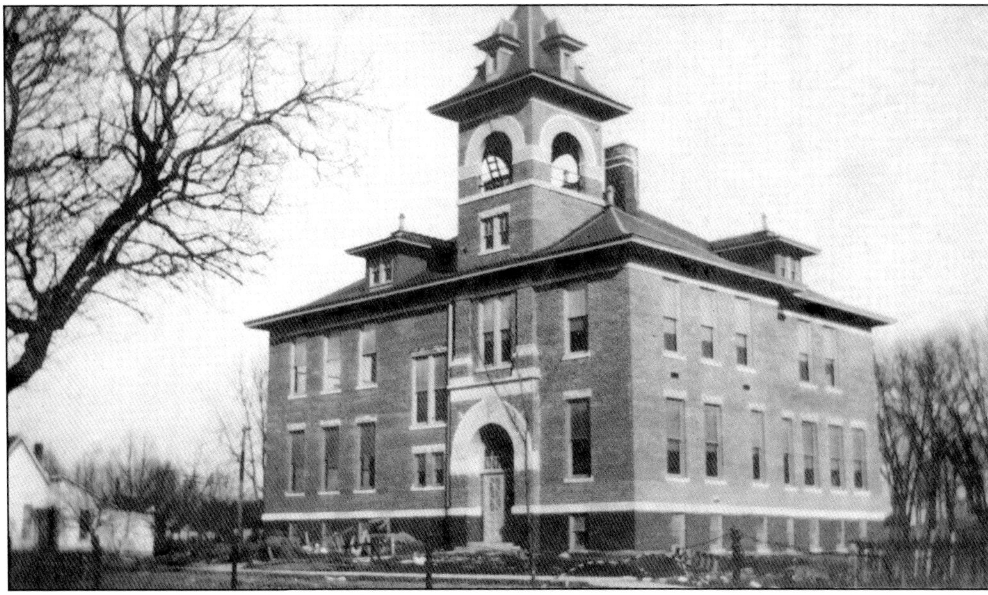

Posing majestically at 261 North Vine Street, the West Grade Elementary School building served a variety of educational purposes during its lifetime. Built in 1907, the structure first housed Plainfield High School, then Plainfield Junior High, and finally was designated as West Grade Elementary School. The building and land were sold at auction on March 12, 1969, to Ray and Edna Wernke and Gene and Mary Lou Coleman for $14,600. The Wernke/Coleman group razed the building to make way for a small, single-story apartment complex, which still stands today.

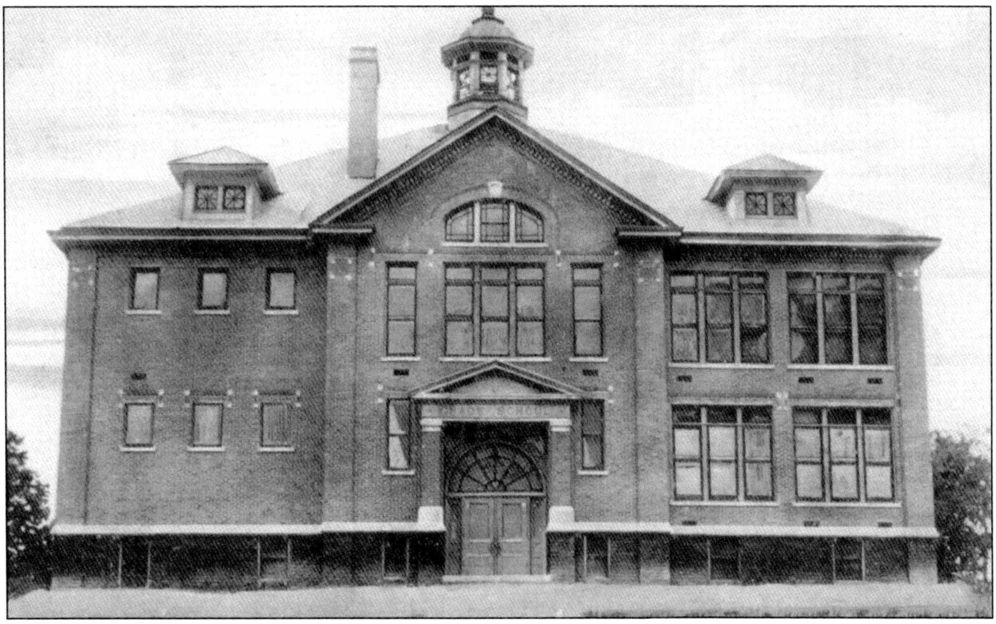

East Grade Elementary School, located at 202 North East Street, had a very auspicious beginning. This photograph shows the third building that occupied the spot. The first building, erected in 1867, burned down on April 7, 1888. The town rebuilt the school, which again burned down on December 30, 1909. The third structure was built in 1910 and remained an elementary school until the mid-1970s. East Grade was razed in March 1981 to make way for apartments.

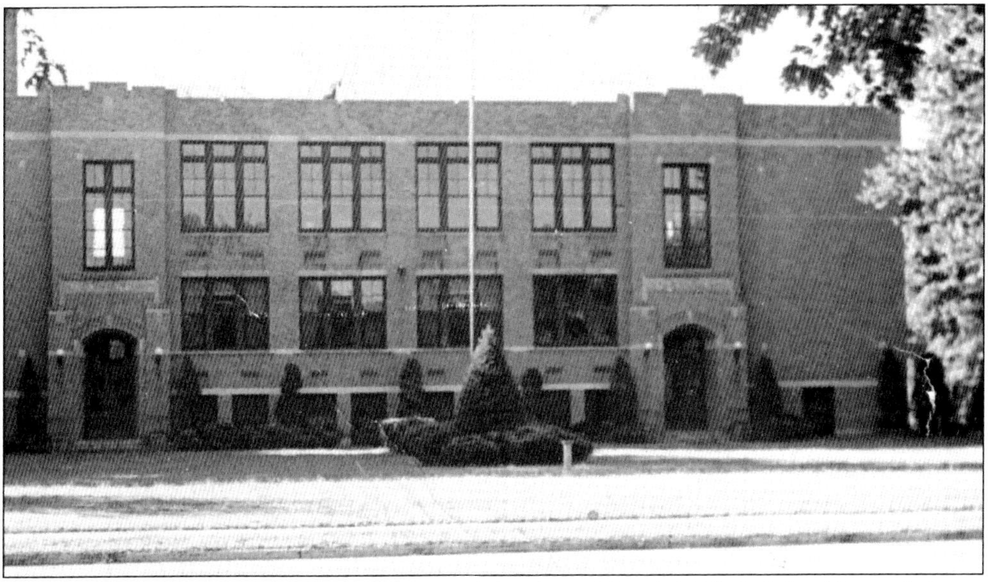

Built in 1931 on the site of the original Central Academy, Plainfield High School housed classes here until 1958, when the new school was built on Stafford Road. Taken a few years after the school was completed, this photograph shows the grounds after the well-known pine tree was planted in front of the school, along Main Street. A Christmas tree–lighting ceremony around the stately pine still occurs every December.

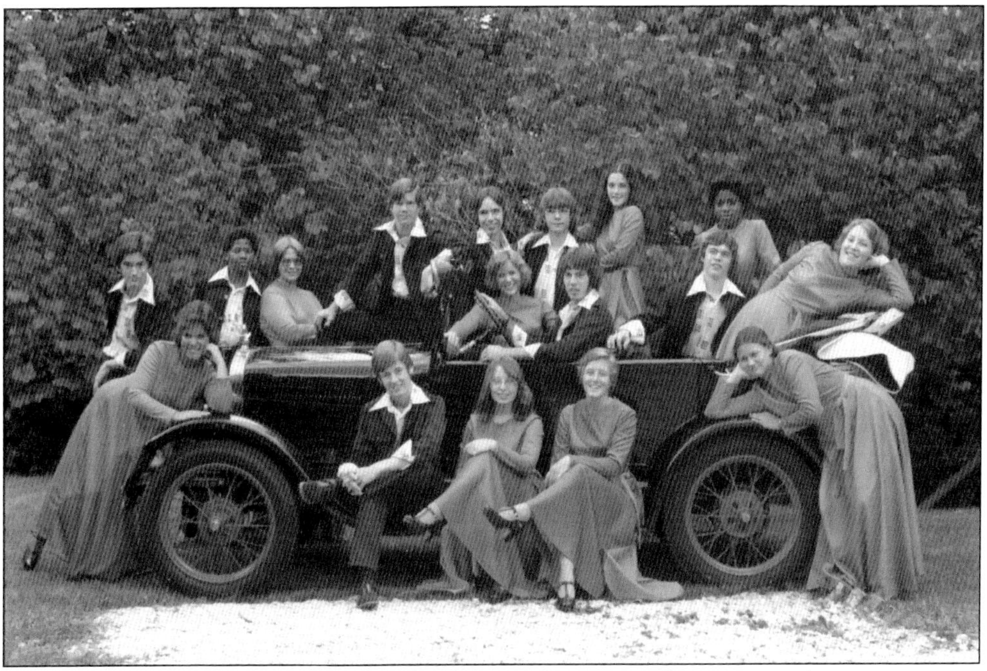

For many years, the Plainfield High School music department has sponsored a singing group called the Belles and Beaux Swing Choir. Seen here in 1975, the show choir members included Sue Badanek, Chris Carr, Wayne Smith, Cindy Peters, Mike Smith, Lisa Bennett, Teri Reynolds, Rhonda Robinson, Wes Bennett, Steve Sigmund, Paul Hays, John Kivett, Becky Stapf, Dana Urshel, Kevin Wright, Miranda Hampton, and Julia Adams.

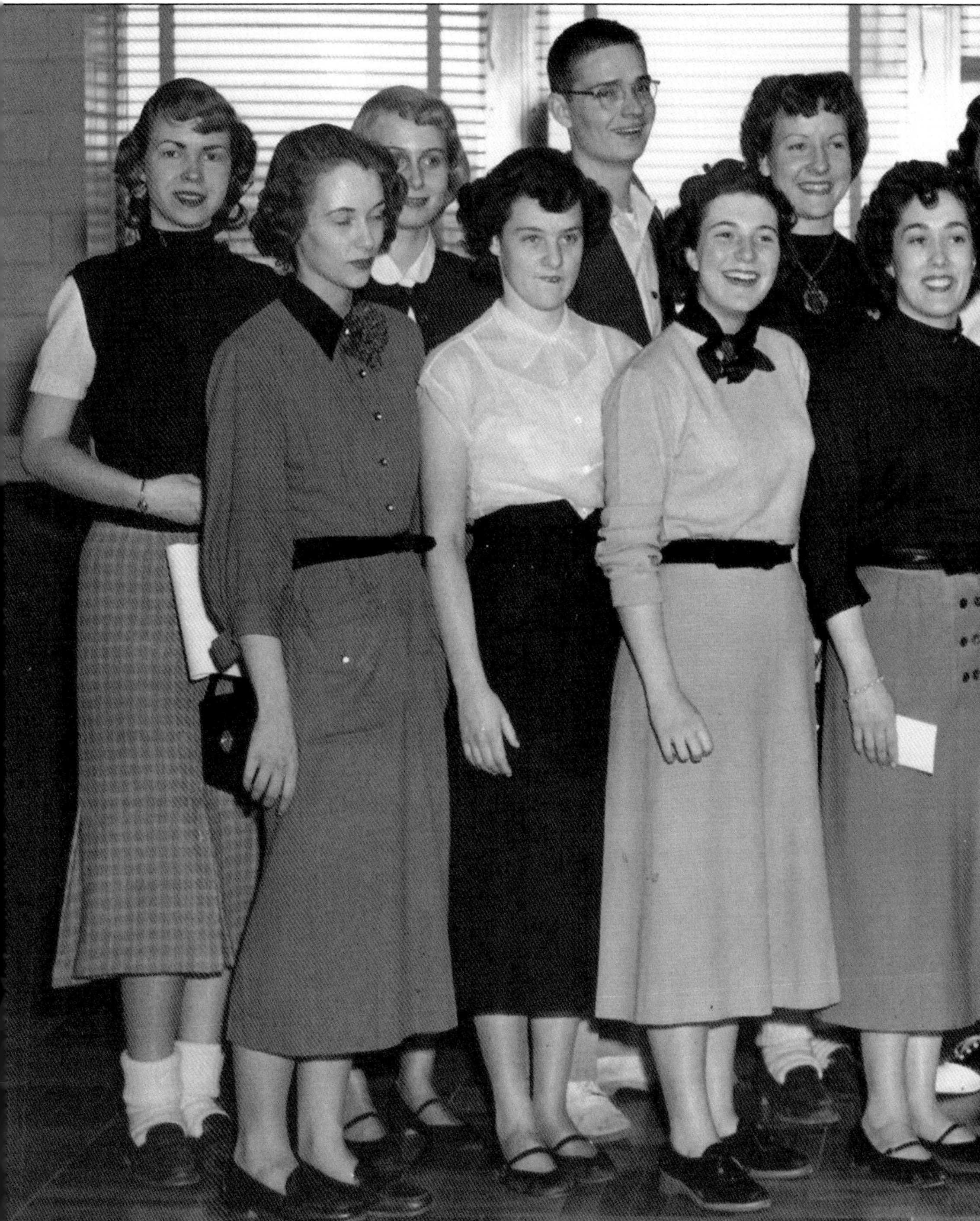

Members of Howard Pike's business class from the Plainfield High School class of 1952 took a field trip to the headquarters of Public Service Indiana to get a firsthand look at the electric utility. Public Service Indiana (now Duke Energy) was located at 1000 East Main Street in Plainfield. Those in attendance from left to right are (first row) Carol Johnson, Wilma Skirvin, Virginia

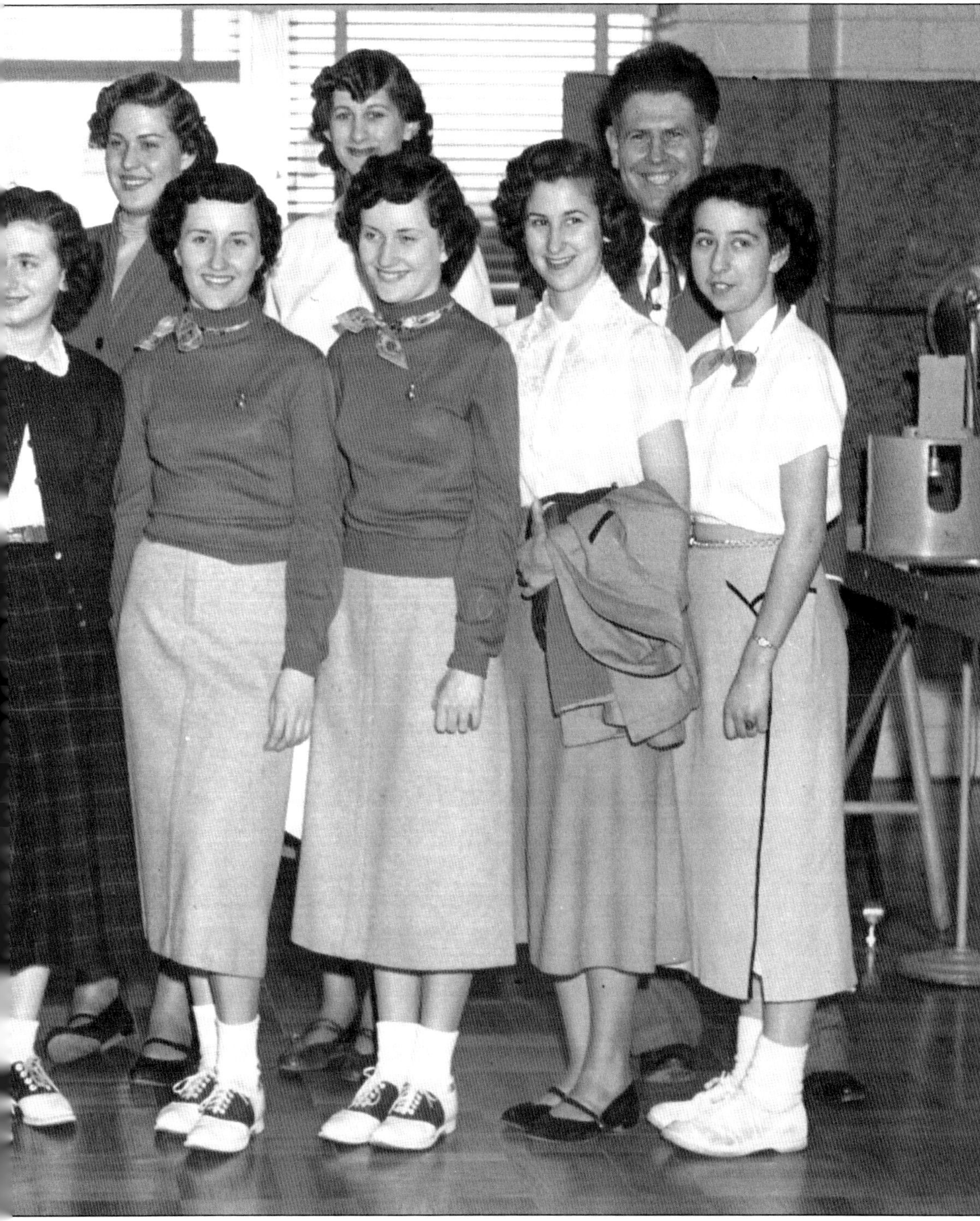

Brown, Barbara Trent, Beverly Martin, Janet Murphy, Phyllis Murphy, Eileen McNelley, and Patty Warner; (second row) Barbara Asher, Diane Hughes, Jack Albright, Rowena Dietz, Virginia Cokain, Claudetta Parker, Esther Daum, and teacher Howard Pike.

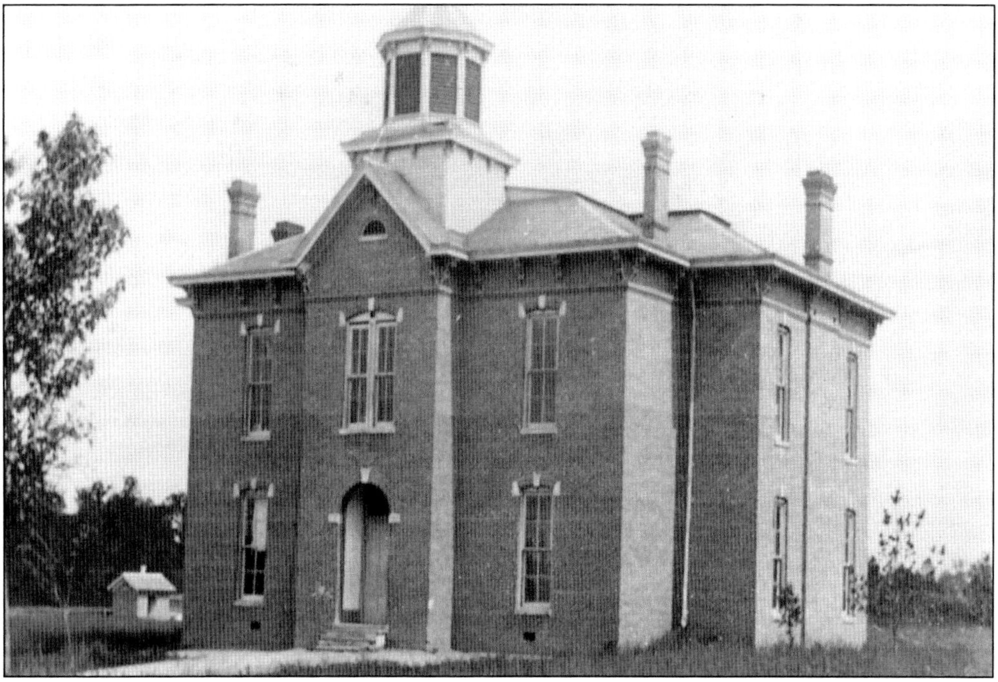

Central Academy, a secondary high school, was owned and operated by the Western Yearly Meeting of Friends. Located on the site of the current Central Elementary School in the 300 block of East Main Street, the school offered students a private education experience. This photograph shows the first Central Academy building, which was erected in 1882 and burned down on January 23, 1906.

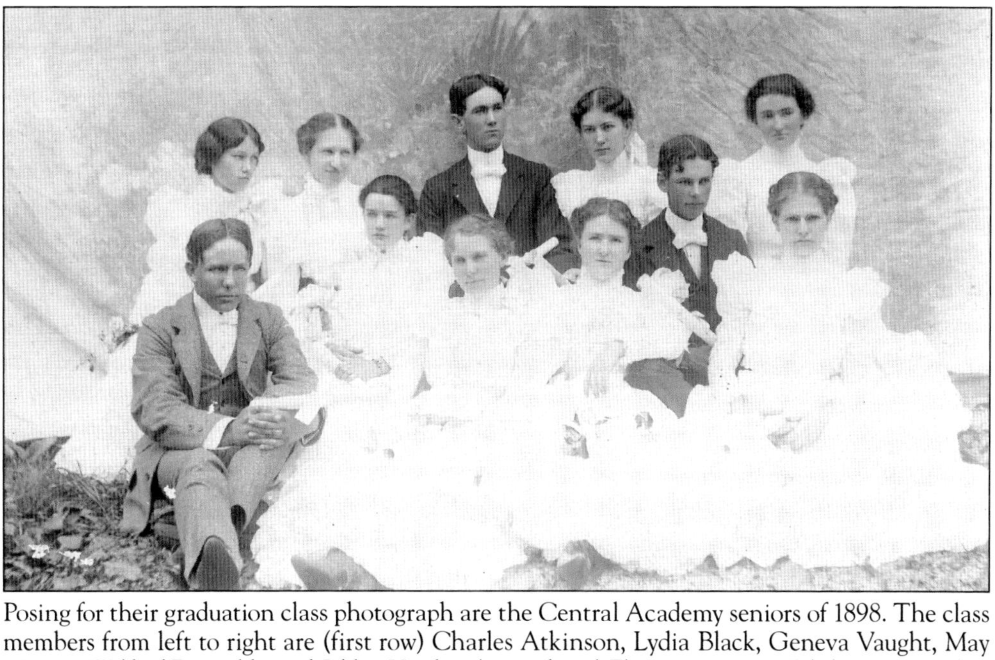

Posing for their graduation class photograph are the Central Academy seniors of 1898. The class members from left to right are (first row) Charles Atkinson, Lydia Black, Geneva Vaught, May Merritt, Wilfred Reynolds, and Sibbie Henley; (second row) Florence Hanna, Edith Rains, Walter Guyer, Emma Dillon, and Ella Hadley.

Shown here are two views of the shattered shell of the original Central Academy building, which caught fire and burned on January 23, 1906. These photographs illustrate the devastation the fire had on the school and on the community. Central Academy was a well-respected secondary school, and to see it burned to the ground must have been heartbreaking. Curious onlookers stand on the frozen ground, transfixed by what was once the impressive school building. The *Friday Caller* newspaper headlines proclaimed, "Academy Is In Ruins . . . Origin of the Fire Unknown . . . Loss Estimated at $10,000 With But $3000 Insurance." The fire started in the west room on the second floor and had likely ignited in a defective flue.

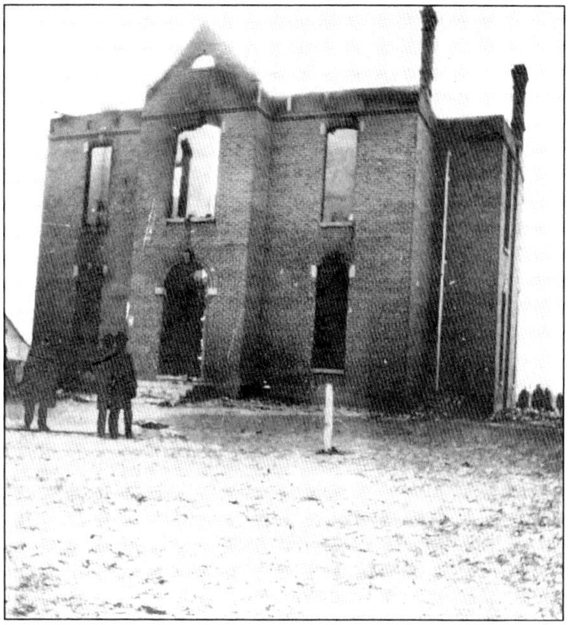

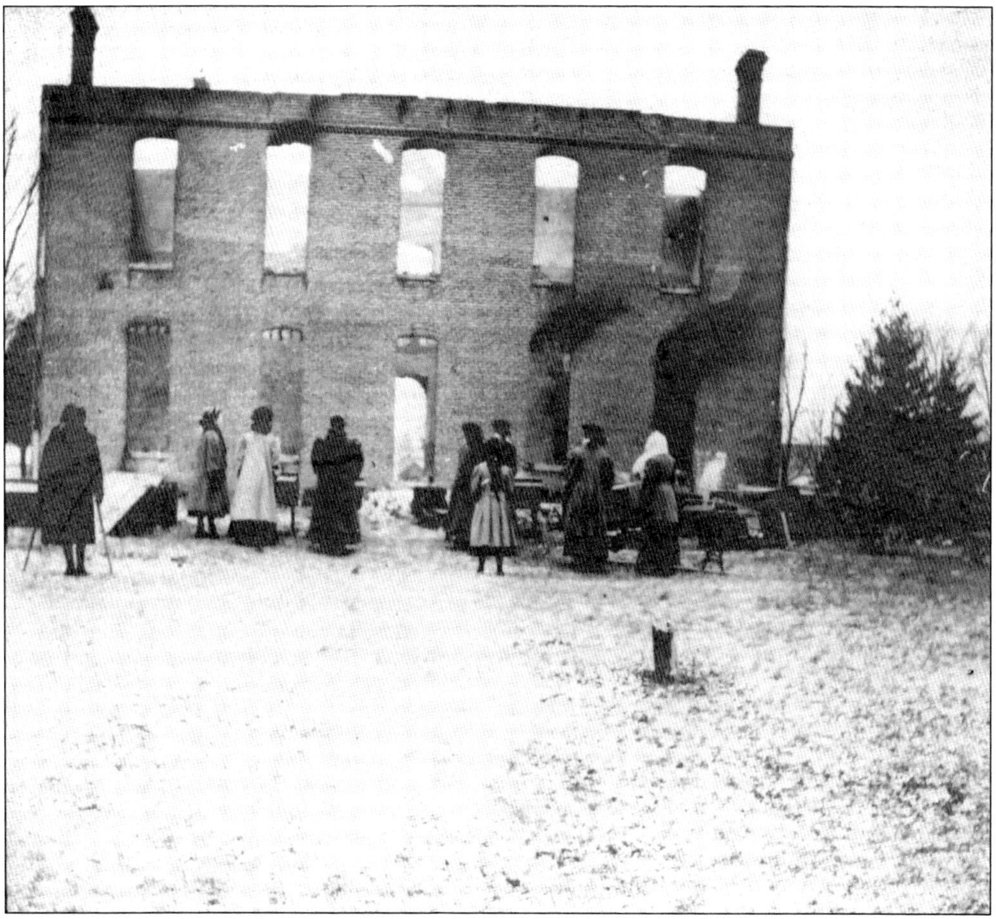

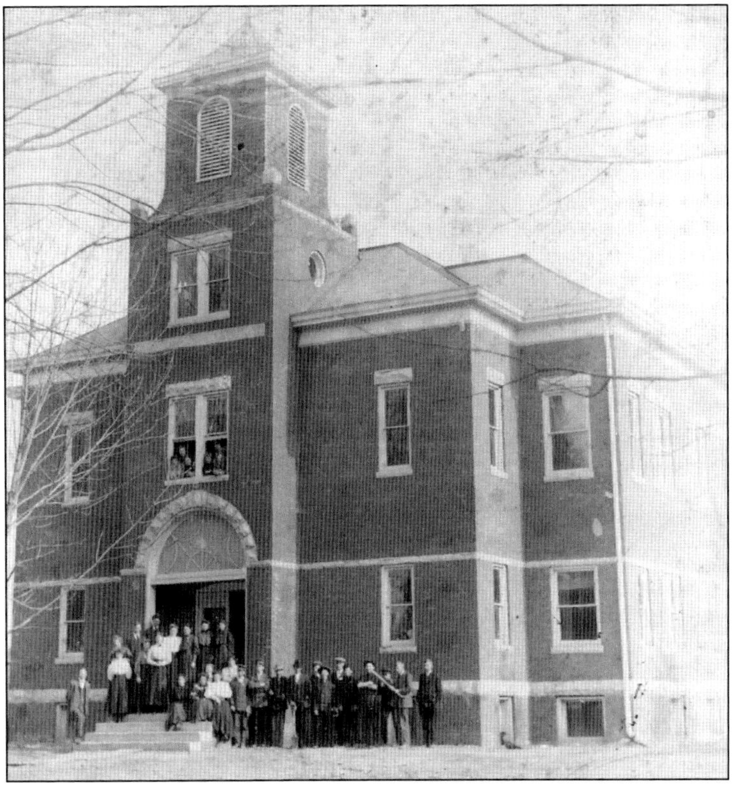

The Western Yearly Meeting quickly rebuilt the burned school the same year, and by September 1906, the students returned to find a very similar architectural design to the first building. Noticeable changes included the square cupola on the roof and the enlarged main entrance, adorned by an archway of limestone.

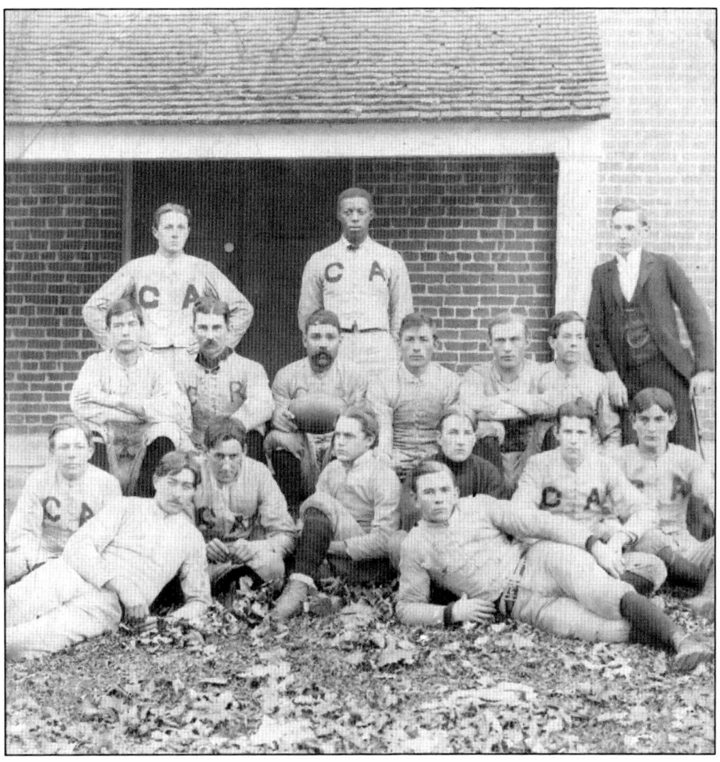

During the fall of 1894, the Central Academy boys' football team posed for their team picture. Members of the team included, from left to right, (first row, lounging) Ernest Swindler, and Charlie Vestal; (second row) Charlie Atkinson, Joe Dennis, Ralph Morgan, Ralph Swearingen, Ernest Carter, and Jess Hadley; (third row) Ernest Cooper, ? Uestal, ? Blair, Horace Sellars, Wils Loy, and Lawrence Hadley; (fourth row) Elvin Carter, Bob Miller, and Will Hiss.

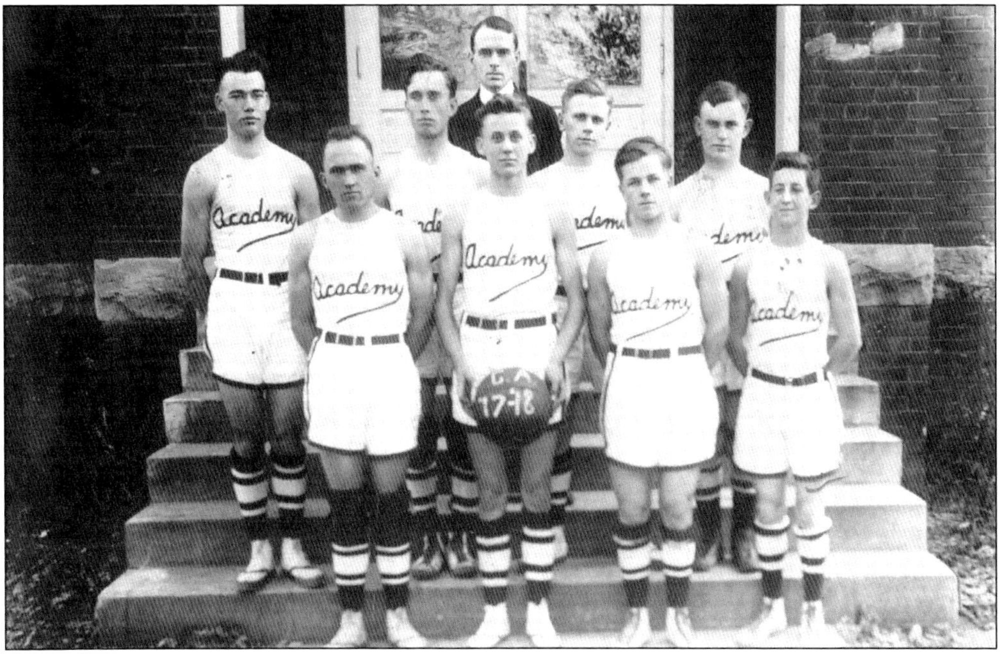

Wearing their full uniforms, the boys of the 1917–1918 Central Academy basketball team pose on the front steps of the school. The team members from left to right are (first row) forward Morris Barker, captain George Hadley, substitute Ralph Hawkins, and substitute Russell Hawkins; (second row) guard Leon Fields, center Wendell Loy, Coach Kelsey, guard Wendell Dixon, and forward Wayne Hevland.

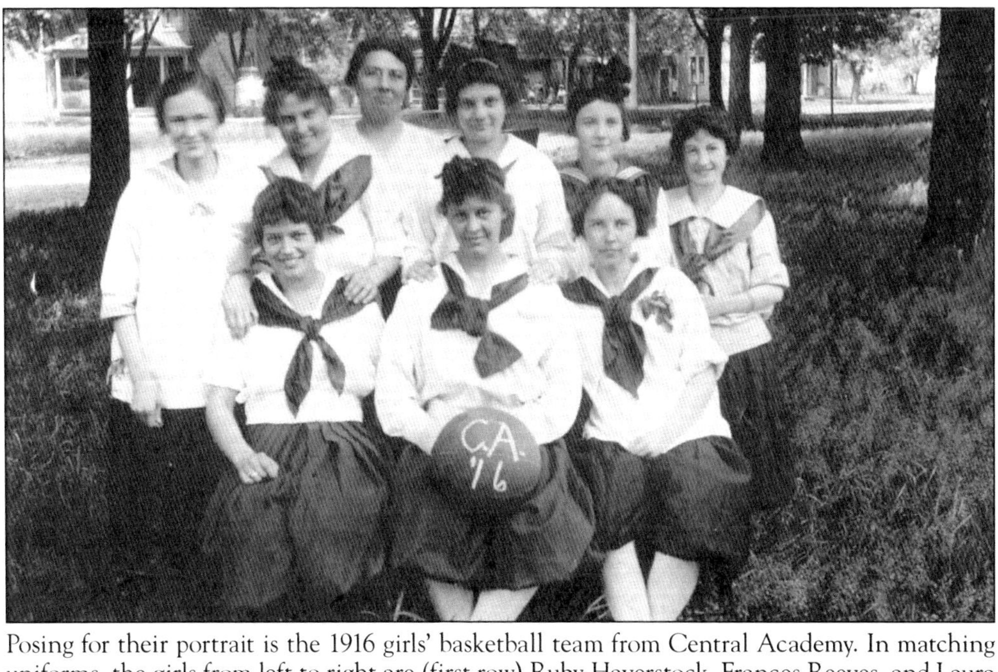

Posing for their portrait is the 1916 girls' basketball team from Central Academy. In matching uniforms, the girls from left to right are (first row) Ruby Haverstock, Frances Reeves, and Laura Cook; (second row) Gladys Powers, Reba Bradford, coach Osia McClain, Doris Hagee, Esther Vestal, and "E. M."

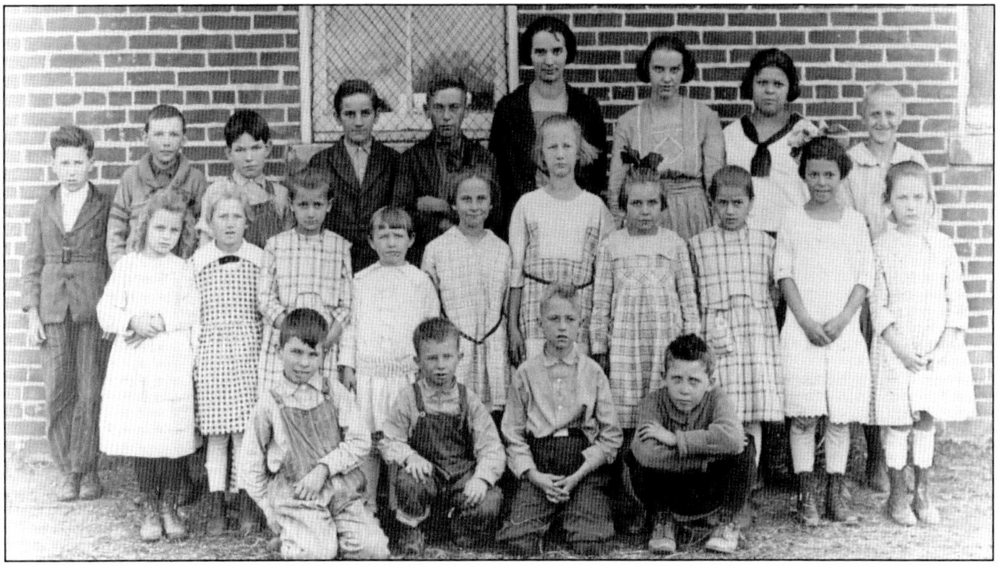

The Black Rock School was located on old Indiana State Road 267 at the intersection of 800 S. This photograph shows the class of 1921–1922. Posing for the portrait from left to right are (first row) Elmer Chandler, Albert Chandler, Cecil Vanwinkle, and Bennie Poff; (second row) Marie Chandler, Ladema Vanwinkle, ? Greeson, ? Cartwright, Dorothy Frank, Isabell Vanwinkle, Dorothy Sheets, ? Greeson, Hildred Walls, and Doris Pike; (third row) Harold Atkinson, Harold Sheets, Bill Baldwin, Carl Greeson, Harlan Beau, teacher Lillian Chandler, Marcella Sheets, Gladys Walls, and Dora Greeson.

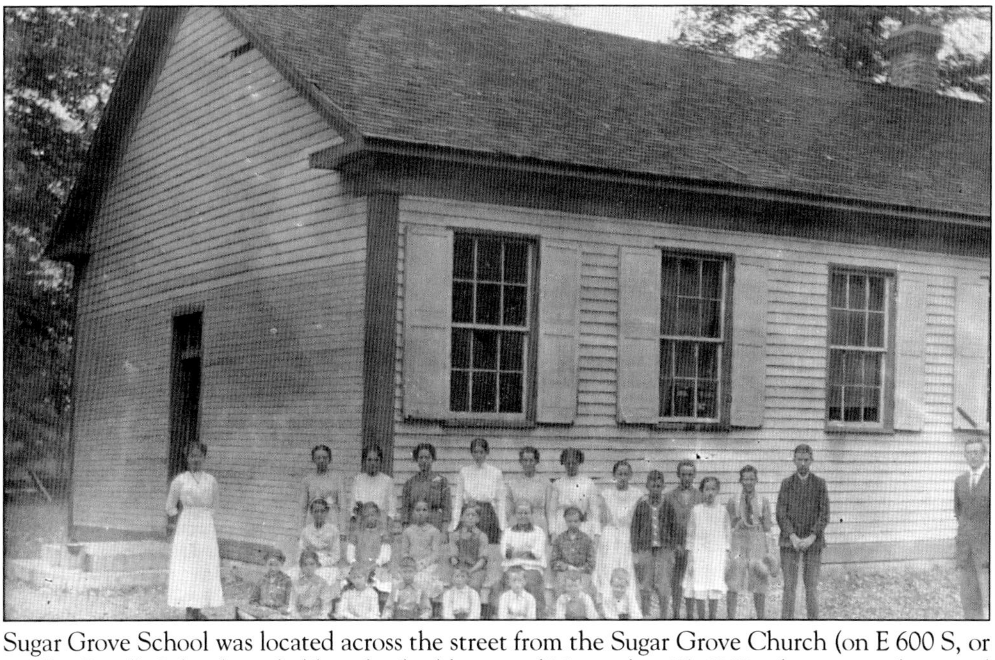

Sugar Grove School was located across the street from the Sugar Grove Church (on E 600 S, or Hadley Road). School was held in this building until November 25, 1929, when it was destroyed by fire. Records indicate that 196 children from 17 families attended the school at Sugar Grove. This photograph has no date or student identifications but does reflect a diverse group of children attending the Quaker school.

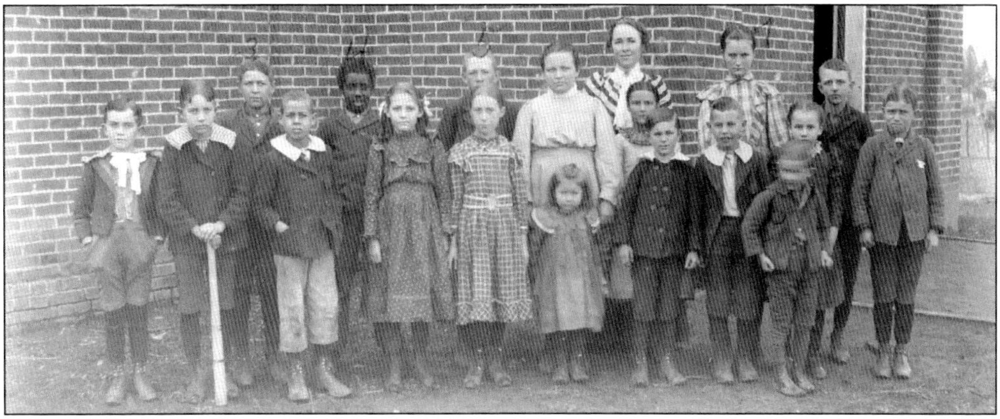

In this photograph, the students of the Friendswood School class of 1899–1900 pose with their teacher. Included in this photograph are teacher Anna Hornaday, Donald Jessup, Minnie Squires, Halstead Jessup, Oscar Kays, Rosco Hampton, Harrison Peterson, Grace Kennecky, Mary Clark, Albert Hampton, Louise Jessup, Fay Shelley, Zelphia Kays, Chestney Shelley, Walter Jessup, Edna Hite, Elso Fritche, Walter Fritche, and John Fritche. Friendswood School was located on 800 S (locally known as Mooresville Road) and was discontinued in the fall of 1939.

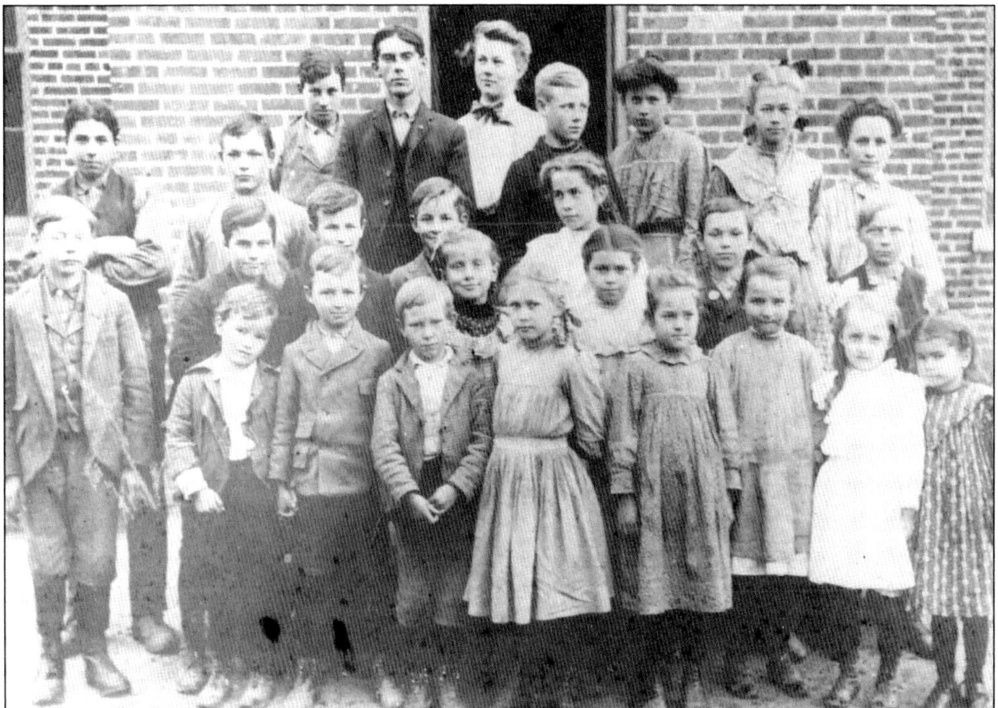

The Buttonwood School was located on Joppa Road, west of old Indiana Road 267 south at 525 E and 800 S. The students seen here attended the school in 1903. Shown here from left to right are (first row) William Chandler, George Sellars, Ray Walls, two unidentified children, Hazel Head, Lillian Chandler, Ethel Sellars, and ? Walls; (second row) Louis Hadley, Simeon Chandler, Joel Chandler, two unidentified children, Gladys Sellars, Chauncey Walls, and Leonard Hadley; (third row) Alex Chandler, George Walls, Manual Chandler, ? Smitherman, two unidentified children, ? Smitherman, Mary Farmer, and Elizabeth Chandler.

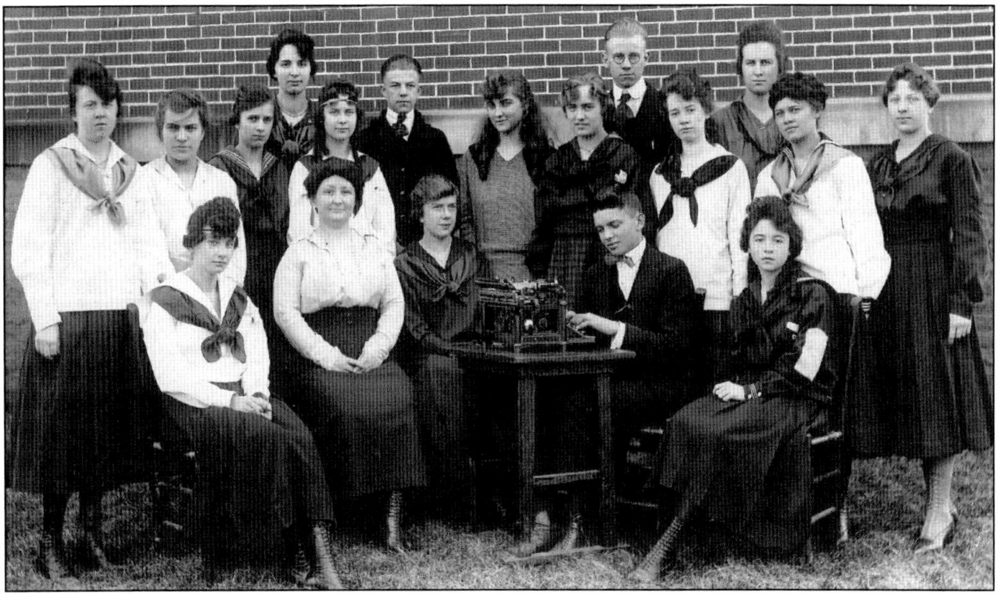

Showing off their typewriter in this photograph is the 1919 Plainfield High School commercial class of students. Those pictured are, from left to right, (first row, seated) Edna Carr, Cora DeWiese Hack (instructor), Mary Pritchett, Adna Moon, and Mary Lucille Judd; (second row) Helen Coble, Mabel Compton, Pauline Spears, Pearl Allen, Edith Marshall, Olive Seaman, Esther Hadley, and Dorothy Broyles; (third row) Lillian Chandler, Pierre Herringlake, Roy Cooper, and Ella Chandler.

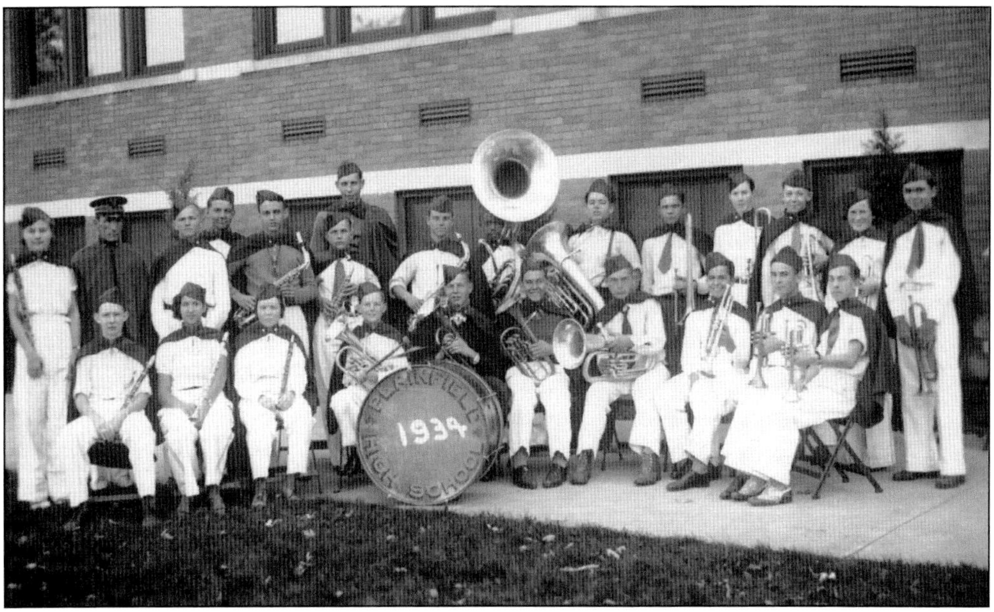

All smiles, Plainfield High School band members proudly pose in their uniforms and with instruments outside their school in 1934. The white shirts and pants, along with the capes and beret hats, made for a crisp-looking group. The band consisted of four girls, twenty boys, and one band director.

Four

Religious Life

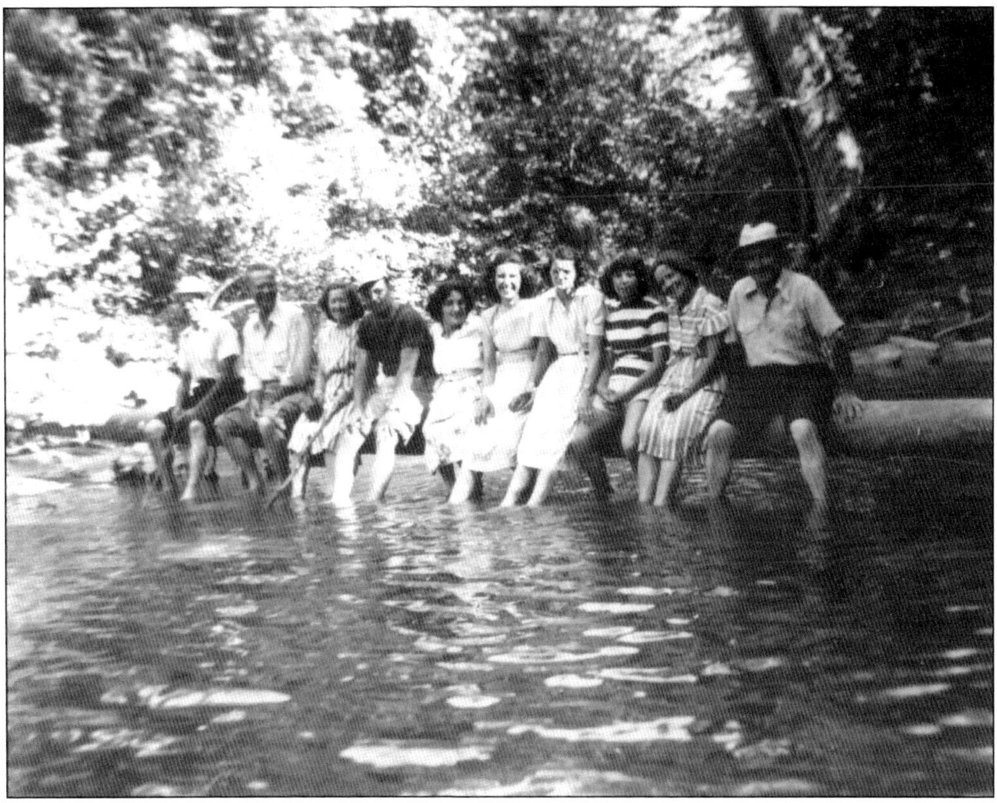

Enjoying a lazy summer afternoon is one of the Sunday School classes from the Plainfield Friends Meeting. Sitting on the downed tree-trunk bench from left to right are Ben Anderson, Paul Doan, Margaret Atkinson, Jack Miller, Frances Drake, unidentified, Martha Doan, unidentified, Miriam Atkinson, and John Peacock. The photograph is undated.

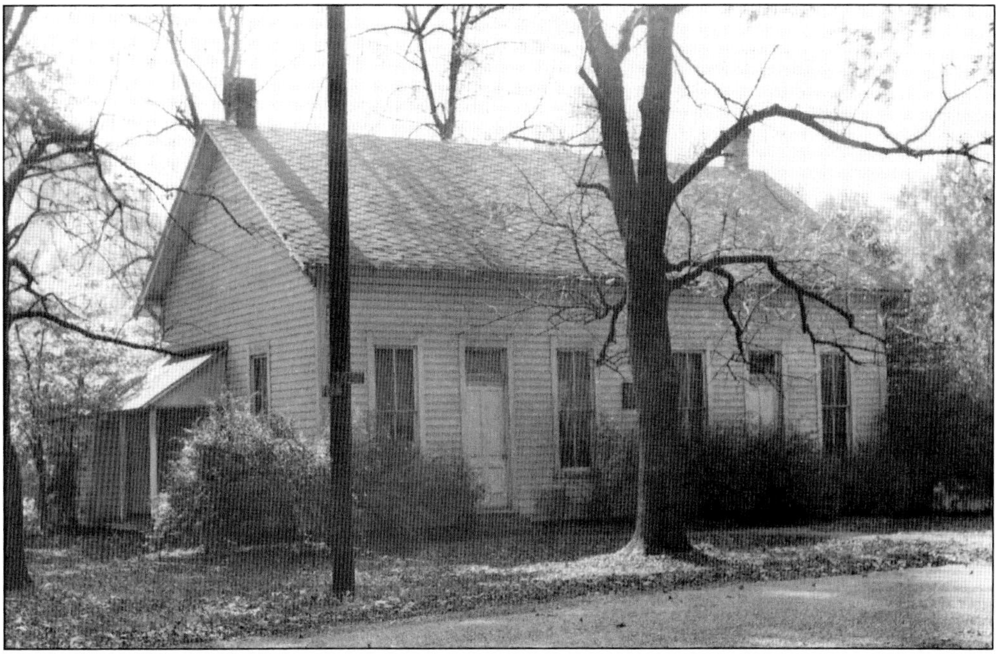

The Plainfield Friends Meeting has a long history in Plainfield. The first Quakers came to the area from Guilford County, North Carolina, around 1832. The Friends quickly established several meetinghouses in the area, including the one seen here at 105-107 West South Street. This home, which was the original Conservative Friends Meeting House, is currently a residence.

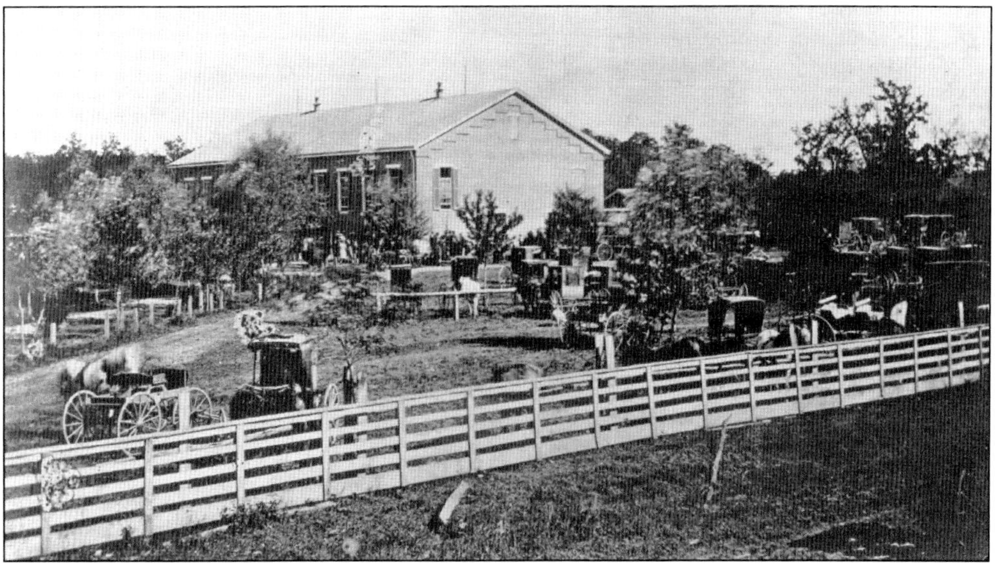

The Plainfield Friends Meeting House was built in 1858. Seen here around 1860, the grounds, located at 105 South East Street, look oddly vacant without the numerous, stately trees that would eventually provide beauty and shade to this tranquil setting. This is the view of the original Plainfield Friends Church, which was later renovated after a fire destroyed part of the building.

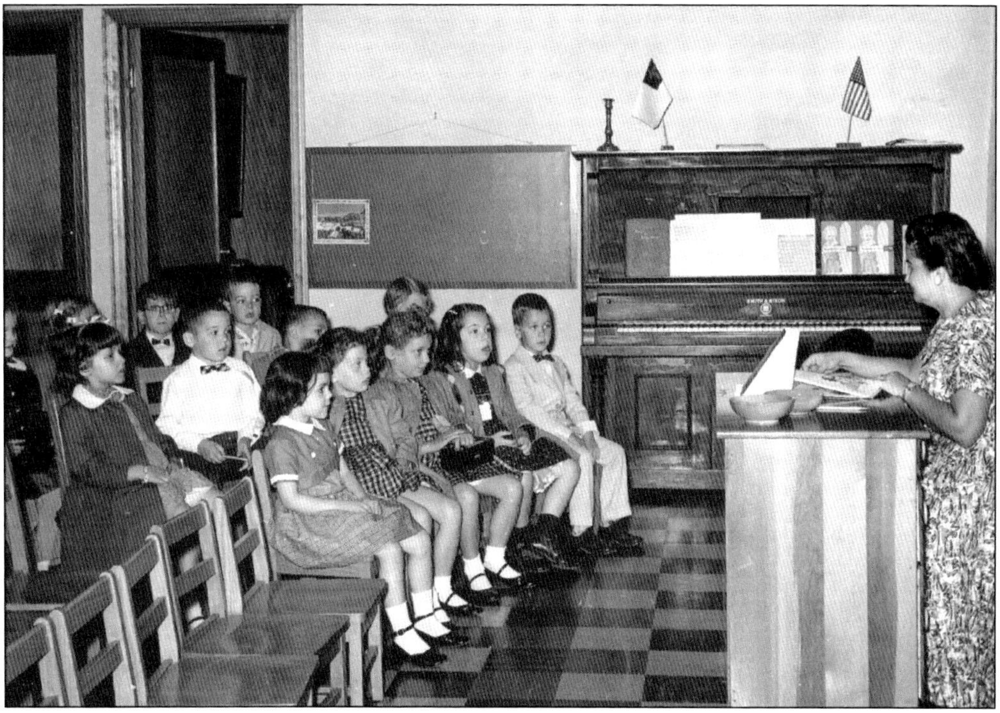

This photograph from around 1958 shows young members of one of the Plainfield Friends Sunday School classes. Some of the attentive children listening to teacher Nadine Kemp are Holly Ramsey, Bobby Gray, Georgia Gaddie, Jerilyn Gaddie, Susan Miller, and Jay Lee Ellis.

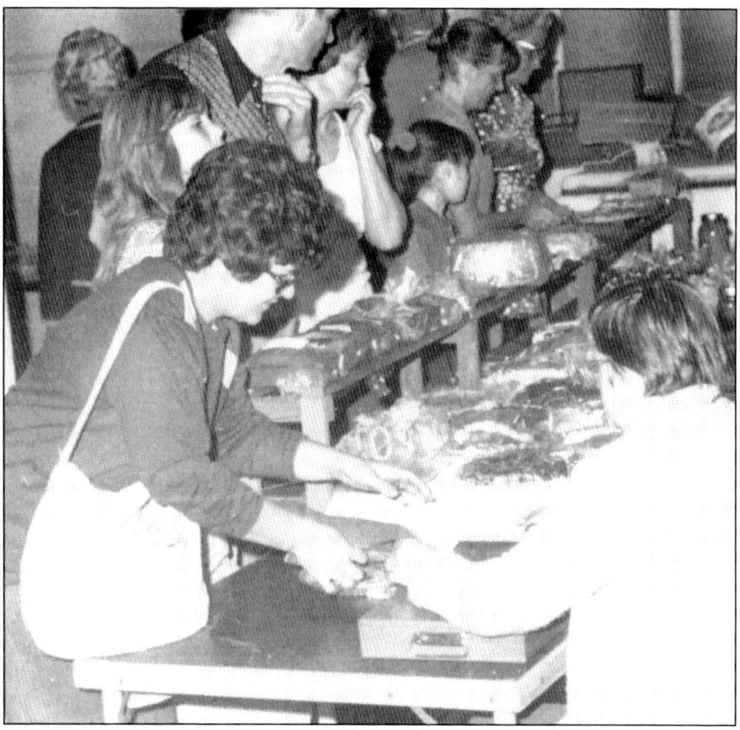

One of the highlights of the fall festival season was the Church Mouse Sale, held at the Plainfield Friends Meeting House. Local church and community members would create, bake, and construct a wide variety of craft and food items to sell. In this photograph from October 1977, customers contemplate their purchases at the sale, which was held in the basement of the building.

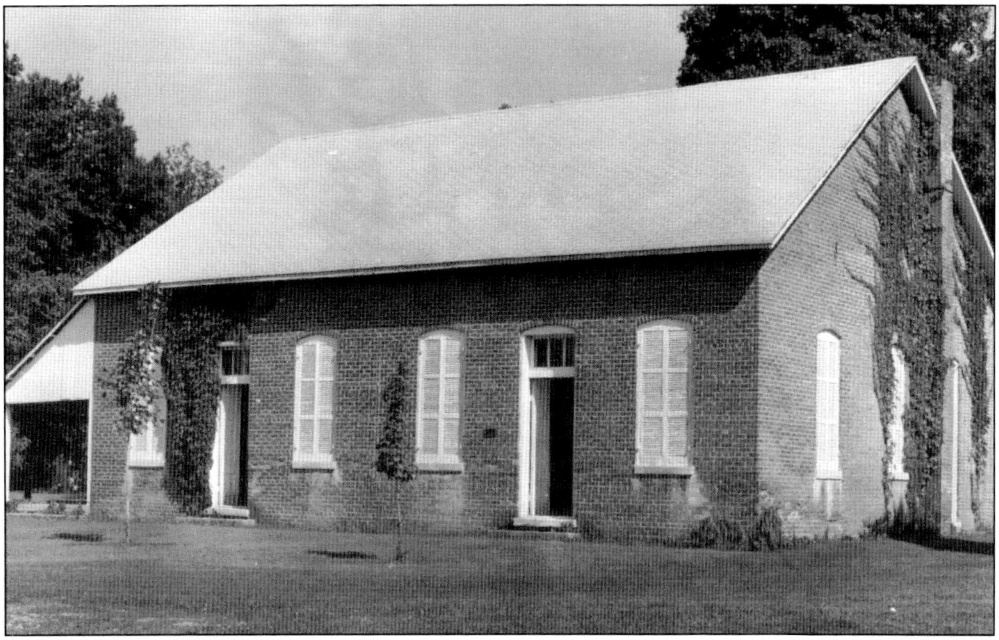

The Sugar Grove Meeting House, located at the intersection of E 600 S and S 700 E (formerly Hadley Road), is characterized by its simplicity. Situated among a grove of sugar, walnut, and yellow poplar trees and near a pioneer cemetery, the meetinghouse was constructed between 1870 and 1872 at a cost of $1,500. Seen in the photograph below, the interior is one of solemn silence and simplicity. The pews were constructed out of yellow poplar. The meetinghouse was used by worshipers for the last time on September 5, 1962. Available today for special events and occasions, the property was deeded by the Friends of Sugar Grove to Western Yearly Meeting in 1969, with a trust fund to maintain the building and grounds.

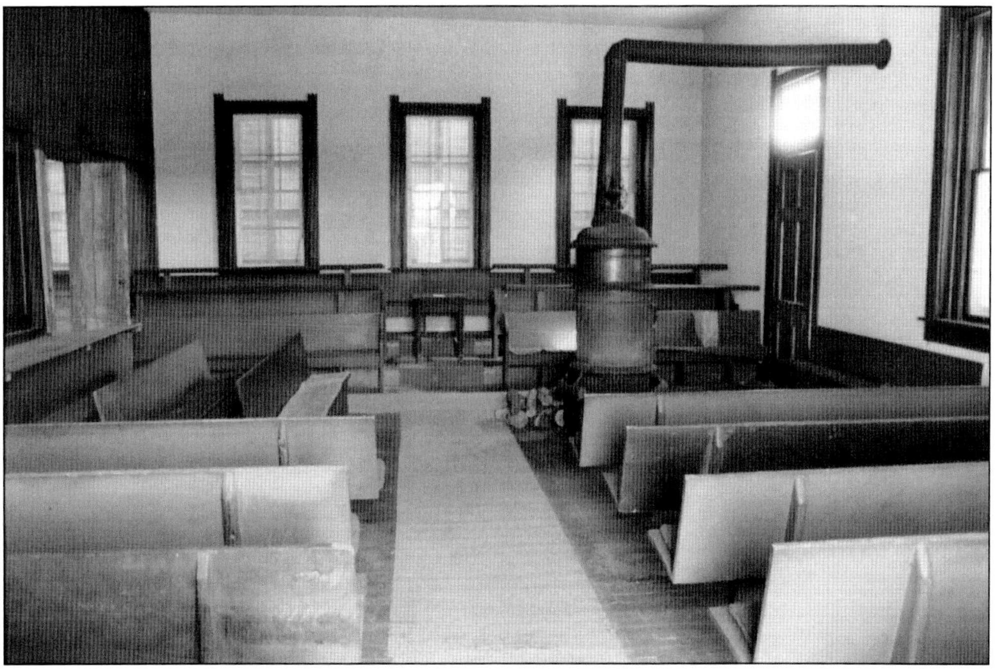

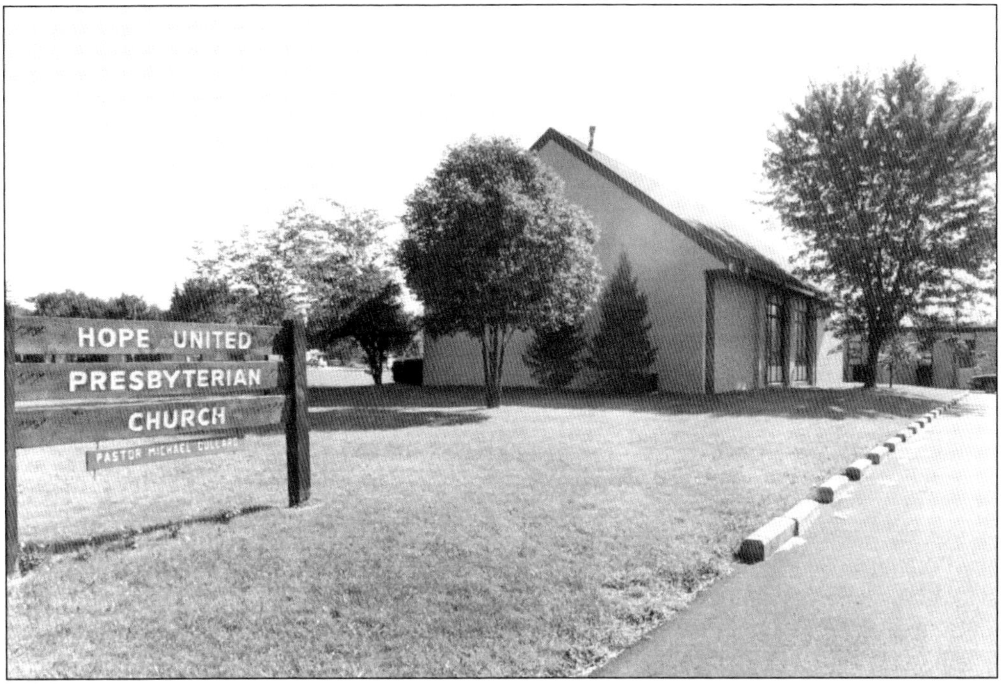

Located at 1331 Section Street, the Hope United Presbyterian Church's origins in Plainfield date to 1959, when a group of interested persons made plans to hold Sunday services. The first services were held in the Carnegie Library building in February 1959. The formal organization for the church was conducted on March 12, 1961, with 66 charter members. After constructing the building on Section Street, the first service was held there on February 3, 1963. The church has been a steady part of the community ever since, holding a craft sale each fall. In the below photograph, members prepare for the 1979 annual bazaar. Pictured around the table clockwise from lower left are Mrs. Merle Moore, Dixie Duncan, Annabelle Walters, Judy Harvey, Virginia Pemberton, Dee Anderson, Virginia Brunson, and Anne Krause.

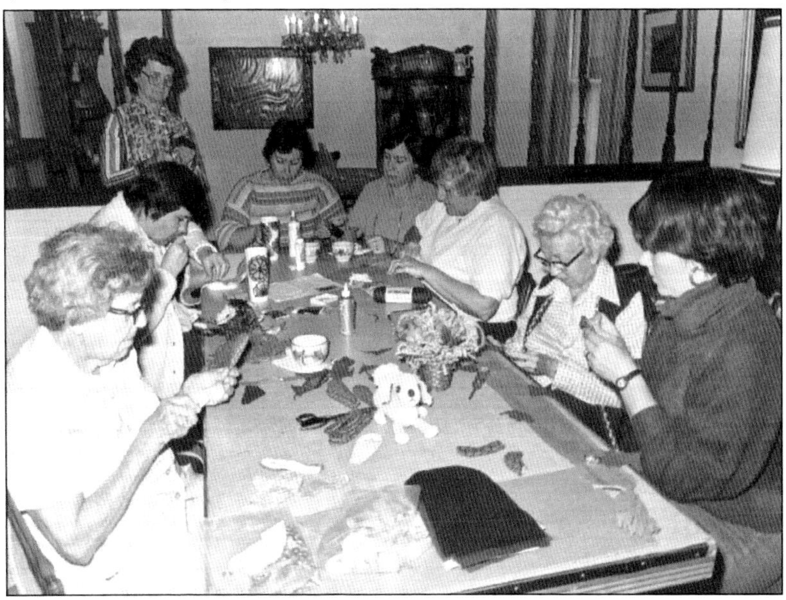

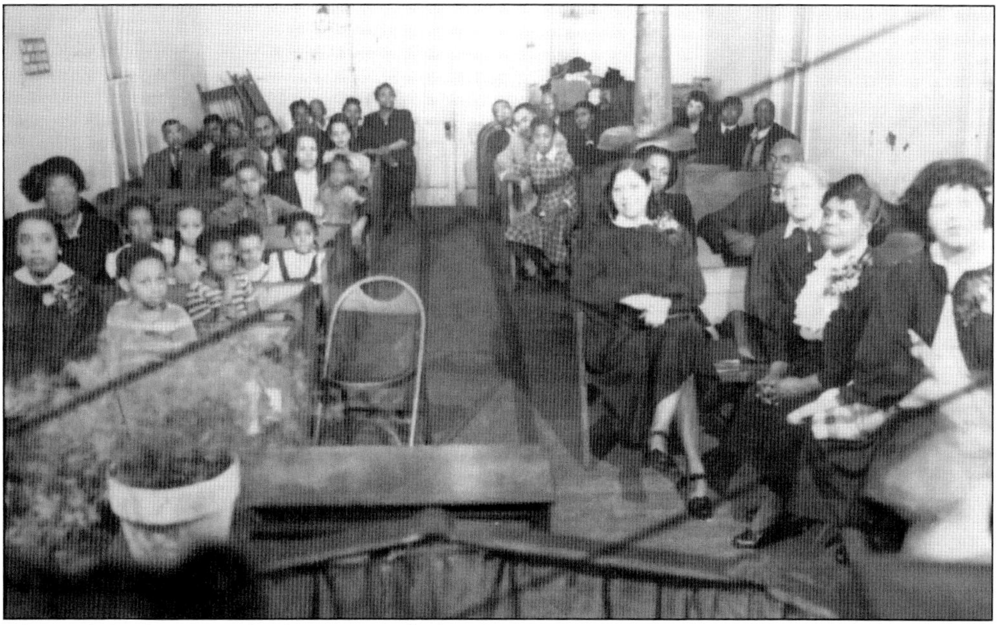

The Bethel African Methodist Episcopal Church was the first AME church in Hendricks County. The original church was located south of Plainfield on old Indiana Road 267 and named Black Rock Church, since the land was near a huge black rock. In 1879, the church moved into Plainfield and occupied an old blacksmith shop on North Vine Street. Seen here in the 1940s are members of the AME fellowship. (Courtesy of James Gilbert Sr.)

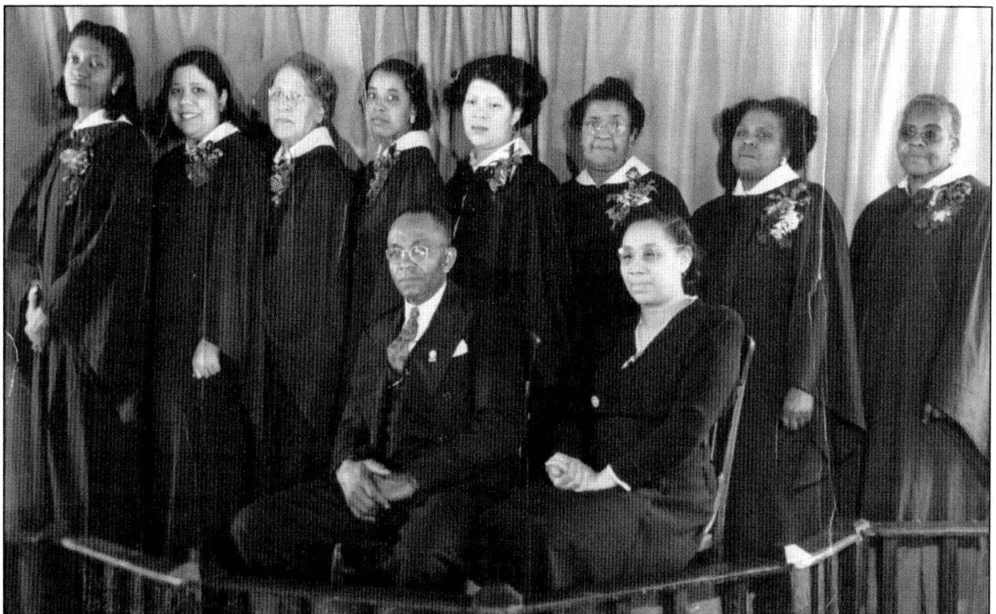

Members of the Bethel AME church choir join the minister and his wife at the front of the church on the chancel in 1950. Shown from left to right are (first row) Rev. and Mrs. J.C. Mitchell; (second row) Cassie Swarn, Grace Yost, Martha Davis Goss, Katherine Cullins, Gladys Gilbert Carbin, Anna Cullins, Laura Cloud, and Alice Carbin. (Courtesy of James Gilbert Sr.)

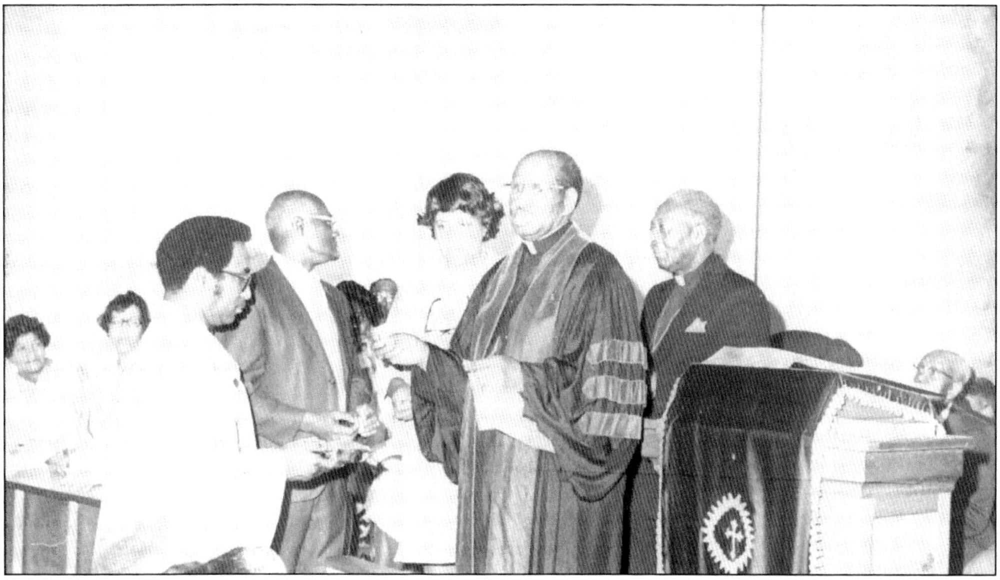

In 1968, the Bethel AME congregation moved from their renovated blacksmith shop into a newly constructed brick church building at 304 North Vine Street. Faithful members of the church gave financially and, by November 1974, they were able to pay off the mortgage. Seen here at the "mortgage destruction" ceremony are AME trustees and Bishop Thomas Primm.

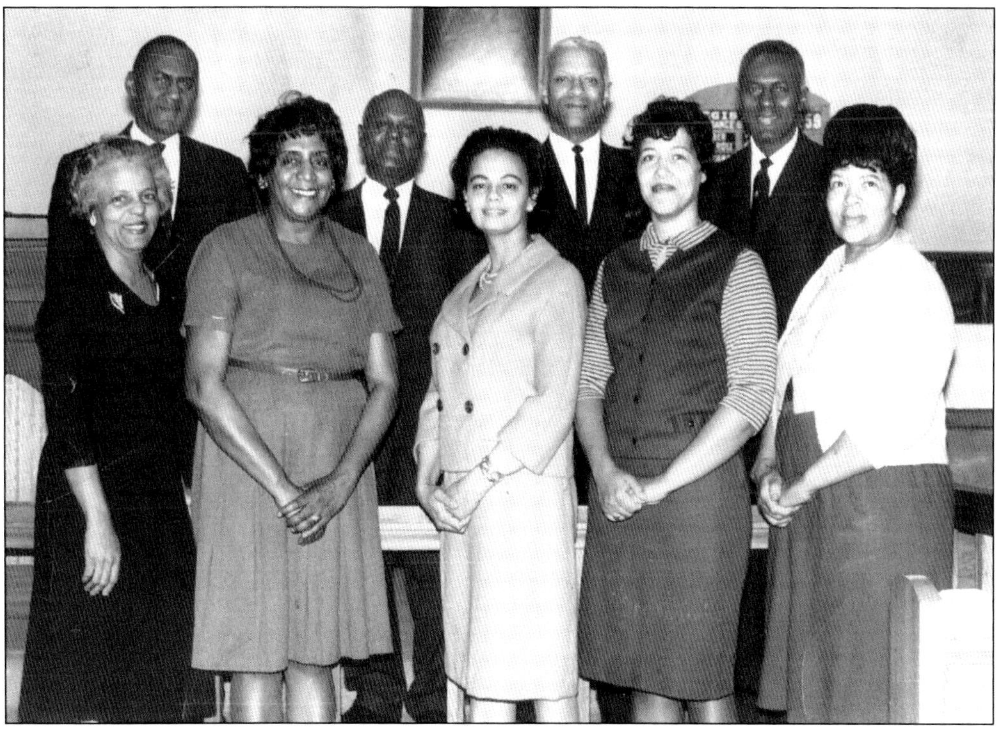

Standing proudly on the altar of the new AME church are, from left to right, (first row) Nancy Swarn, Charlotte Horn, Rose Swarn, Catherine Gilbert, and Gladys Gilbert Carbin; (second row) Churchel Swarn, Edgar Swarn, James V. Gilbert Sr., and Herbert Swarn. These families represent a long, rich history of the black community in Plainfield. (Courtesy of James Gilbert Sr.)

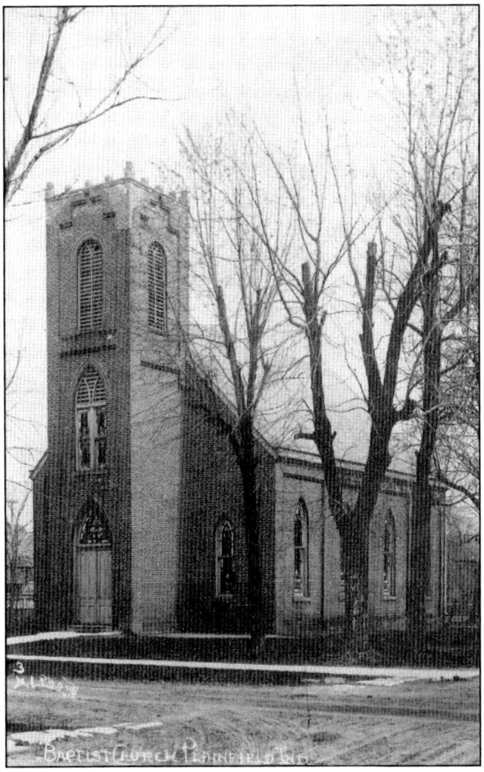

Located at 201 North Vine Street is the original First Baptist Church building, shown in the photograph to the left. The congregation had previously met in a frame building on Krewson Street. Currently a residence, the church was used for worship by First Baptist from 1884 until 1964, when the congregation moved to its new building at 1012 Stafford Road. The first service at the new Stafford Road building, seen below, was held on Easter Sunday in 1964. Members recall that on the Thursday prior to that Easter Sunday, the new church was empty with no pews to sit on. The seating miraculously appeared by that Sunday morning.

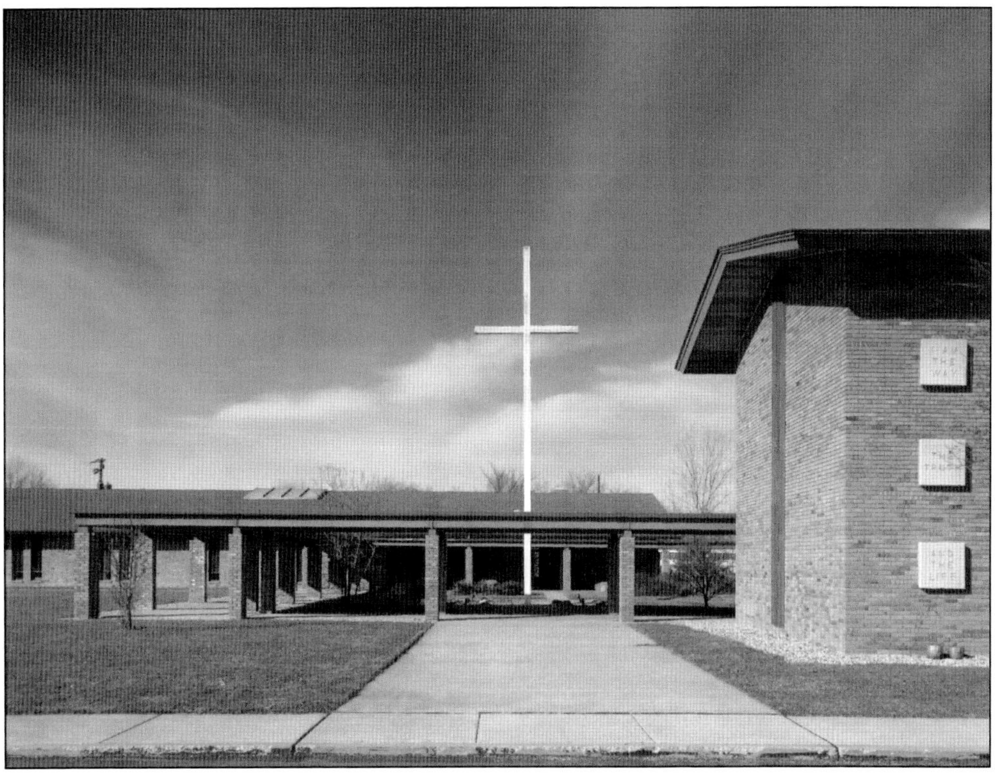

In 1979, the First Baptist Church embarked on a unique fundraising activity. The Multiply Your Talents program encouraged members to use their skills to increase a church-approved investment of $10 and donate their proceeds back to the church. The church invested $1,200, and members raised over $10,000 in return. In the photograph to the right, Lori McComb and Larry Lydick visited the First National Bank & Trust Co. to get a look at the original investment, consisting of 1,200 silver dollars. The successful 10-week program ended in August 1979. In the photograph below, Pastor Marc Hays congratulates Leva Spencer on the success of her pie- and pickle-making venture. She raised $510.

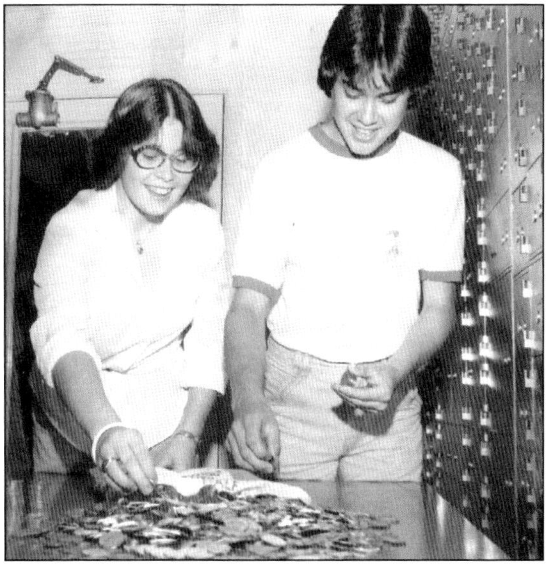

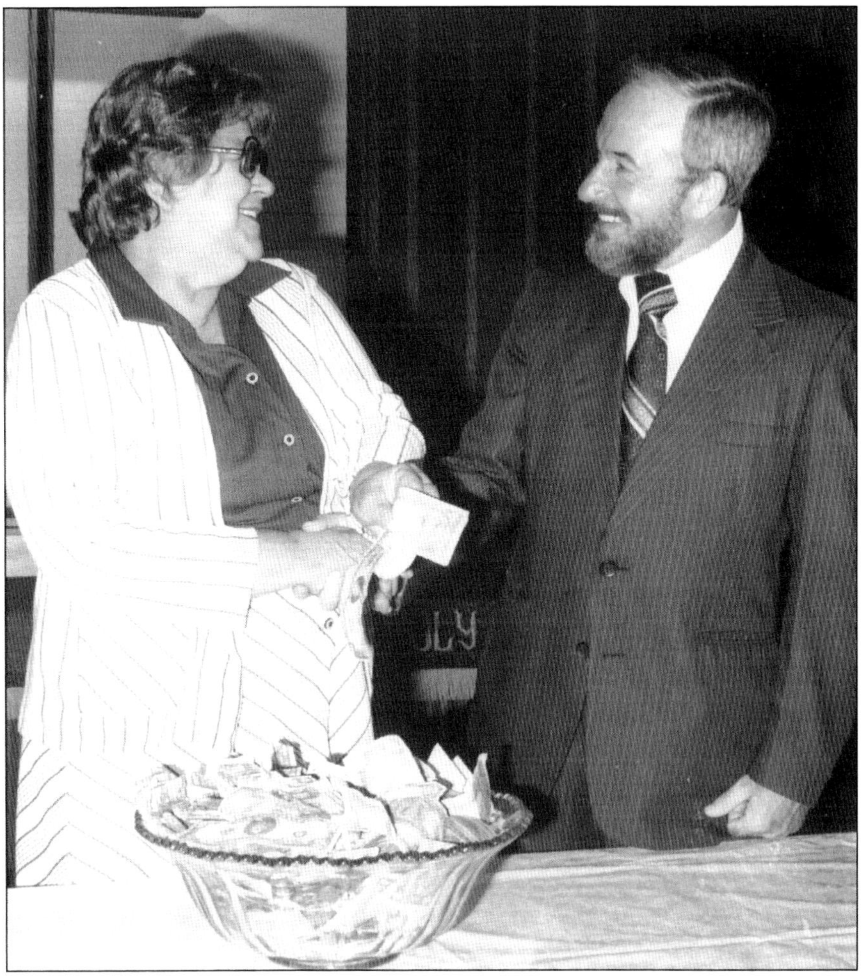

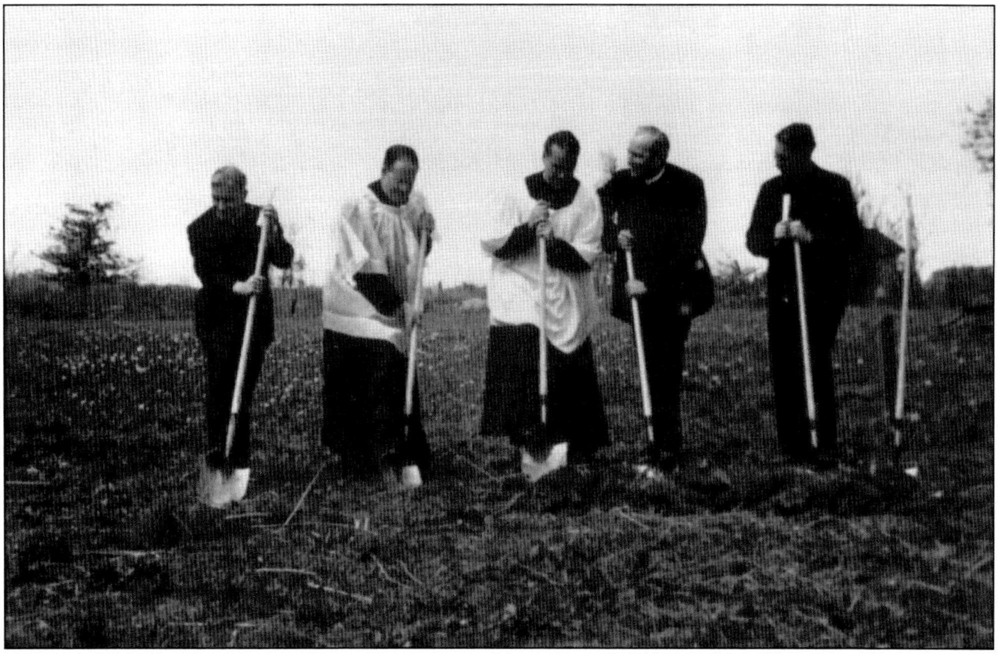

Ground breaking for the new St. Susanna Catholic Church and School occurred on May 3, 1953. Seen in the above photograph from left to right are Father A. McLaughlin, Father Cleary, Father Reidy, Monsignor Goosens, and an unidentified fifth person. Just five months later, the building and school, shown below, were complete. About 1,000 people attended the open house of the church and school on October 17, 1953. Archbishop Paul Schulte of Indianapolis conducted the dedication ceremony, and the *Friday Caller* reported that Maude Hall played the organ. The familiar white church building is located at 1210 East Main Street in Plainfield.

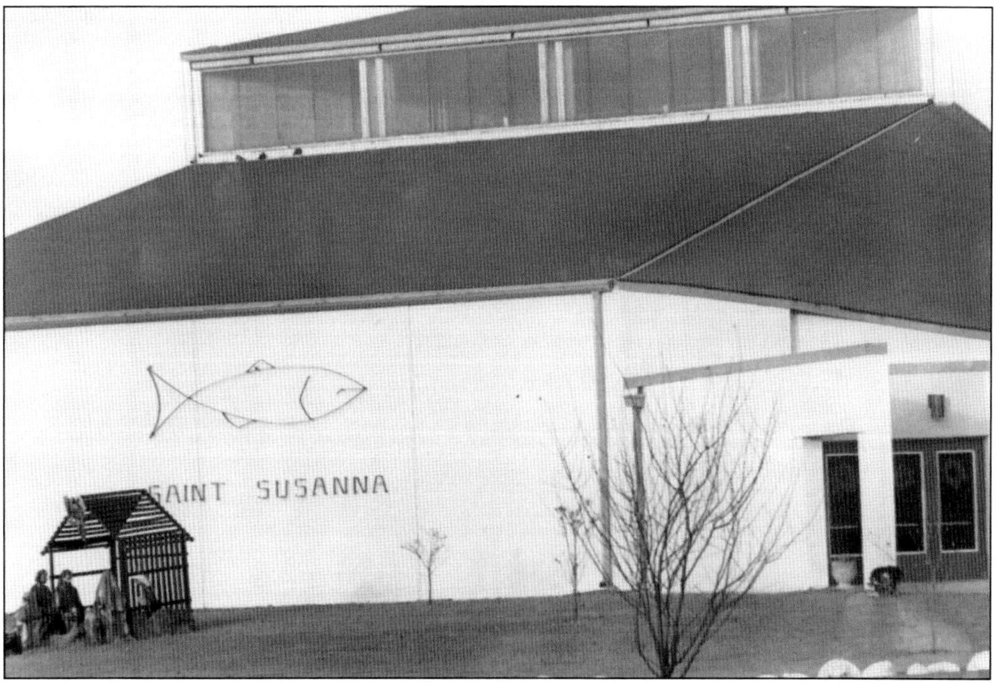

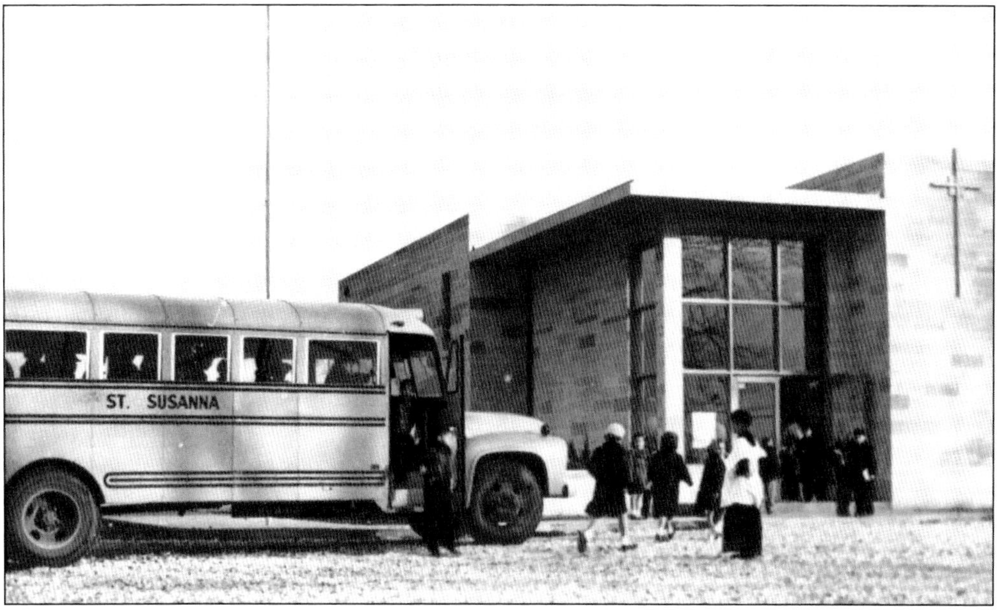

When the St. Susanna School opened on October 13, 1953, about 80 children attended. Today, over 300 students are enrolled in St. Susanna. This photograph shows students arriving on that first day. In its almost 60-year history, St. Susanna has educated hundreds of children in Plainfield and Hendricks County.

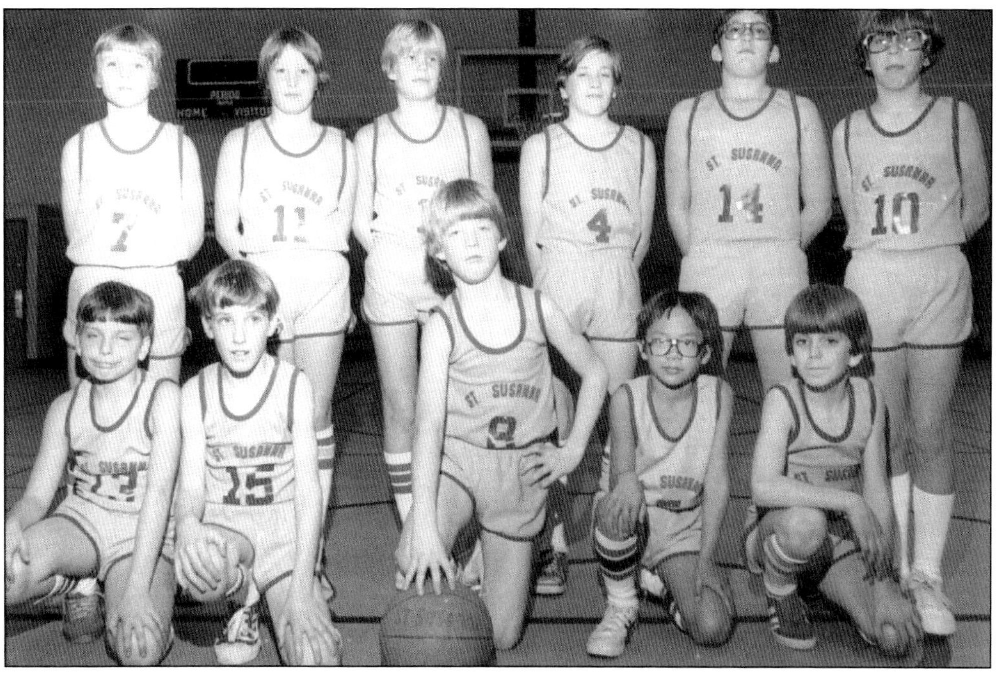

Education involves more than just book learning! This photograph shows the St. Susanna boys basketball team from 1980. The team, which was undefeated, included, from left to right, (first row) Nicky Weiss, Nathan Coleman, Patrick Costello, Chris Darroca, and Chris Dages; (second row) Mike Eickholtz, Brian Satterfield, Kevin Hickam, Arthur Caldwell, Chuck Schooley, and Mike Hummel.

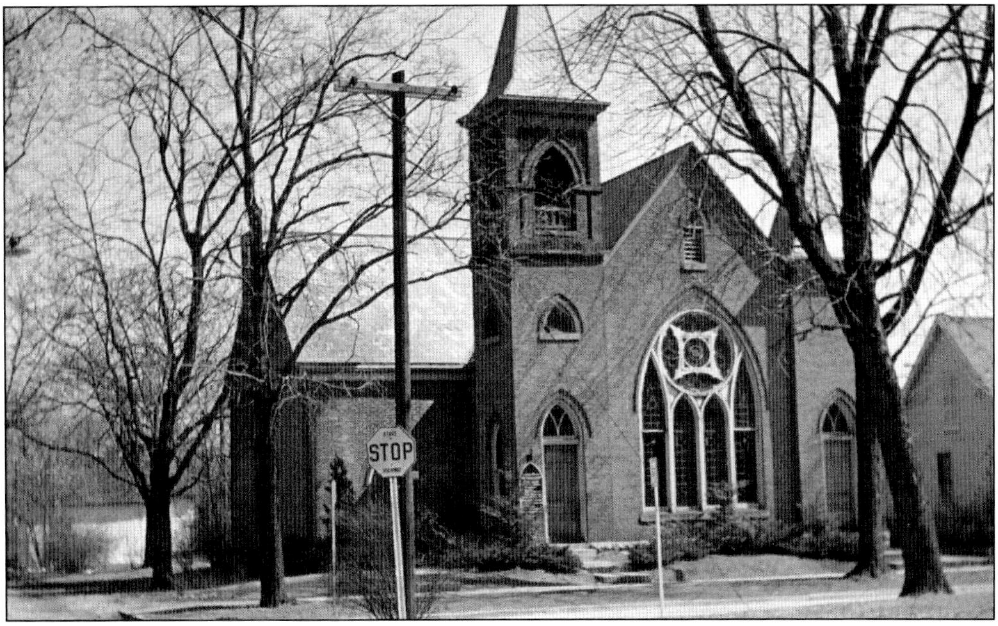

The Plainfield United Methodist Church congregation worshiped at this building, located at 301 South Center Street, from 1891 until 1958. Two other churches have also met in this building—the Plainfield Baptist Church and St. Mark's Episcopal Church. Currently, this building is used as a wedding chapel. From 1845 to 1891, the Methodist members met in a small frame house at 208 S. Mill Street, which is now a residence.

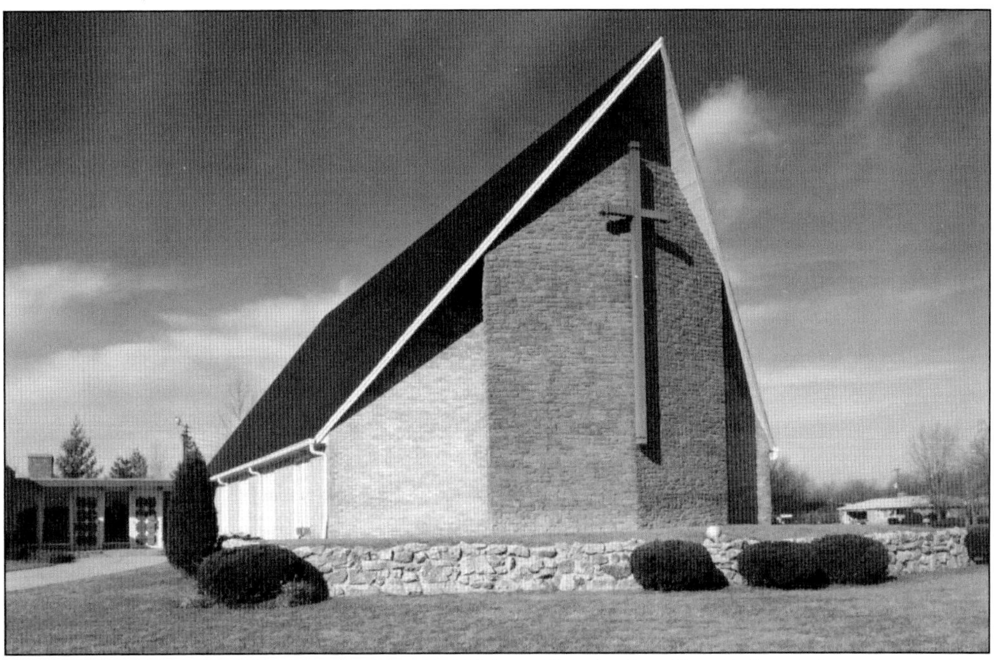

Because of growing membership, the Plainfield United Methodist Church decided to relocate their building. The decision was not without much thought and concern. Church leaders purchased land on the outskirts of Plainfield, and construction began in 1957. Dedicated on September 7, 1958, the current Plainfield United Methodist Church is located at 600 Simmons Street.

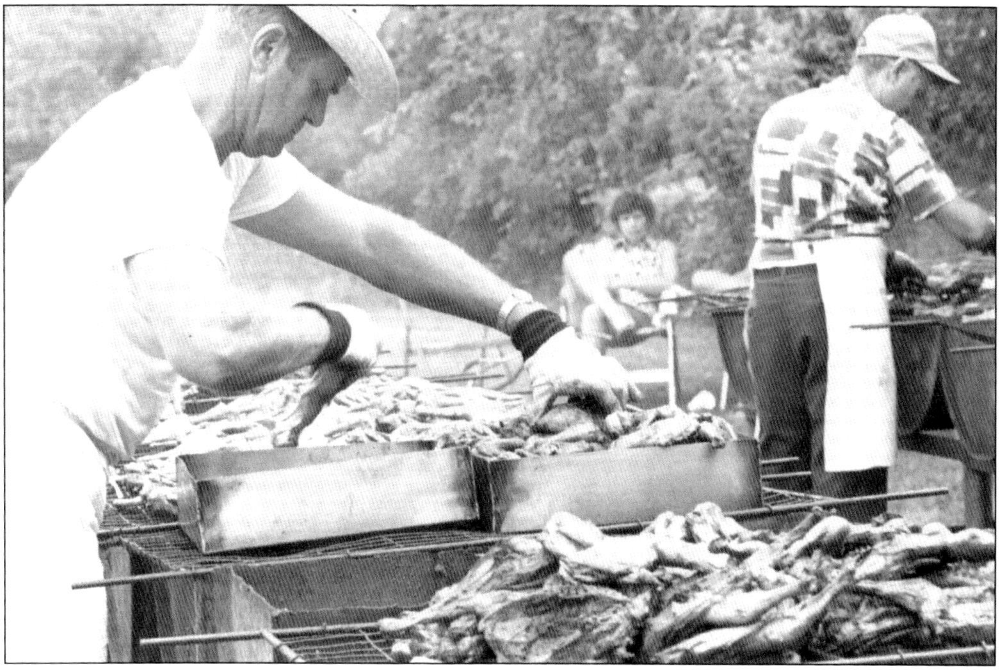

Each year, during the first weekend in August, the Plainfield United Methodist Church hosts a very popular fish fry. Long lines can always be expected, as people anticipate good food and good community fellowship. These two photographs show some of the hard work involved in producing a quality event. The above photograph from August 1977 shows Bill Earl skillfully handling the barbeque chicken. The image below from August 1989 shows John Tate (left), Bill Dalton (center), and Cory Shaffer coordinating the rotation of the chicken on the grill. The event remains a highlight of the summer and has proved so successful that drive-thru lines have been added for those who can't stay to eat.

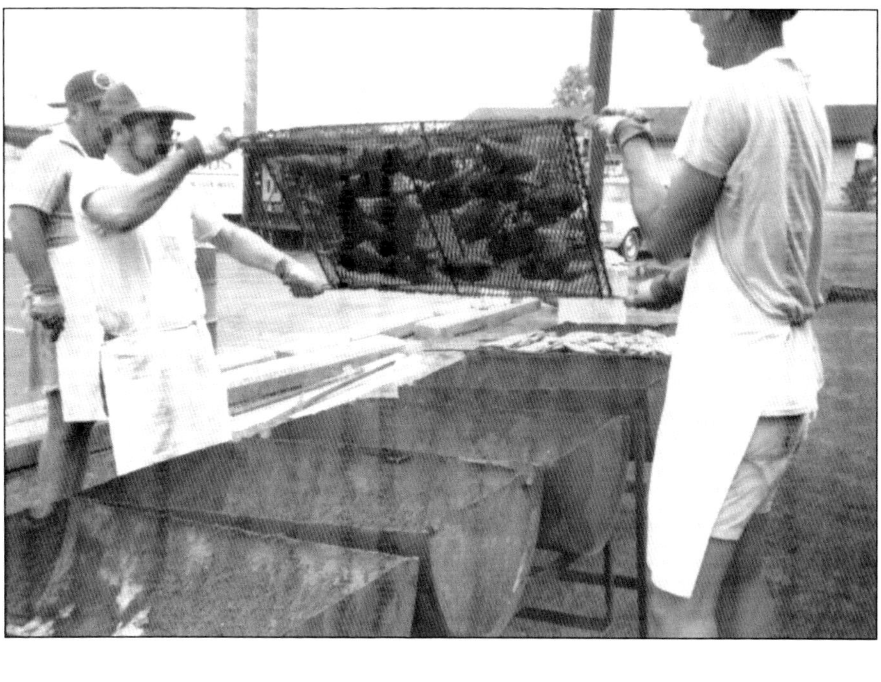

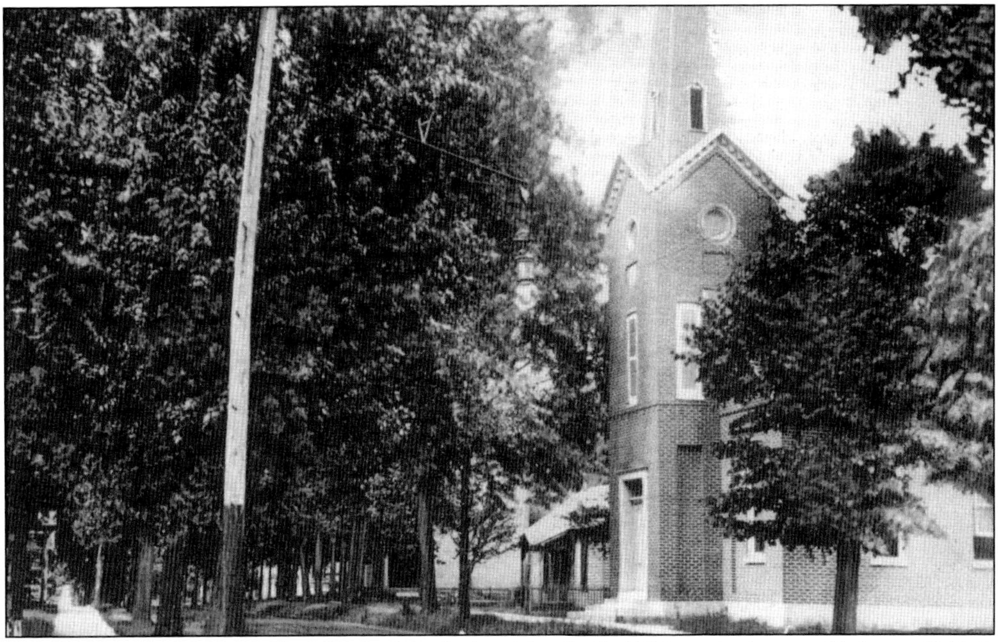

The Plainfield Christian Church was founded on March 29, 1829, in the home of John and Edith Hadley. In 1840, the congregation purchased the site at 201 North Center Street. This photograph shows the tree-lined street and stately brick church building. The Plainfield Christian Church is recognized as Plainfield's oldest established congregation.

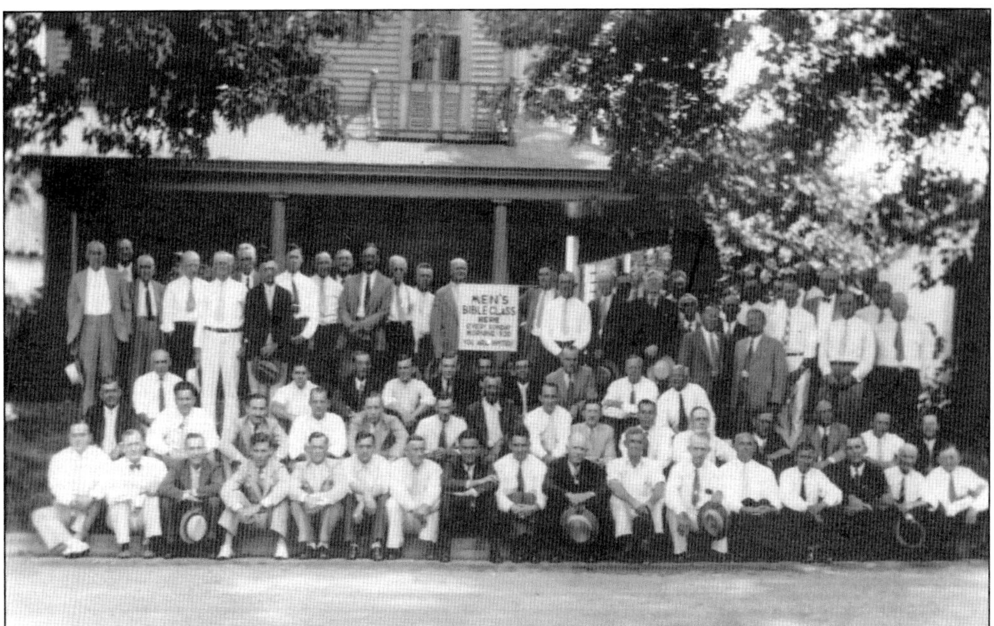

This impressive group of men is the 1933 Plainfield Christian Church men's Bible class. In this photograph, taken on North Center Street, the sign reads "Men's Bible Class Here every Sunday morning 9:20. You are invited!"

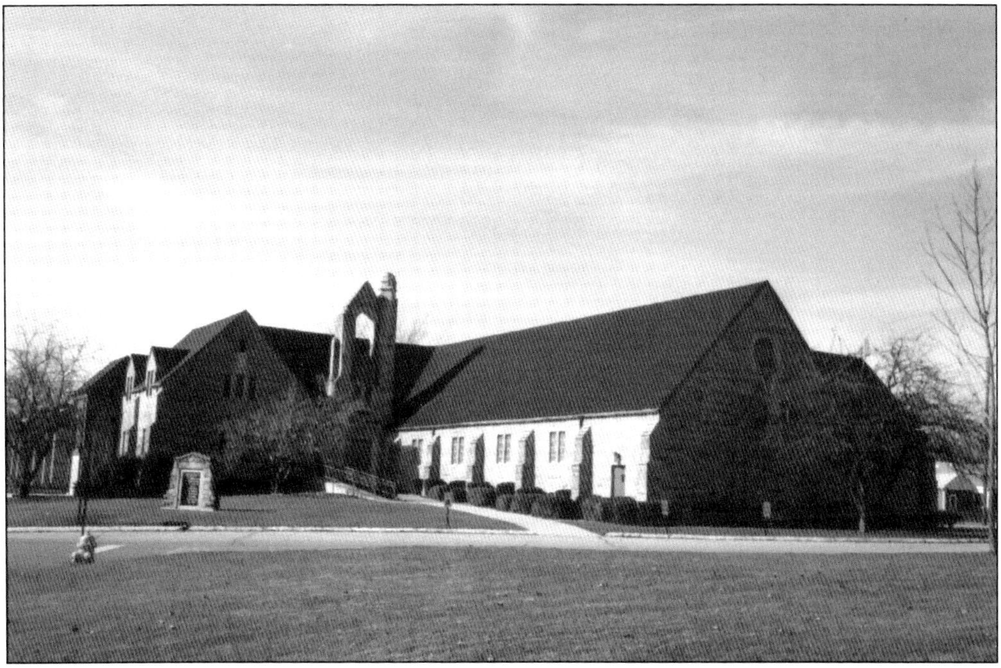

The Plainfield Christian Church relocated to 710 East Buchanan Street in 1955 after purchasing land at the corner of Masten and Buchanan Streets. This new building would provide much needed space for the church, which had outgrown the North Center Street building. The church ground-breaking ceremony was March 28, 1954, and the first service was held on Easter Sunday in 1955.

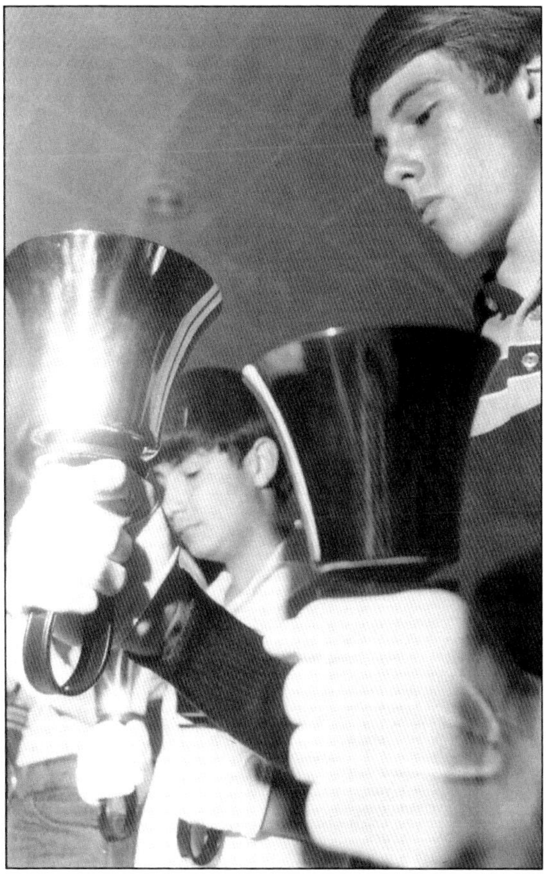

Among the many musical opportunities offered at the Plainfield Christian Church is the Praise Ringers handbell choir, which has been ringing for over three decades. The bell choir was formed in 1978 by then director Nancy Bennett. This photograph from October 1978 features Andy Richmond (right) participating in a rehearsal session.

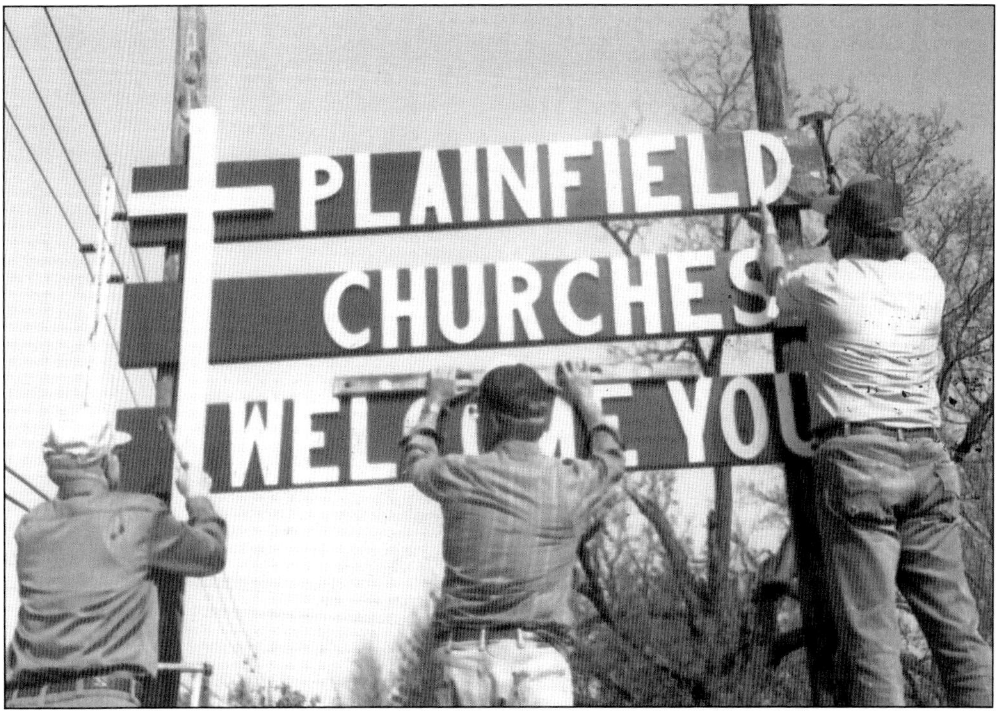

The Plainfield Federation of Churches is an organization that was created to foster interdenominational fellowship and support to the residents of Plainfield. In 1989, the federation members built and erected welcome signs at two locations in Plainfield. Travelers coming into town on State Road 267 or US 40 (west, near the Indiana Boys' School) were greeted with the words "Plainfield Churches Welcome You," as seen in the above photograph. The federation, which is still active, supports many different ministries, including the Weekday Religious Education (WRE) program. WRE provides fourth-grade students the opportunity for nondenominational study of the Bible. In the 1979 photograph below, Anne Rudy teaches a group of young children attending the program at the Plainfield Friends Church.

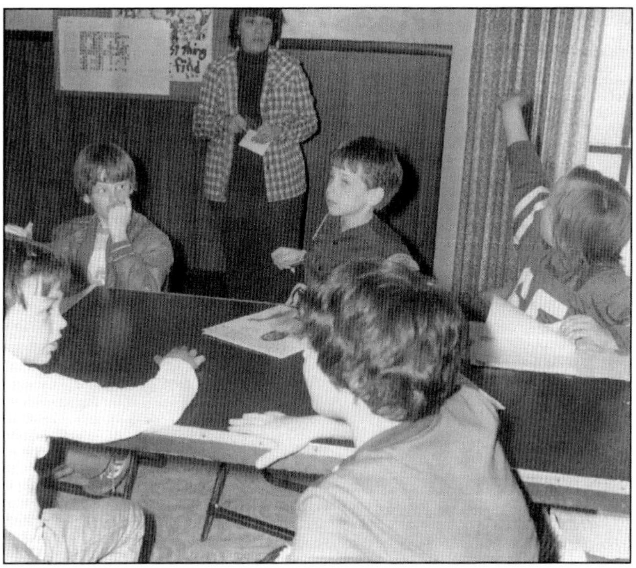

Five

BUSINESSES

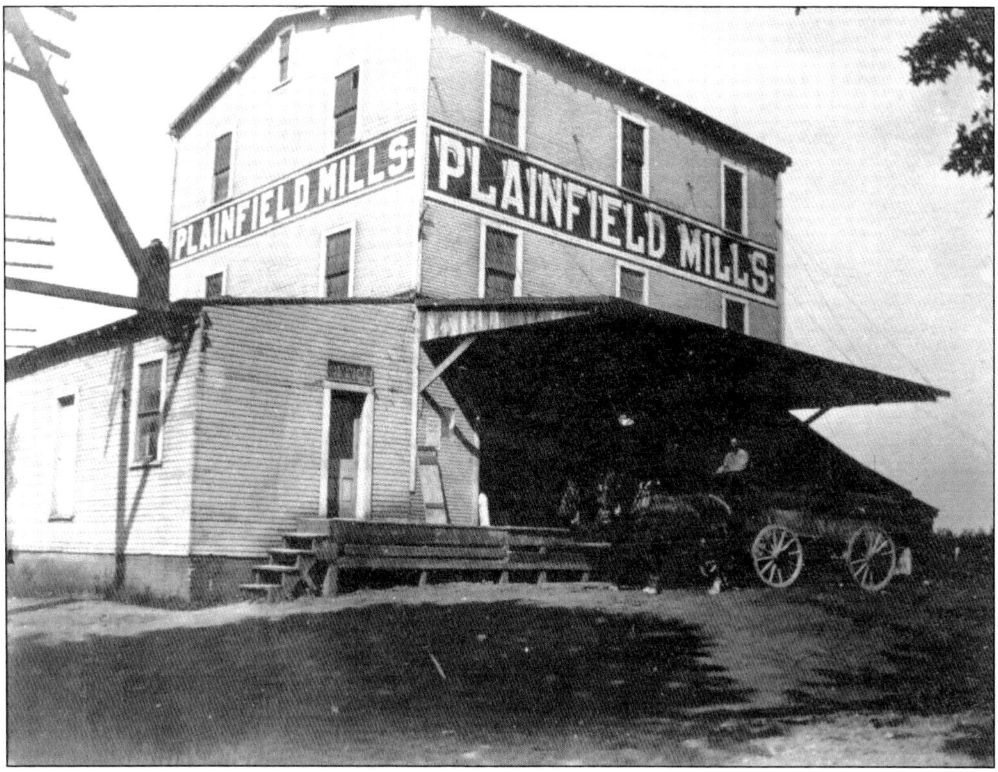

The Plainfield Mill was a grain and flour mill that operated on what is now North Mill Street. Built around 1889, the Plainfield Mill was a 50-barrel mill that handled the grain from area farmers. This photograph shows an unidentified man sitting atop his horse-drawn buggy in front of the mill. The structure was razed in 1958 to make way for the construction of a new post office.

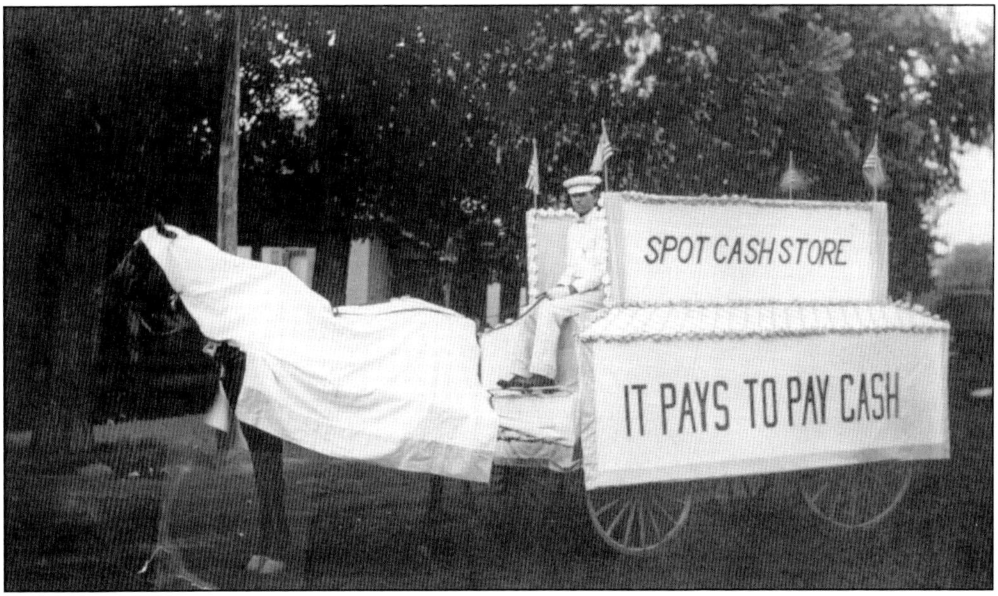

The Spot Cash Store, located in the lower level of the Knights of Pythias building at 115 West Main Street, was a popular dry goods emporium. In 1910, Fred Breedlove formed a partnership with Albert Barlow and purchased the Spot Cash Store from Joseph Prewitt. Barlow died in 1928, and Breedlove then acquired sole ownership of the store. In 1945, Breedlove sold the store to L.B. Hundley, who sold it to a Mr. Davis, who then sold it to Frank and Stella Smith. Except for a brief time, it was always known as the Spot Cash Store. The two photographs seen here show the store during different periods. The horse-drawn wagon float, shown above, is ready for a parade in Plainfield. Pictured below in the interior view of the store from left to right are shopkeepers Nona Lisbee, Albert Barlow, Emma D. Stone, and Fred Breedlove.

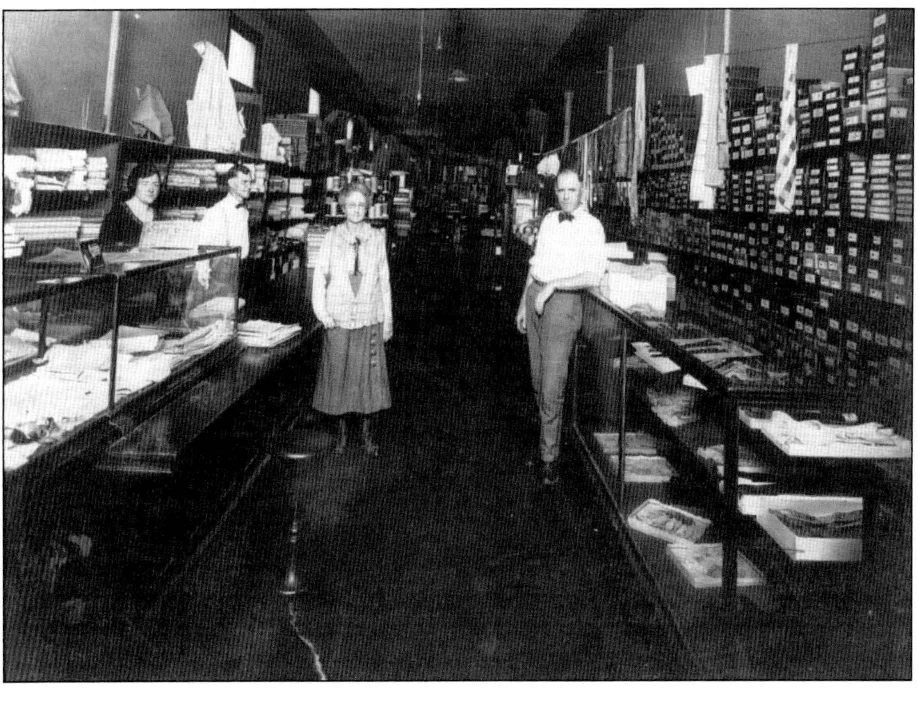

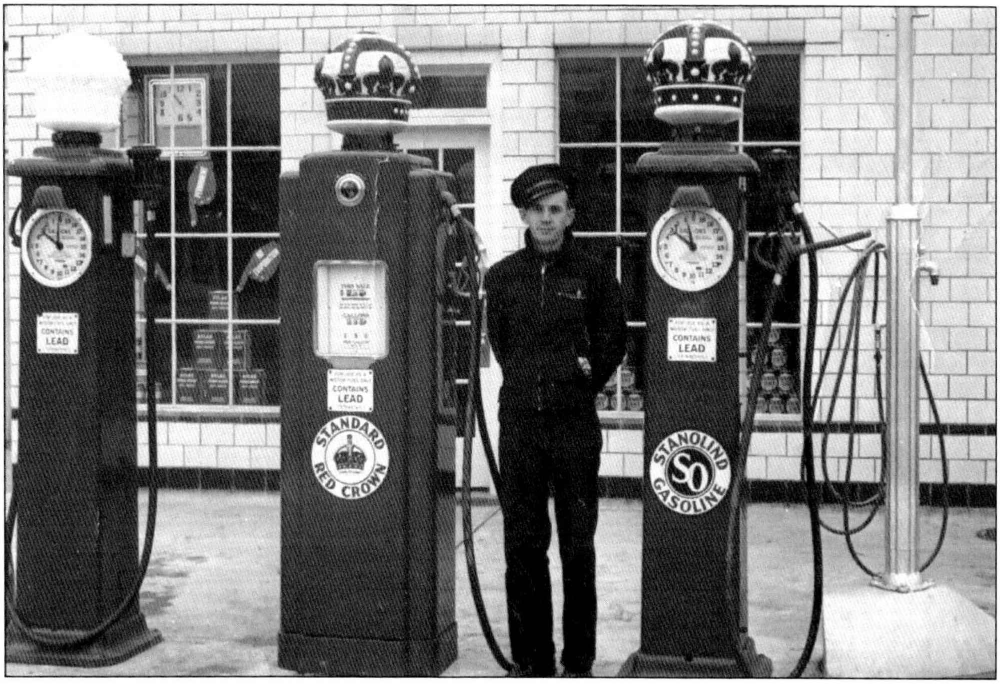

Owner George Sims proudly stands outside his service station in this 1940 photograph. The Sims Station was located at 326 West Main Street (on the northeast corner of Main and West Streets) and opened for business in December 1940. Notice that Stanolind gas is offered for sale. Stanolind Gas formed in 1931 and was a subsidiary of Indiana Standard Gas.

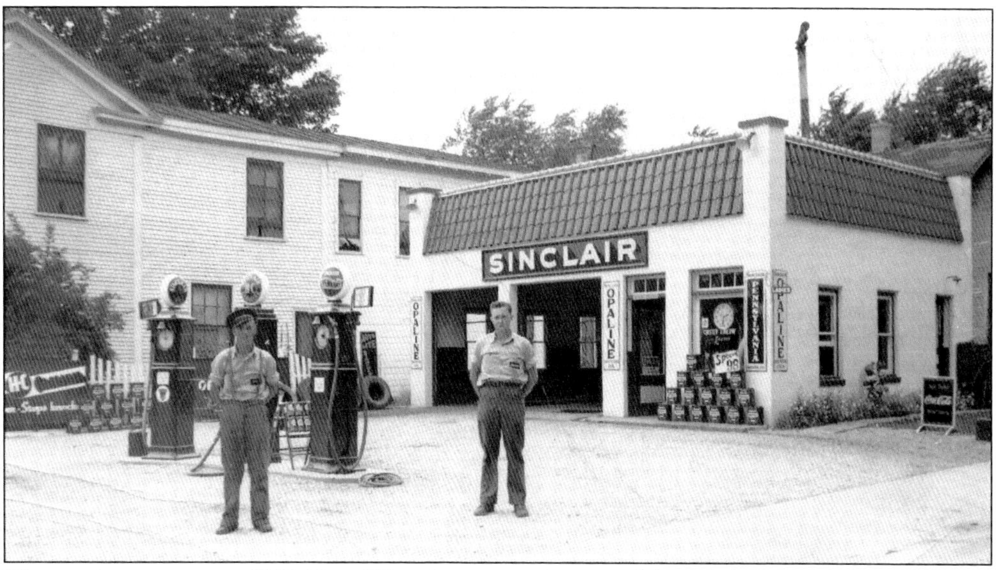

The northwest corner of US 40 and East Street was the site of the Sinclair Gas Station. First run by Paul Hardin, the station was taken over in February 1941 by Charles Springer and renamed Springer's Sinclair Station. The station sat on the site that previously housed the first Plainfield Public Library, Dr. J.C. Stafford's medical office, Oris Jordan's tailor shop, and the Green Tea Pot restaurant. Most residents will recognize this as the corner where Hill's Cobbler Shop now stands.

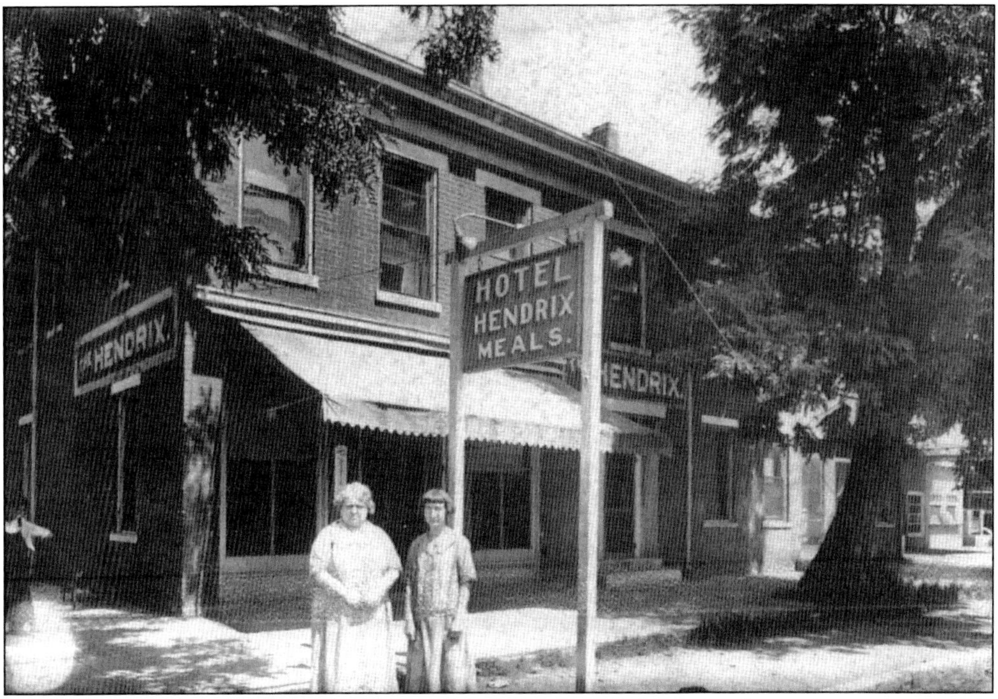

Originally erected around 1855, the building located at 104 East Main has housed many businesses, most of which were hotels. Known as the Commercial Hotel, the Hendrix Hotel, and the Van Buren Hotel, the building has retained its imposing look over the years. The hotel had several owners, including William Fawcett, Isaac Holton, and John McClain, and was known as the Commercial Hotel. The hotel was remodeled in 1915, at which time a heating plant was installed along with modern appliances. The 26-room hotel also got a new name: the Hendrix Hotel. Later, the name was changed to the Van Buren Hotel. The above photograph is from 1916, when the building was renovated and renamed the Hendrix Hotel. Minnie Richardson (left) and Vera Kersey stand near the new hotel sign. The late-1930s photograph below shows the building when it was the Van Buren Hotel. The Plainfield Post Office, with its door on the corner, shared space with the hotel. Residents will recognize this as the current location of Headquarters Barbershop.

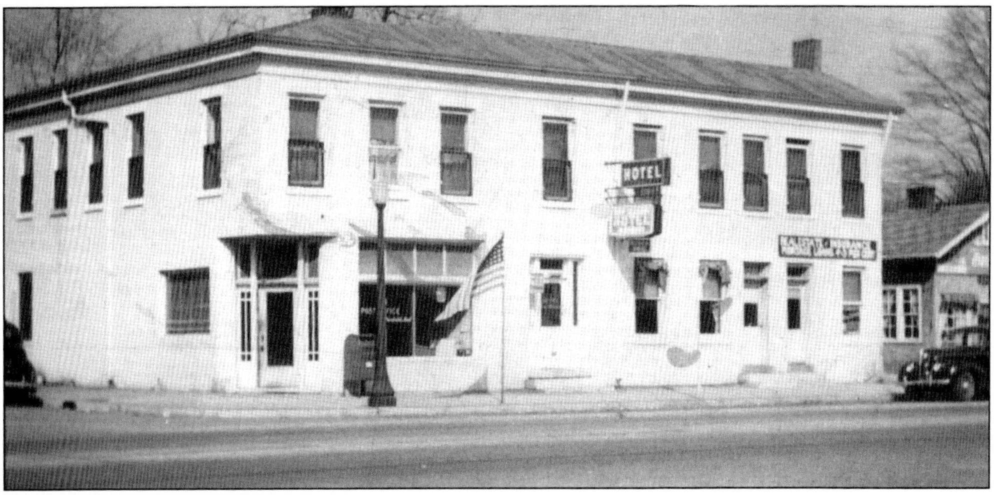

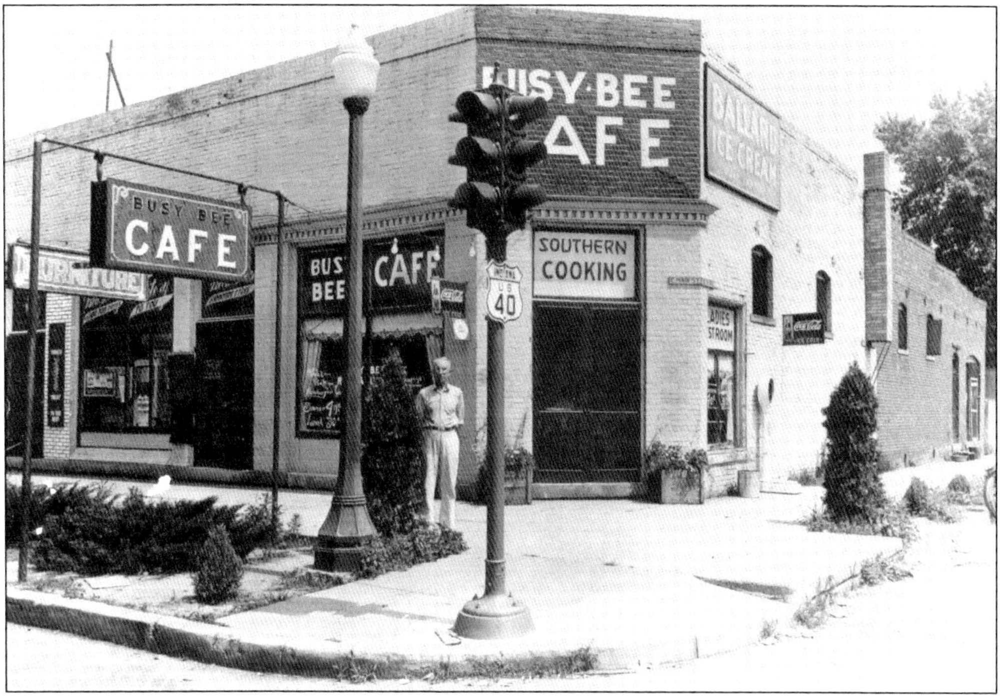

One of the more popular locations for a restaurant in Plainfield was the southeast corner of Main and Vine Streets. In 1905, Roy Hiatt moved a home from this site and erected the building with the familiar angled doorway. Between 1905 and 1919, this building housed two box ball alleys, a grocery store, and four different drug stores. In 1919, Dr. Shearer established a restaurant in the front part of the building. Seen in the 1934 photograph above, it was known as the Busy Bee Café. Later, it was also known as Chrisman's Restaurant, Randall's Café, and Stacey's Café. The photograph shows owner A.C. Willis standing in front of the Busy Bee. Pictured below is the interior of the Busy Bee restaurant. Employees of the establishment from left to right are Anna Whitt, unidentified, A.C. Willis, unidentified, and Mary Ellen Douglas King. Willis sold the store to Jesse Chrisman in 1939.

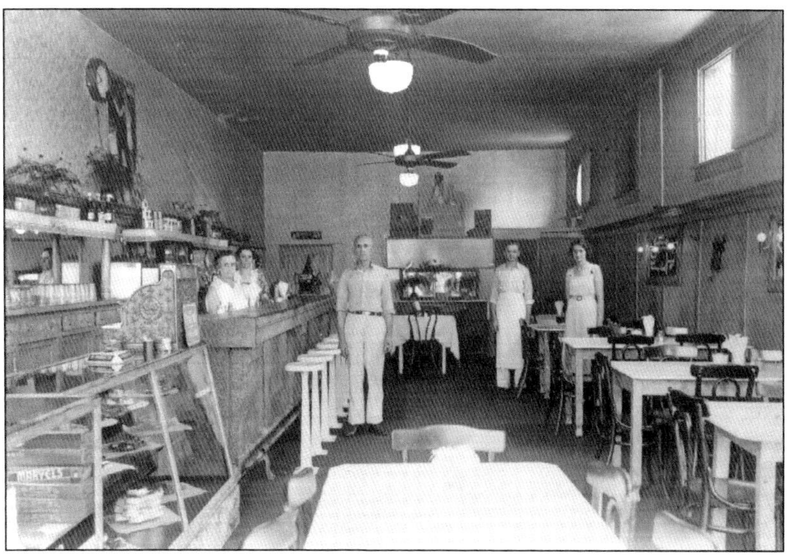

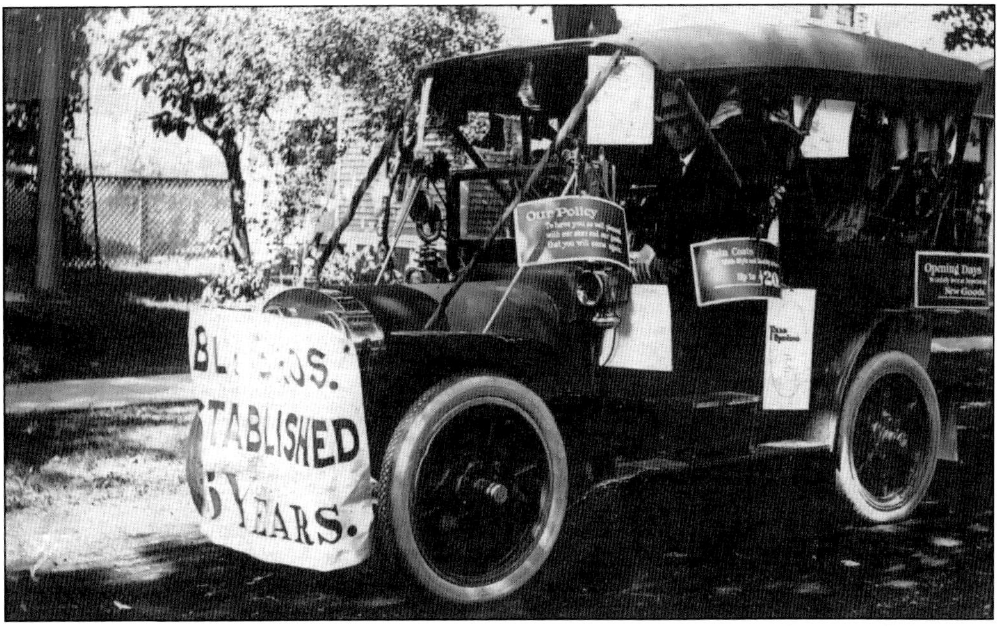

On August 13, 1896, brothers Emmett and Dot Bly, ages 18 and 19 respectively, opened their first store, Bly Bros. Dry Goods. The store's first location was at 104 West Main Street, and by August 1897, sales had increased their business so much, they relocated a few doors down to 120 West Main Street. Dot became ill and died in 1905 at age 28. His brother continued to run the business, keeping the name Bly Bros. Emmett Bly is seen here driving their "float" in a local parade.

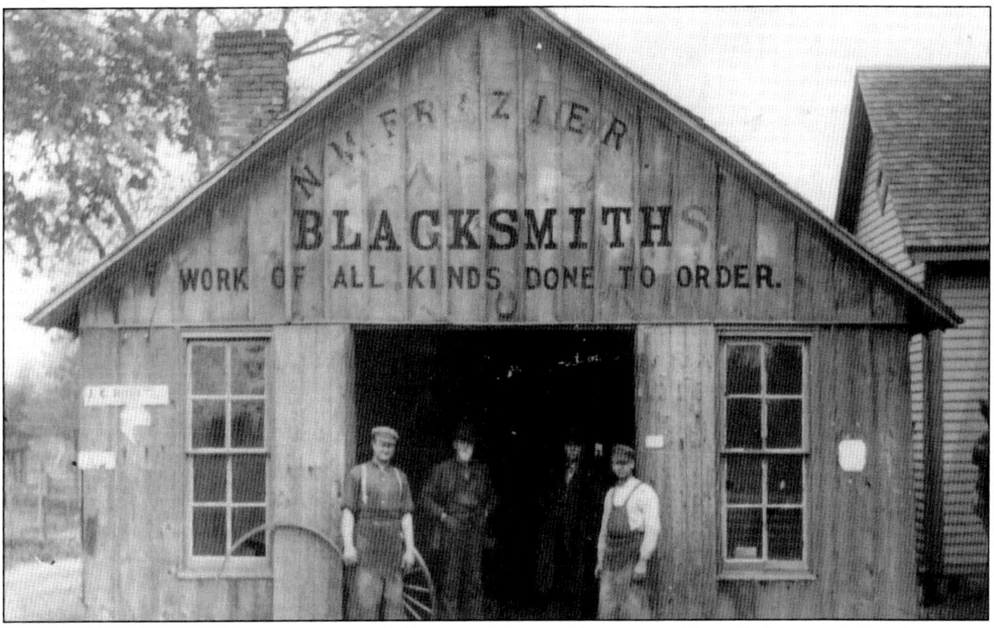

Located on the northeast corner of West and Main Streets in Plainfield was N.M. Frazier's blacksmith shop. Frazier was born in Guilford County, North Carolina, in 1849 and moved to Plainfield at age three. He was in business in Plainfield for over 40 years. Seen in this photograph from left to right are Frank Frazier, Nehrus Frazier, unidentified, and Ivy Newby. Note the lucky horseshoe hanging above the doorway.

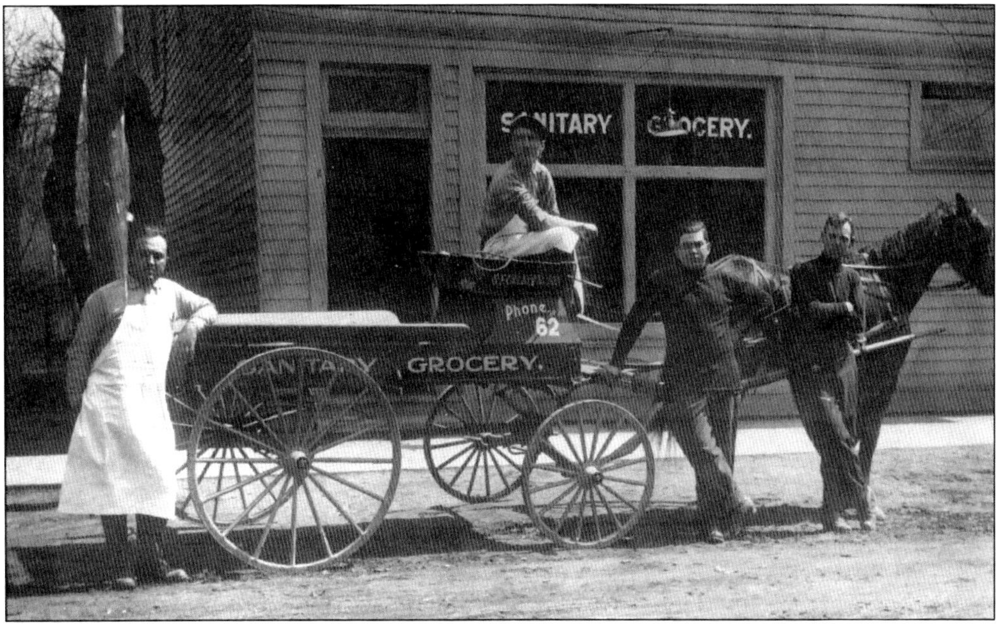

Making its debut on September 30, 1911, was the Sanitary Grocery, owned by G.F. Calbert and his son. The store was originally located near 117 South Vine Street in the old Red Man's Hall, which no longer exists, but eventually moved north one block to the southeast corner of Vine and Main Streets. Shown in this 1911 photograph from left to right are Fred Calbert, Oscar Kanter, Todd Calbert, and Orla Johnson. The store was sold to Harry E. Wilson on August 17, 1913.

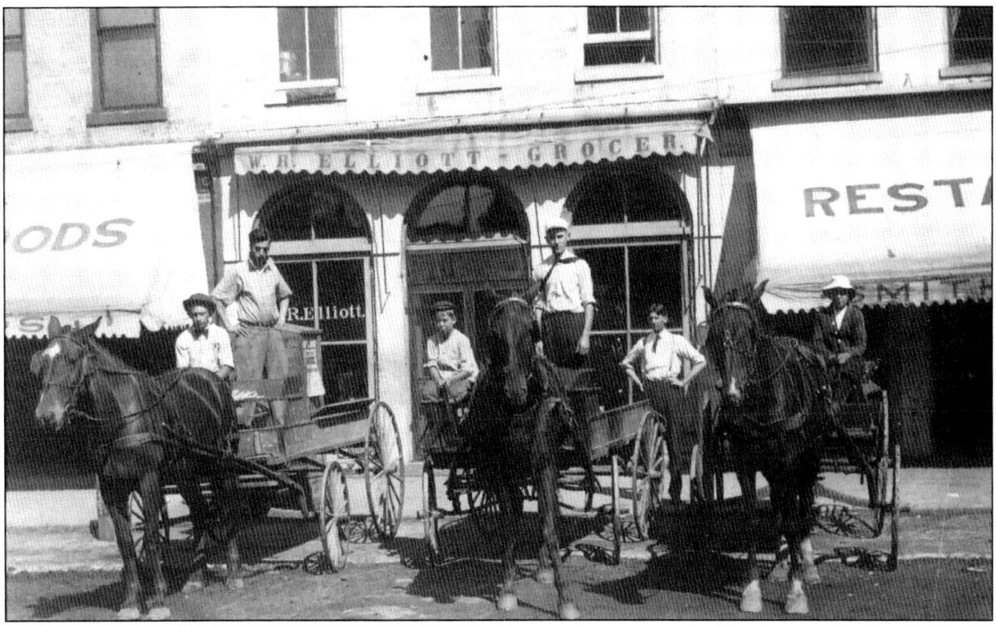

Another local Plainfield grocer was the W.R. Elliott Grocery Store, located at 116 West Main Street. Elliott opened his store on January 11, 1905, and was noted for having stayed in business in downtown Plainfield for over 40 years. In 1947, Elliott sold to Robert Pavy, who opened Pavy's Grocery. This photograph shows Elliott standing on the sidewalk in front of the window. Mrs. Elliott, wearing a white hat, is seated in the wagon on the right.

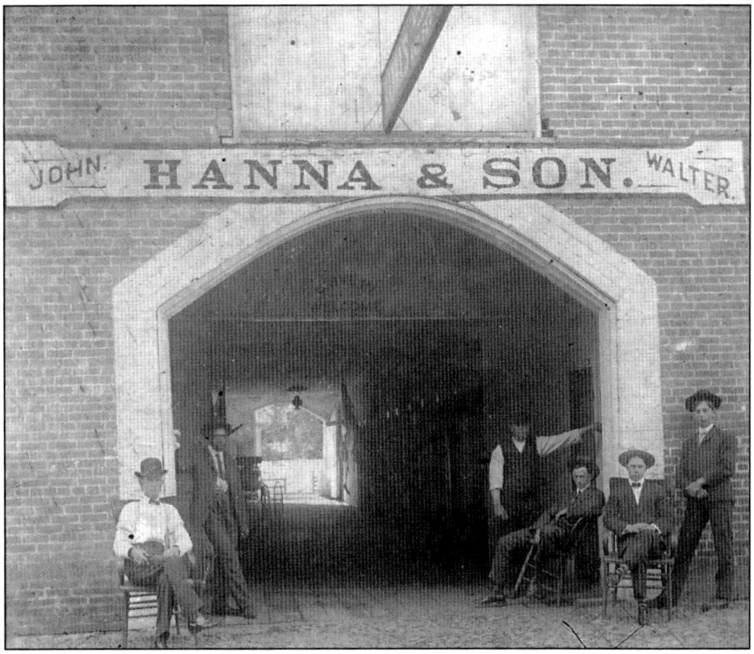

Erected around 1867, the building housing the Hanna and Son livery stable was razed in 1912 to make room for the new Carnegie public library. The structure was built by Alva Gossett especially for use as a livery barn and was not used for any other purpose. John Hanna purchased the barn for $810 in 1900 from the estate of Harlan Hadley. He sold it 12 years later to the library board for $2,800.

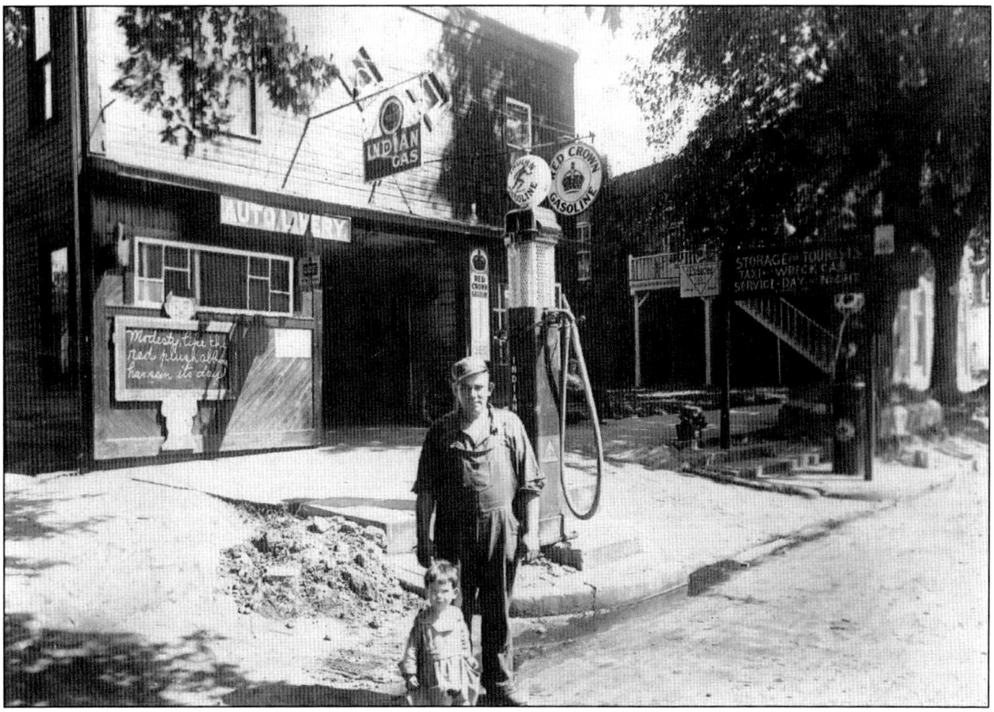

Howard Christopher's Auto Livery was located at 210 West Main Street, next to the Hiss Building. This photograph features Howard and daughter Mary Louise standing in front of the livery. Christopher eventually evolved his business into a wrecking service, which was continued by his son upon his death. One interesting story regarding Howard Christopher Jr. is that he owned a chimpanzee from the Belgian Congo. The chimpanzee would ride with him on his wrecker, and as soon as he stopped, the chimp would hop down and help with the cable and hooks.

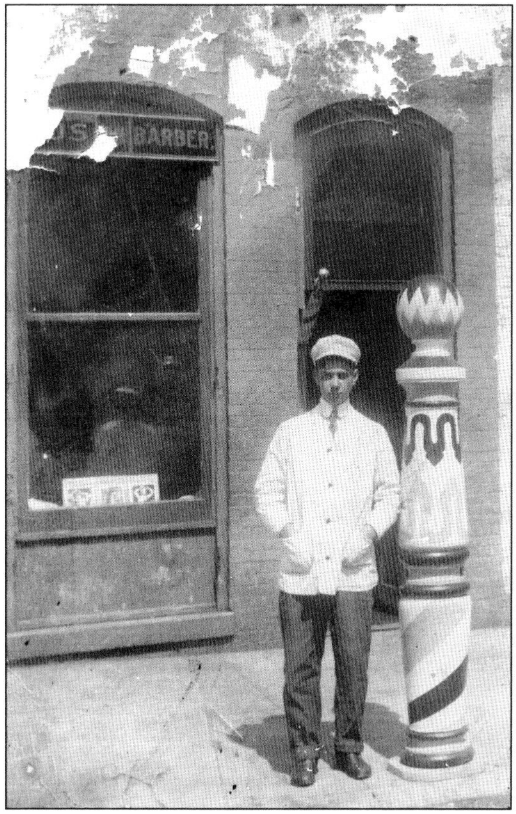

The Krebs men spent many years barbering the hair and faces of the men in Plainfield. The photograph to the right shows a young Gus Krebs in front of his barbershop, on the north side of Main Street in the Symons block about 1917. Later, in January 1925, Gus and Guy Krebs opened a new barbershop across the street. Their store was located on the west side of the first level of the Knights of Pythias building at 115 West Main Street. The image below shows the interior of the store. The barbers from left to right are Guy Krebs, Gus Krebs, and George Krebs.

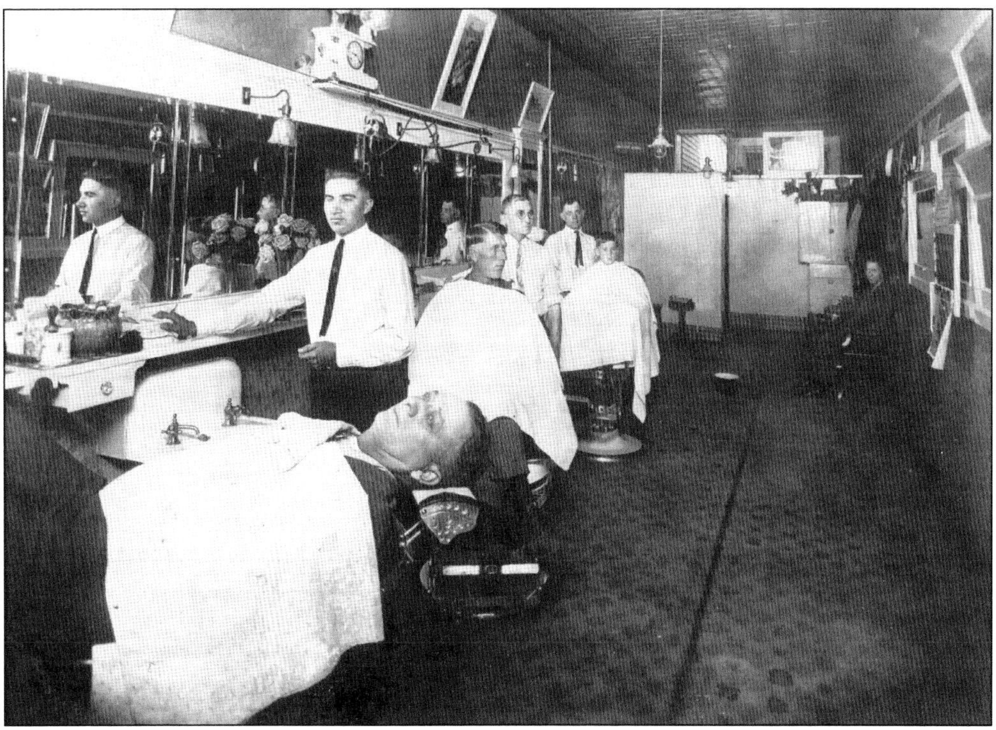

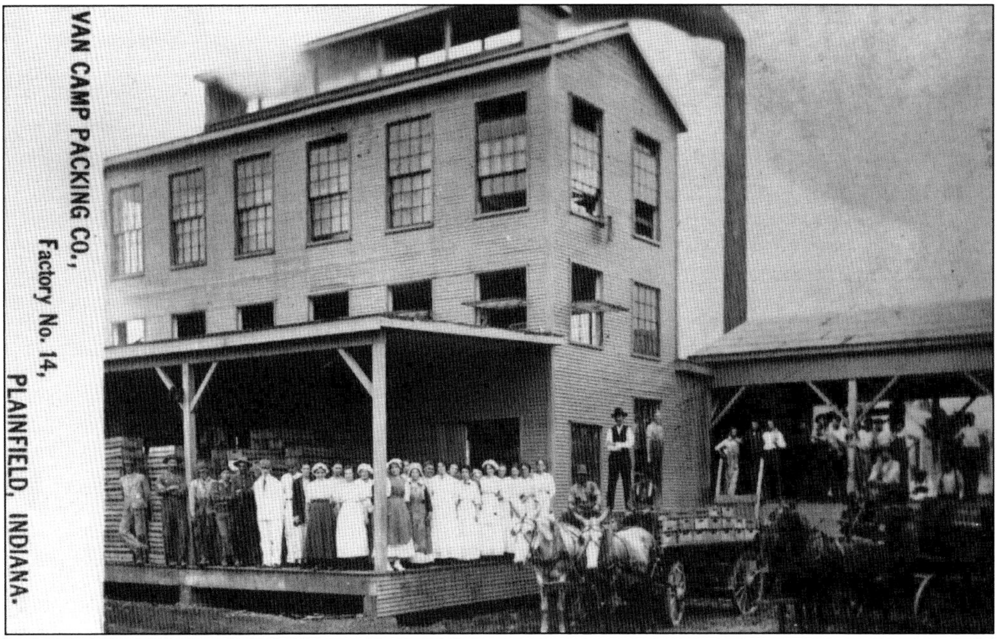

The Van Camp Packing Company was founded in Indianapolis, Indiana, in 1861, when Gilbert Van Camp began his fruit and vegetable canning business. Van Camp Packing Company Factory No. 14 began operations in Plainfield on September 13, 1913. The plant was located in a large building on the east side of North Avon Avenue near the railroad tracks. The plant, which processed tomatoes grown by area farmers, was in business through the late 1930s. Van Camp eventually merged with the Stokely Company in 1933 to form Stokely–Van Camp, Inc. In 1983, the brand passed to Quaker Oats, which purchased it from Stokely–Van Camp. Quaker Oats, in turn, sold the brand to Con Agra in 1995.

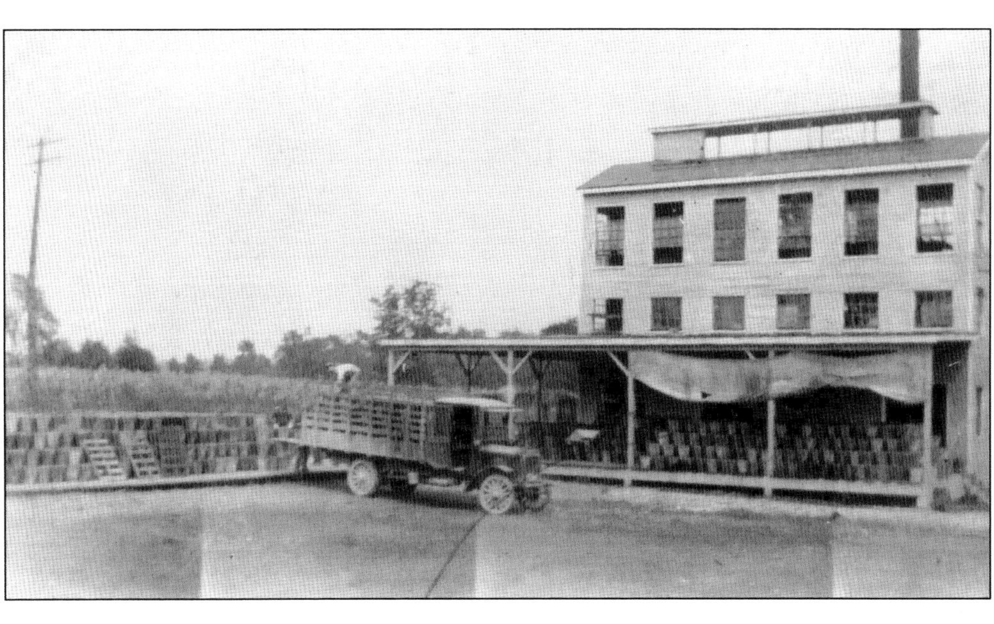

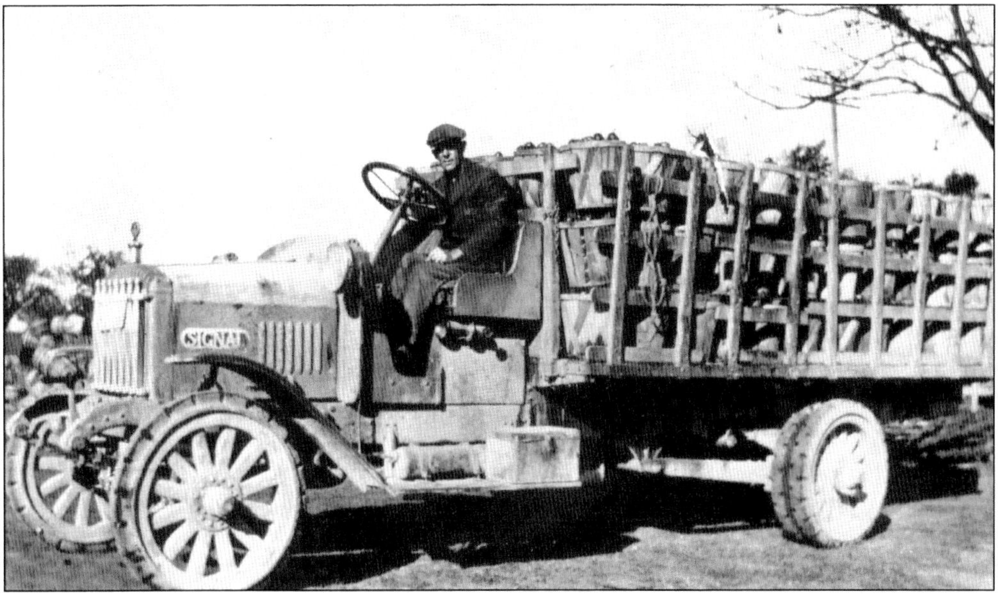

Driver Layton Bradford transports baskets of tomatoes from local farmers to the Van Camp Packing Plant No. 14 on North Avon Avenue. The truck is outfitted with solid rubber tires to better withstand the weight of the tomato freight.

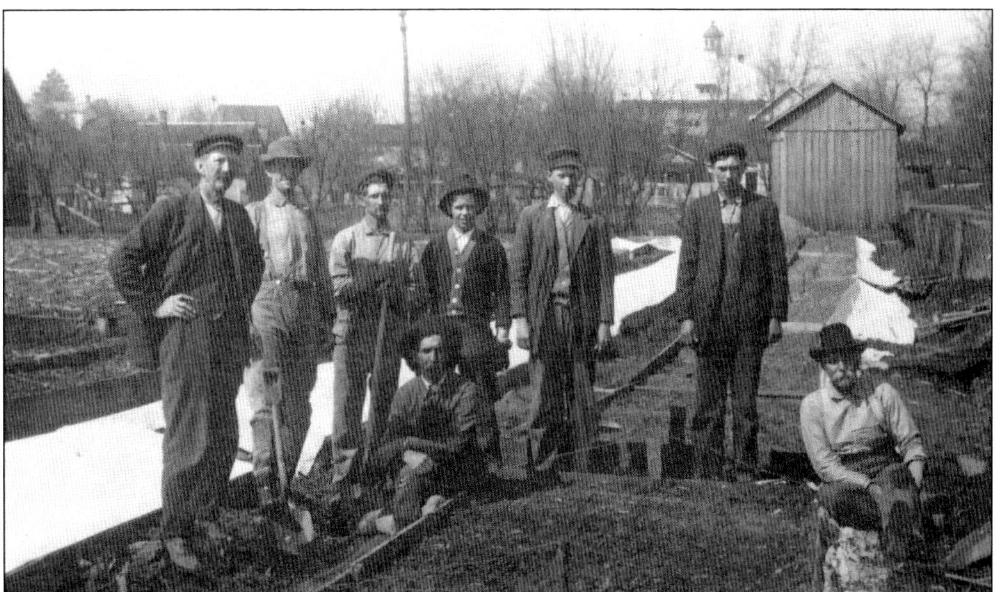

Near the Van Camp packing plant, James Barlow (far left) and crew prepare beds for soon-to-be-planted tomato plants. Other area farmers also grew and sold crops of tomato plants to the Van Camp company. East Grade Elementary School is visible in the background.

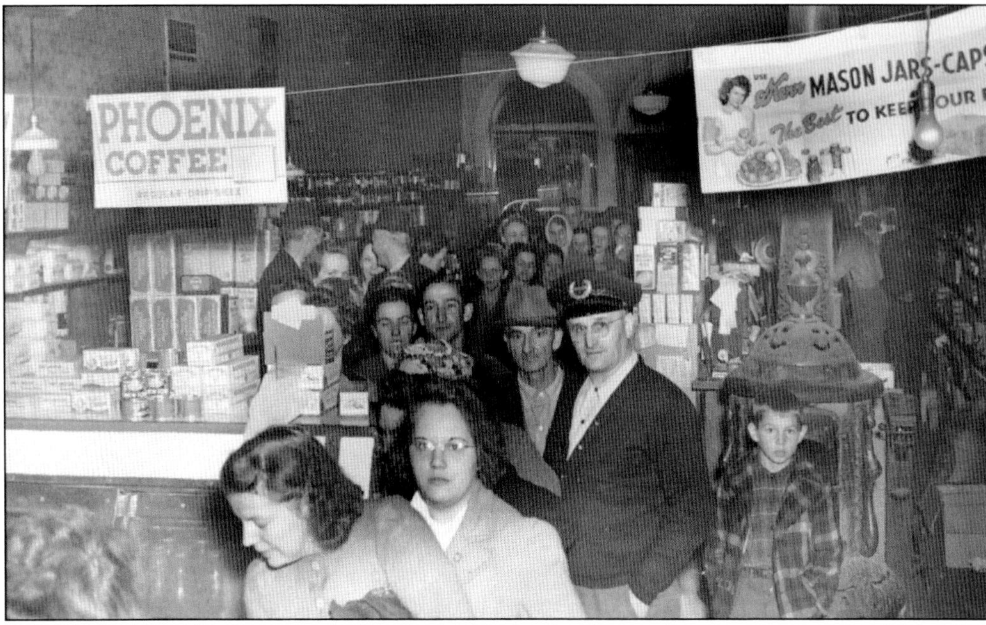

In October 1947, Pavy's Grocery customers celebrate the lessened ration restrictions of the Office of Price Administration (OPA). From 1941 to 1947, the OPA had the power to ration consumer items, including meats, coffee, tires, shoes, nylon, sugar, and gasoline. Joel Chandler, wearing his cardigan sweater and official cap, was the night watchman for the Plainfield Police Department. Pavy's Grocery was located at 118 West Main Street. The store opened on April 7, 1947, and closed in 1954. Robert Pavy had purchased the former Elliott Grocery Store from the estate of W.R. Elliott, who had successfully operated his independent grocery business at this location until his death.

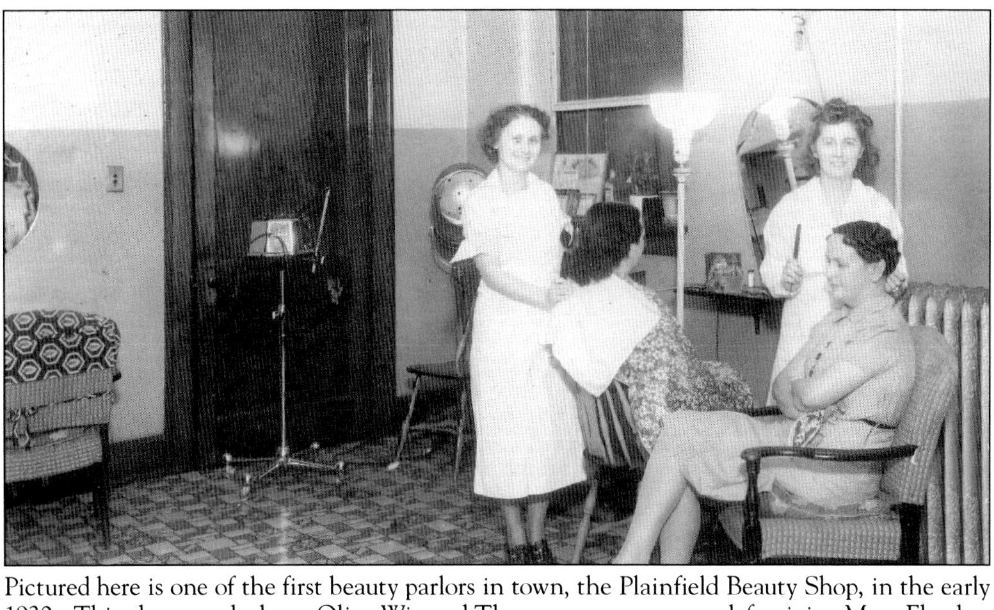

Pictured here is one of the first beauty parlors in town, the Plainfield Beauty Shop, in the early 1930s. This photograph shows Olive Winsted Thompson, operator on left, giving Mary Fletcher a permanent; on the right, Dorothy Winsted Carneal is ready to comb out Mrs. Hansen's hair. The shop was located in the lower level of the Masonic building at 110 South Center Street.

The First National Bank, seen here when it was located at 101 West Main Street, started out in 1903 in a smaller building a few doors west. In February 1930, C.M. Havens, then president of the bank, sold the original lot and purchased the property on the southwest corner of Main and Vine Streets. This photograph shows how the bank looked for many years. First National Bank eventually expanded west and owned half of the block.

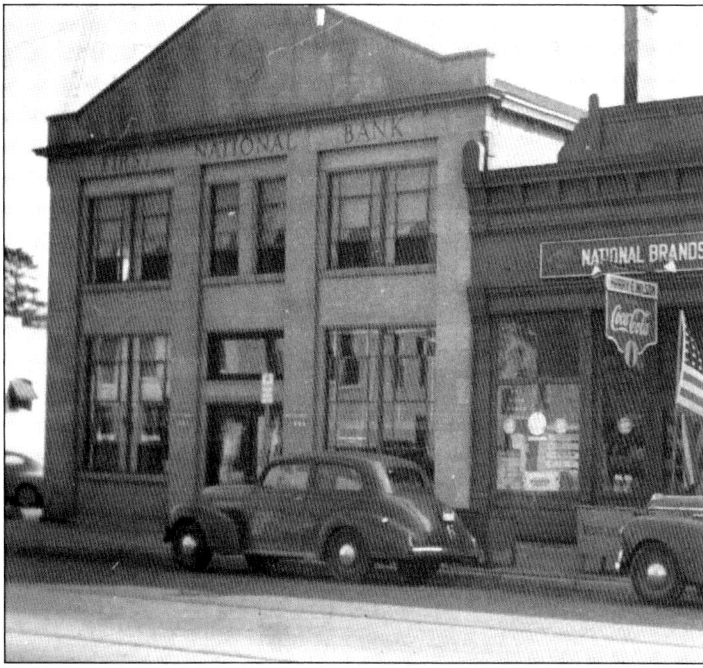

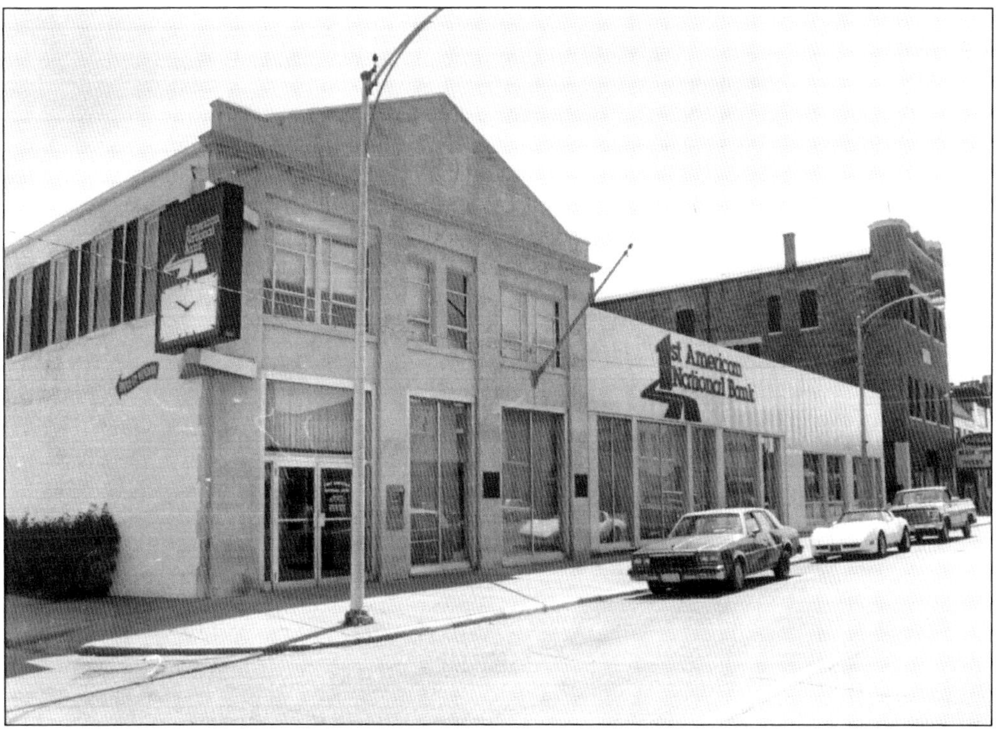

The First National Bank stood prominently on the southwest corner of Vine Street and US 40 at 101 West Main Street. The bank offered one of Plainfield's first drive-up banking windows, which curved inside the parking lot. The bank changed hands several times, and pictured here in 1985, it was the First American National Bank. Eventually, this building was razed to make way for a new bank with the same original name of First National Bank.

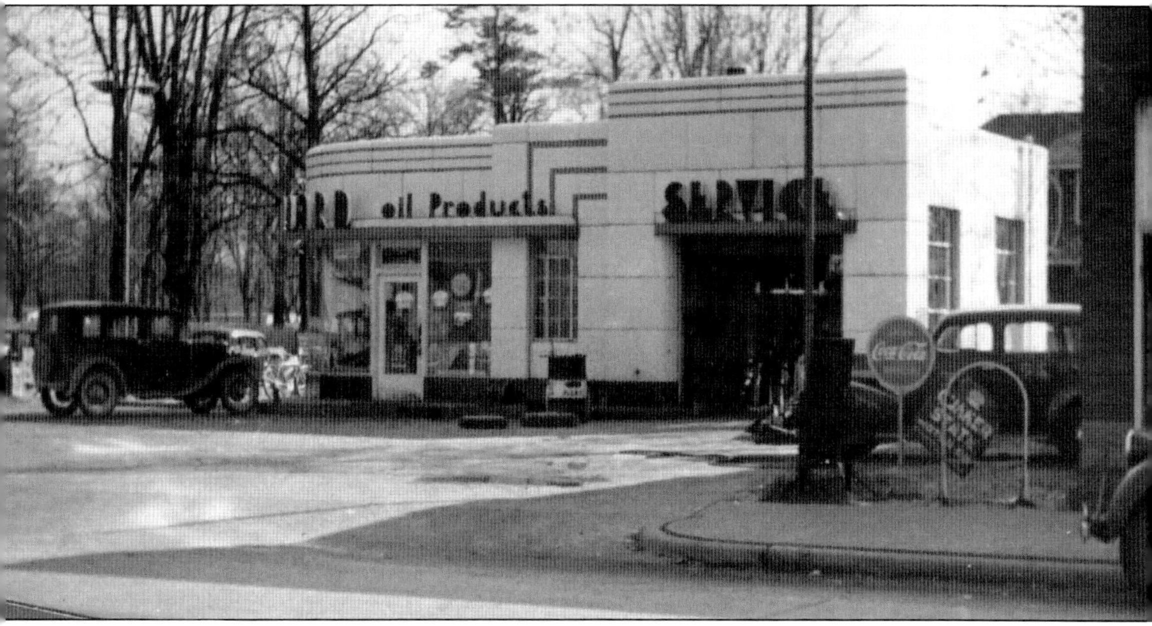

At one time, the southwest corner of Main and East Streets was home to Adna Moon's Standard Service gas station. Moon leased and managed the station from the Standard Oil Company in 1925. In September 1937, Standard built a new and improved building, as seen in this photograph. The design of the station architecture is reminiscent of the Art Deco style. The new station was made of ivory porcelain, enamel, and plate glass, and was trimmed in red and blue. On January 6, 1938, the *Plainfield Messenger* newspaper reported, "The new station is of ultra-modern design and one of the few of this design to be erected in Indiana thus far. The fact that the Standard Oil Co. saw fit to build such a sizable, complete and modern station supplying the newest pumps, indicates in a tangible way the fact that this particular station and location is one of the important units in Standard's distribution system."

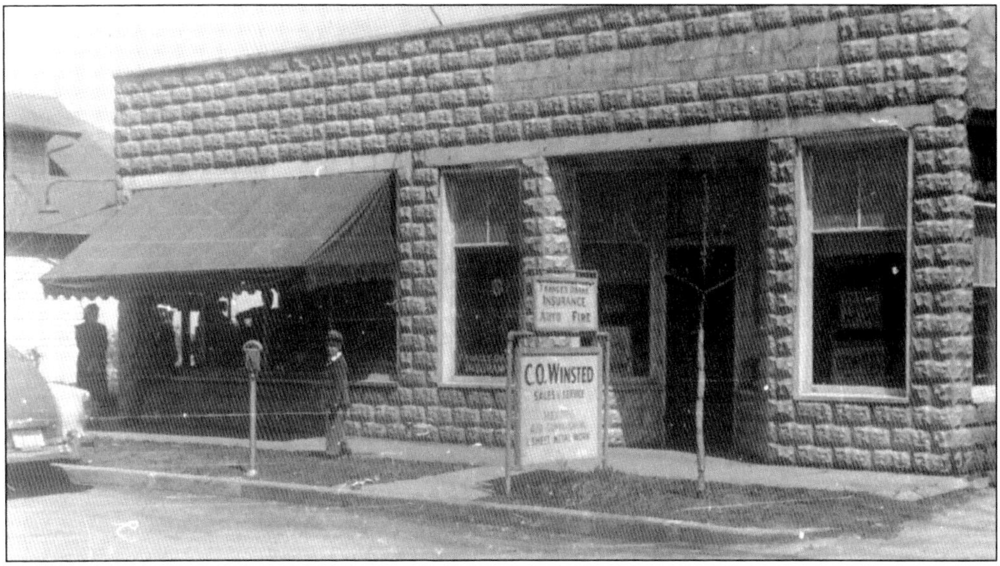

One block off Main Street, on South Vine Street, sat a small cut-stone building housing various businesses. This photograph, taken around 1947, features the following storefronts, from left to right, Mercer/Pomeroy Printers, Frances Drake Insurance, and C.O. Winsted Heating, Air Conditioning and Sheet Metal Works. The building also housed the township assessor's office. The young boy standing in front of the building is Jerry Winsted. His grandmother Hazel Kivett Winsted is standing to the left. Faintly written above the doorway is "Vaughn & Son," a plumbing company, which was the previous occupant.

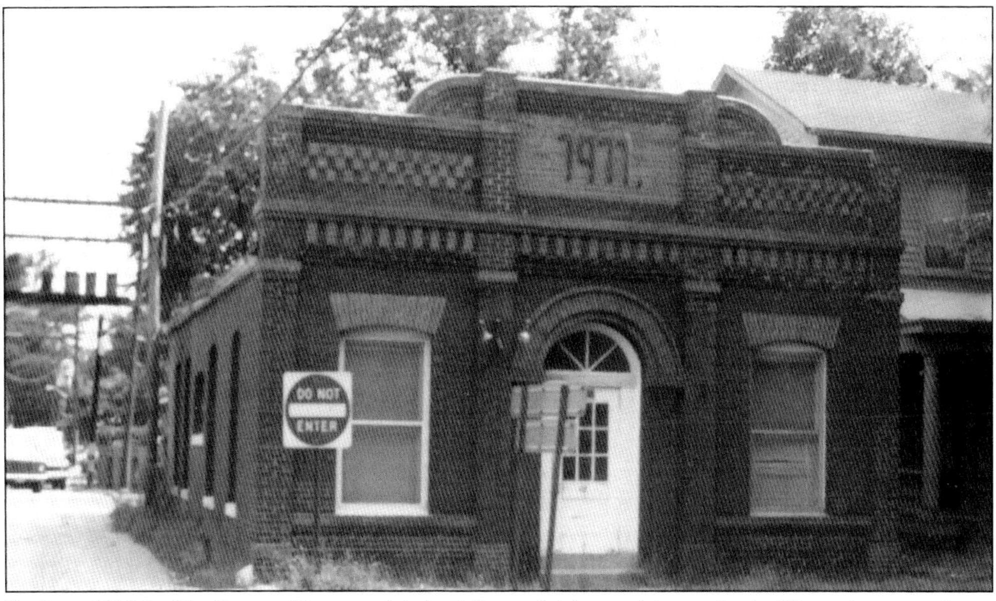

Built in 1911 by Dr. Ernest Cooper, this building, which was his medical office, also served as a location for the Consolidated Telephone Company. Dr. Cooper had the medical facility, located at 115 South Center Street, constructed next door to his home. The facility offered three rooms as "hospital apartments" for patients. In 1924, Dr. Cooper leased the south side of the property to the Consolidated Telephone Company for a new telephone exchange. The building is no longer standing.

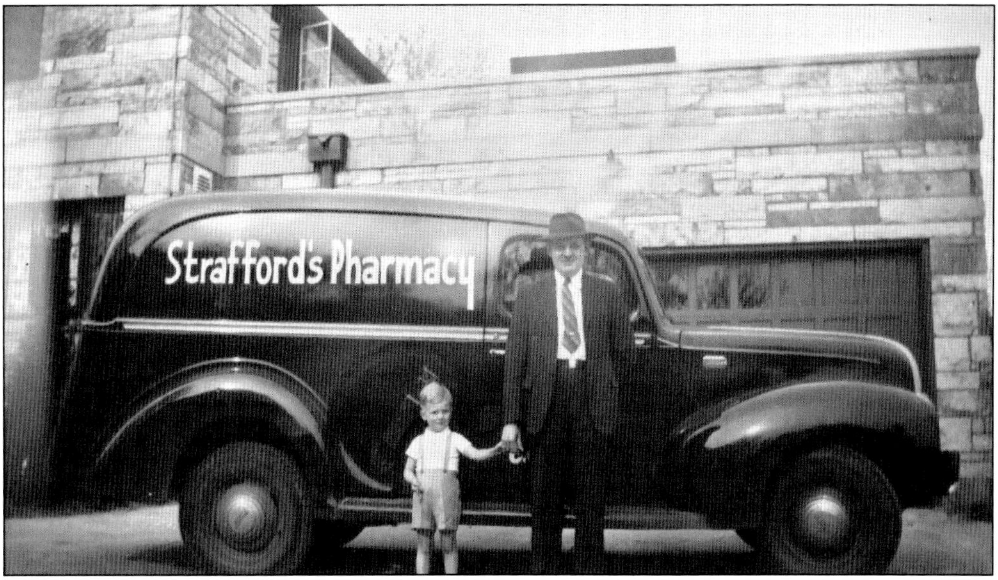

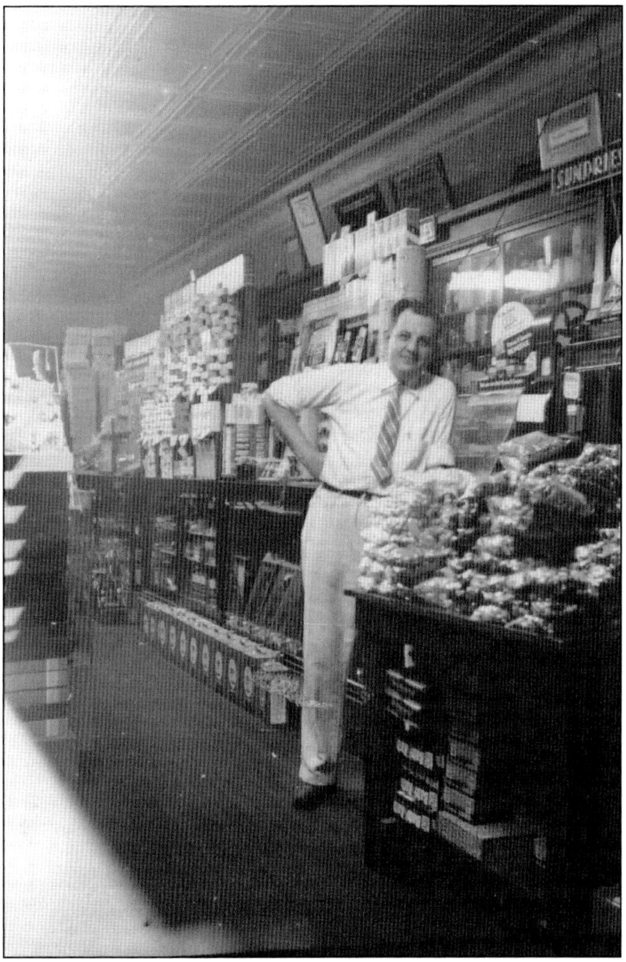

Strafford's Drug Store was a well-known landmark in downtown Plainfield. Located on the northeast corner of Main and Center Streets, the store offered a variety of products for sale. Parked at their home at 907 East Main Street is the Strafford's delivery van. Taken in 1941, this photograph shows Bill Strafford and two-year old Bill Strafford Jr. posing in front of their automobile. (Courtesy of William Strafford Jr.)

Bill Strafford was a very clever marketer of his wares. Here, he stands at the candy display table, which was located at a child's-eye level, near the cash register. He sold so many Hershey candy products that executives from the Hershey Corporation in Pennsylvania actually made a visit to the drugstore to see why; they couldn't imagine a store in Plainfield, Indiana, selling as much chocolate as they did. (Courtesy of William Strafford Jr.)

Surrounded by an array of items for sale, Bill Strafford Jr. stands ready to assist customers at the register. The freshly roasted nuts, which were always on hand, are seen in the bottom right corner of the photograph. (Courtesy of William Strafford Jr.)

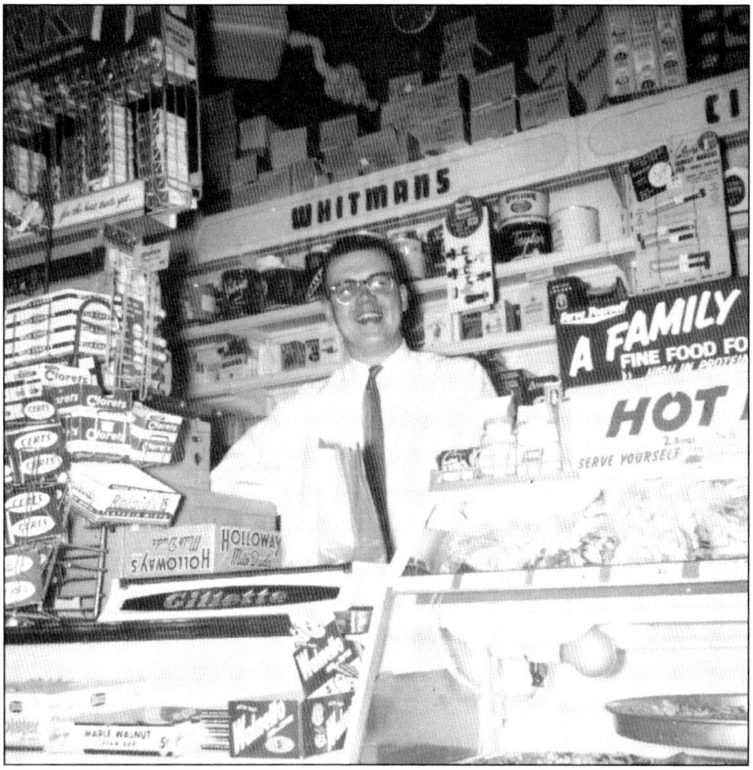

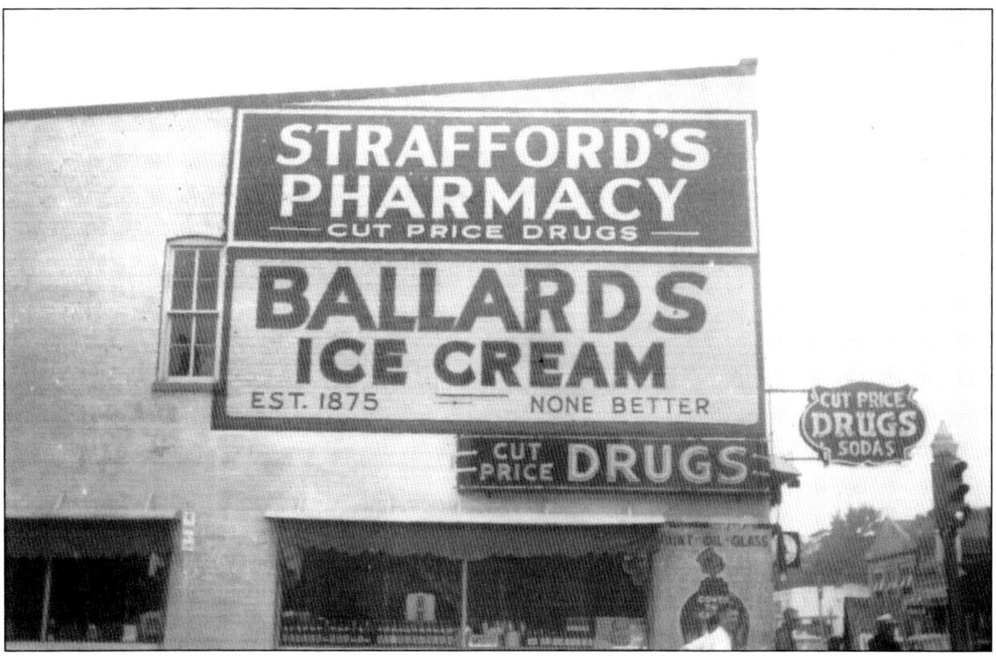

The exterior of Strafford's Pharmacy was a ready-made billboard. Here, the side of the building advertises not only Strafford's, but also the popular Ballard's Ice Cream. Ballard's was later sold to Sealtest. The windows, which were added by Bill Strafford, peek into the back of the soda fountain area. Note the pop bottles lining the windowsill.

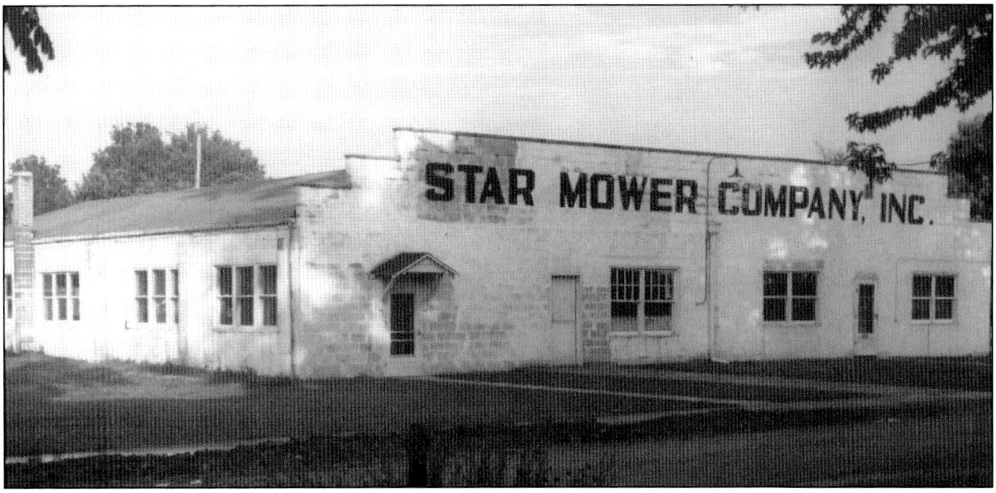

The Star Mower Company, located at 335 North East Street, manufactured hand-built reel lawn mowers. The name "Star" came from a shortened version of owner Lowell Starbuck's name. The company began operations in April 1946 and functioned as the Star Mower Company until it was sold to United Co-Ops on June 9, 1950. The property today is home to the Town of Plainfield's Bob Ward Park. (Courtesy of Sandra Starbuck Norris.)

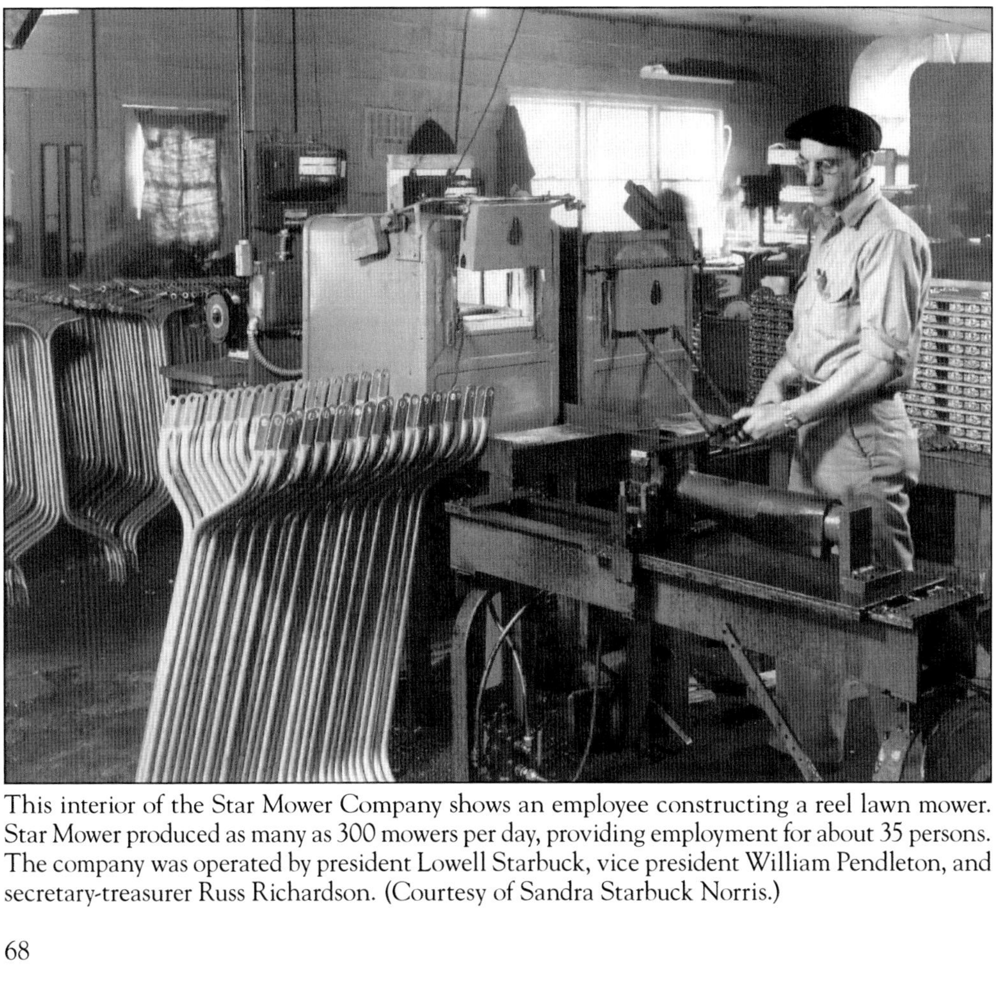

This interior of the Star Mower Company shows an employee constructing a reel lawn mower. Star Mower produced as many as 300 mowers per day, providing employment for about 35 persons. The company was operated by president Lowell Starbuck, vice president William Pendleton, and secretary-treasurer Russ Richardson. (Courtesy of Sandra Starbuck Norris.)

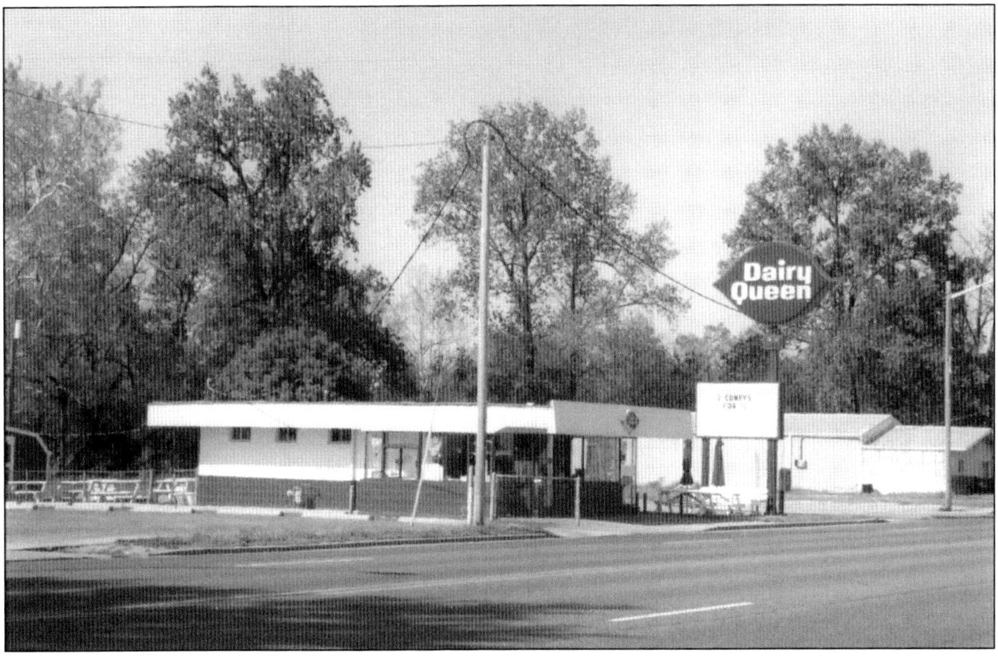

The very recognizable Dairy Queen sign greets US 40 travelers as they enter town from the west. Built in 1952, the Plainfield Dairy Queen has been serving ice cream to residents for over 50 years. This photograph from 2006 predates the building's renovation.

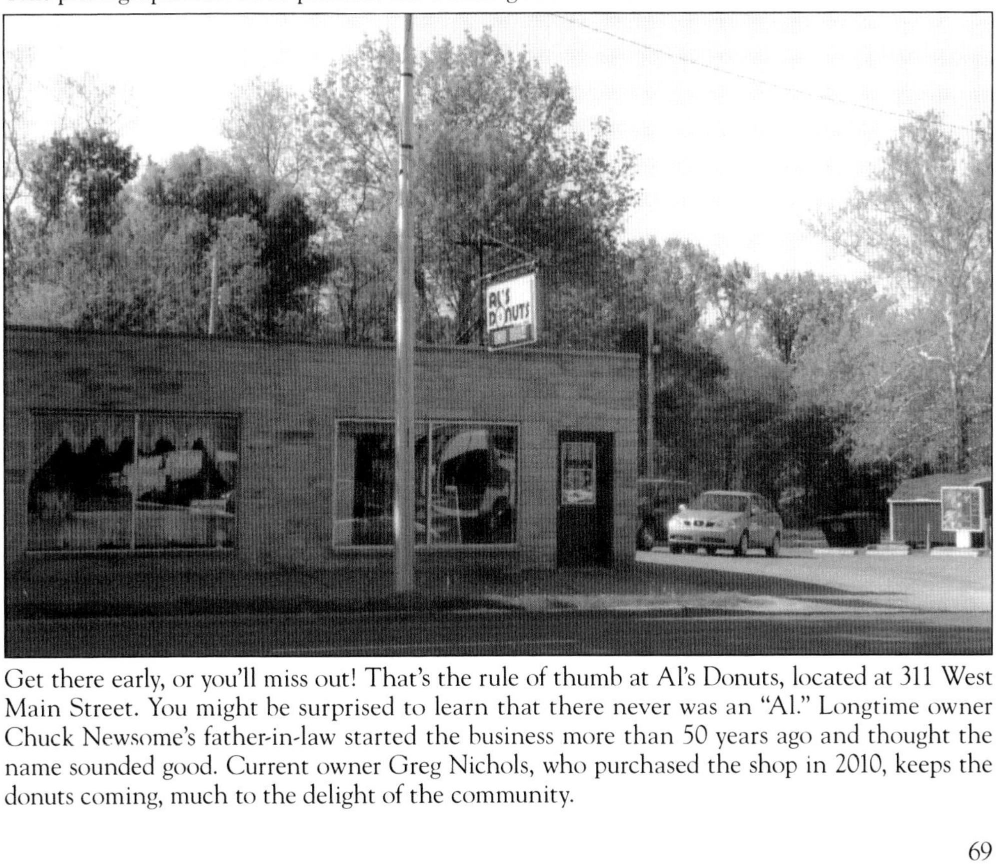

Get there early, or you'll miss out! That's the rule of thumb at Al's Donuts, located at 311 West Main Street. You might be surprised to learn that there never was an "Al." Longtime owner Chuck Newsome's father-in-law started the business more than 50 years ago and thought the name sounded good. Current owner Greg Nichols, who purchased the shop in 2010, keeps the donuts coming, much to the delight of the community.

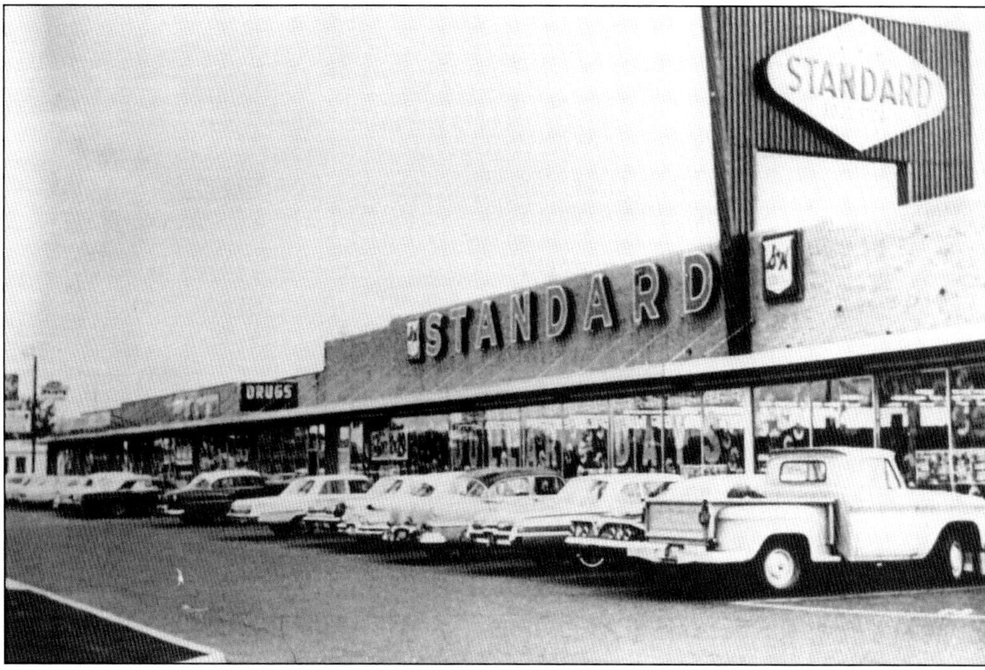

Standard Grocery Store opened its doors to the residents of Plainfield on July 27, 1954. Located in the Plainfield East Hill Shopping Center (1000 block of East Main Street), Standard was an anchor store in the small strip of businesses that were constructed by D.P. Daum. The other stores included Super Drugs, Paul-Harris Department Store, Seneff Hardware, and Price Bros. Furniture Store.

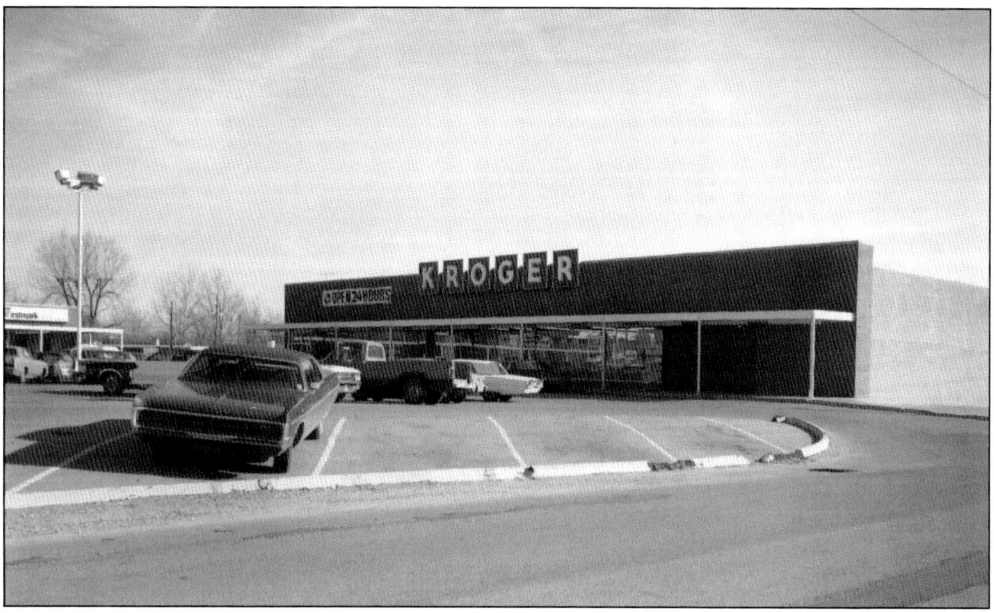

Originally located on Main Street in downtown Plainfield, the Kroger Grocery Store moved to a new location at 1600 East Main Street in 1955. The new spot provided ample parking and moved Plainfield a little closer to suburbia. The store remained there until it relocated again to its present location at 1930 East Main Street.

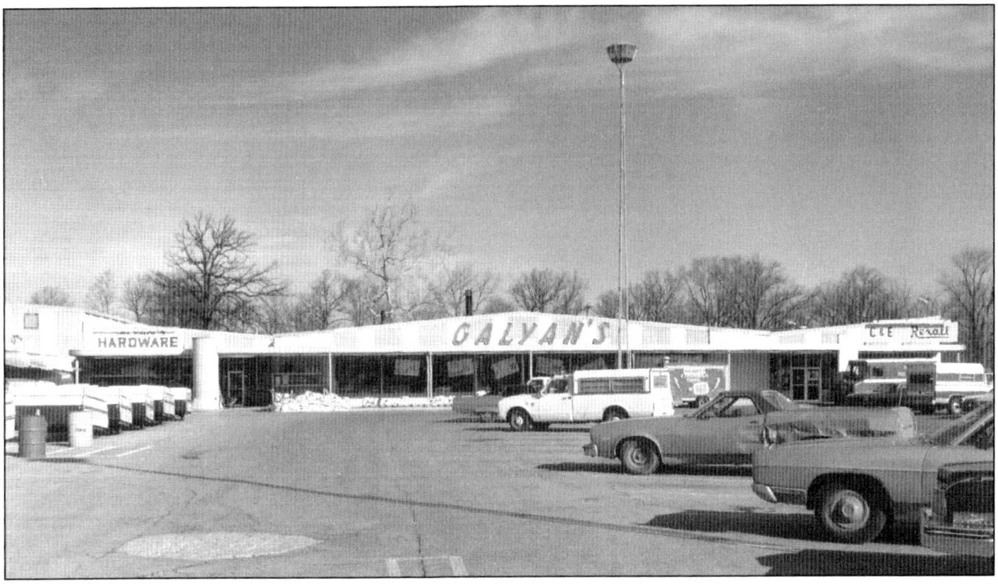

Galyan's Grocery Store began in 1946 by Albert and Naomi Galyan. What began as a supermarket evolved into a well-known sporting goods store. Albert built a log cabin next to the grocery to house what he called the "outdoor store." This photograph shows the Galyan's site when it also included the C & E Rexall Drug Store and Galyan's Hardware. Prior to Galyan's, the property was home to the National Single-Bled Hog Serum Company. The complex was razed in April 2012 to make way for a new bank and grocery store.

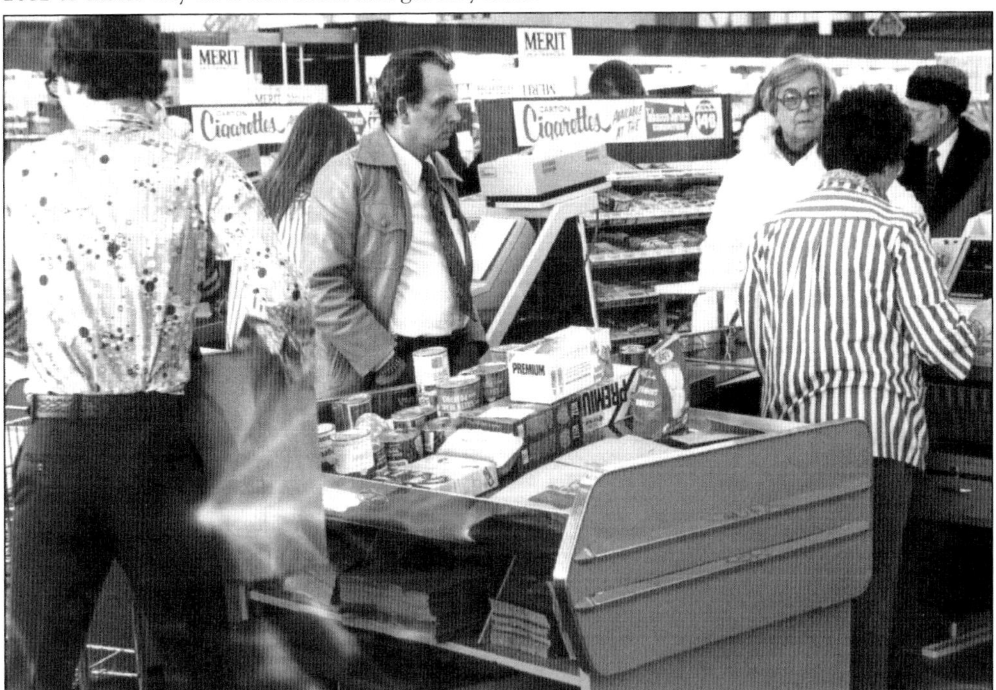

Marsh Grocery was once located in the Plainfield Plaza shopping center before relocating to its current address at 2002 Stafford Road. This photograph from February 1978 shows cashier Ann Vogel and bag boy Jim Covalt ringing up and bagging the purchases of Jack Moore.

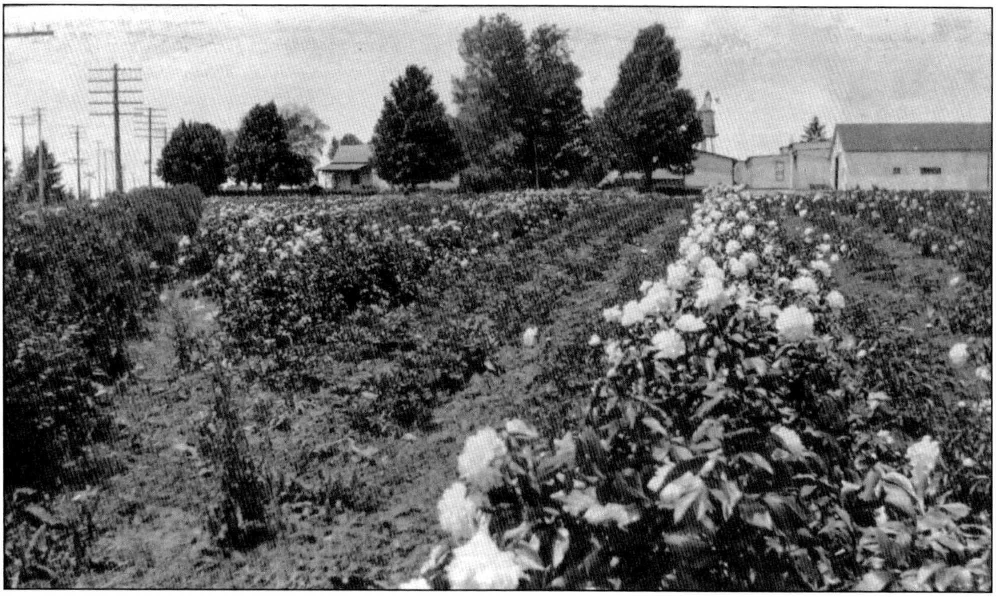

The Hobbs Nursery Company has a rich history in the Plainfield area. In 1875, Oliver Albertson moved his nursery operation from Salem, Indiana, to the Bridgeport area, just east of Plainfield. He was joined in this venture by his son-in-law Cyrus M. Hobbs. Together, they established a thriving nursery operation on over 350 acres, straddling the Hendricks-Marion County lines. Cyrus Hobbs's sons Oliver, Harry, and Fred all followed in their father's footsteps and continued to make the nursery business thrive. Continuing the family tradition, two additional generations of family members—Robert, Thomas and Gordon and then James—carried on the business of C.M. Hobbs and Sons, Inc. These two photographs show rows of established peony plants in bloom and ready to be sold.

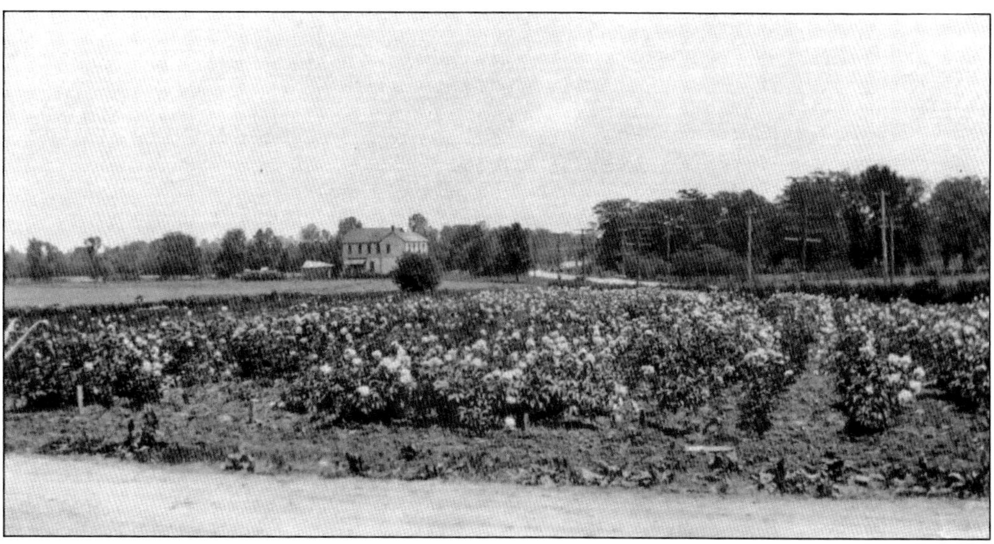

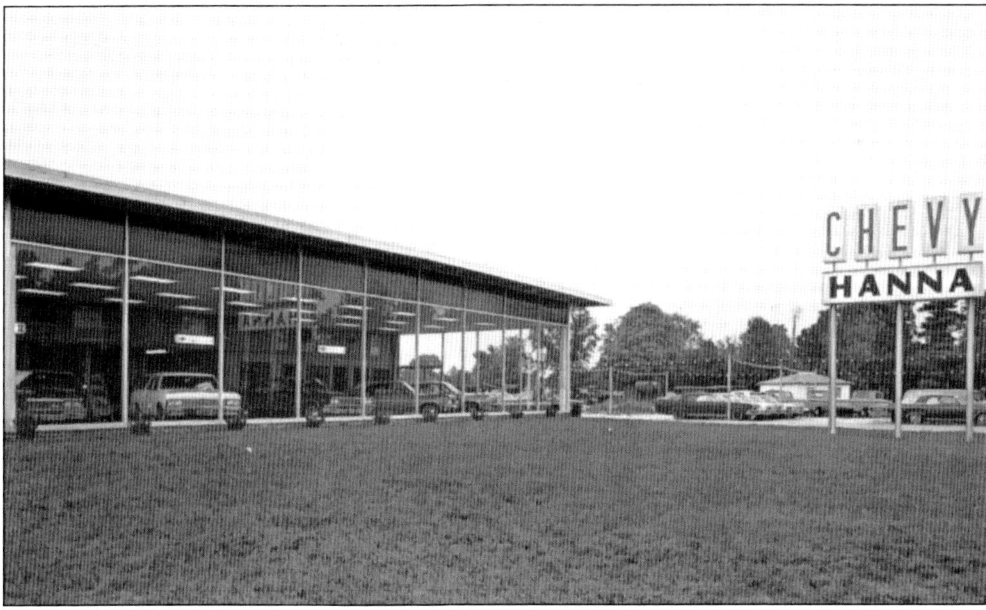

P.W. "Pres" Hanna opened his Chevrolet dealership in 1952 at 131 North Mill Street, in a building owned by John Daum that formerly housed a skating rink. Hanna expanded his business and moved to a larger piece of land on US 40, west of Plainfield, at 704 West Main Street. Hanna Chevrolet was a local landmark at the corner of Vestal and Main Streets until August 2001, when it was sold to Andy Mohr. This mid-1960s photograph shows the dealership during its heyday.

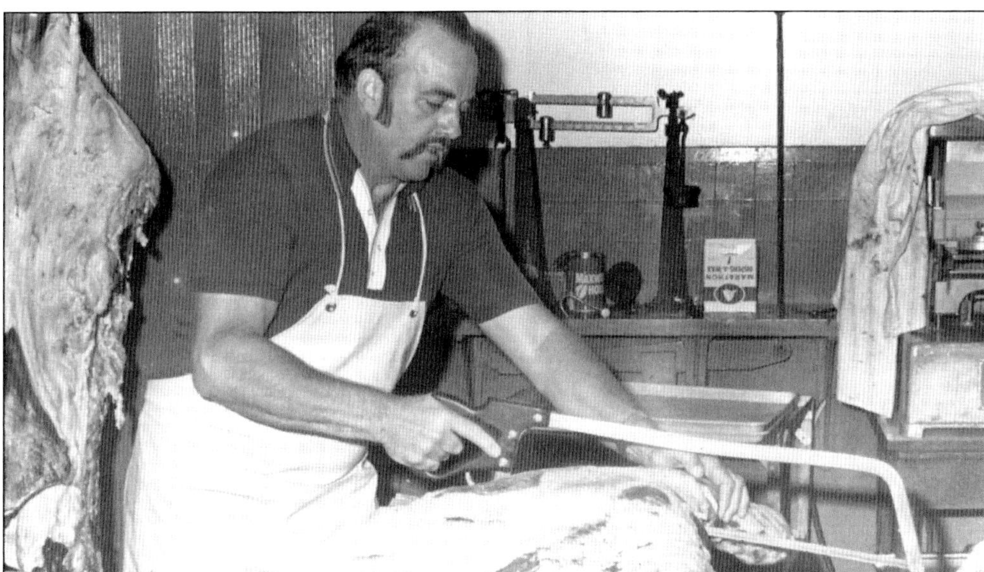

Fulton's Plainfield Locker was located at 226 North Mill Street. Seen here as he prepares a cut of meat is owner Bernie Fulton, who purchased the shop in 1977. Donald Misner originally built the locker plant in 1948 and proudly offered 500 individual meat lockers for persons to rent.

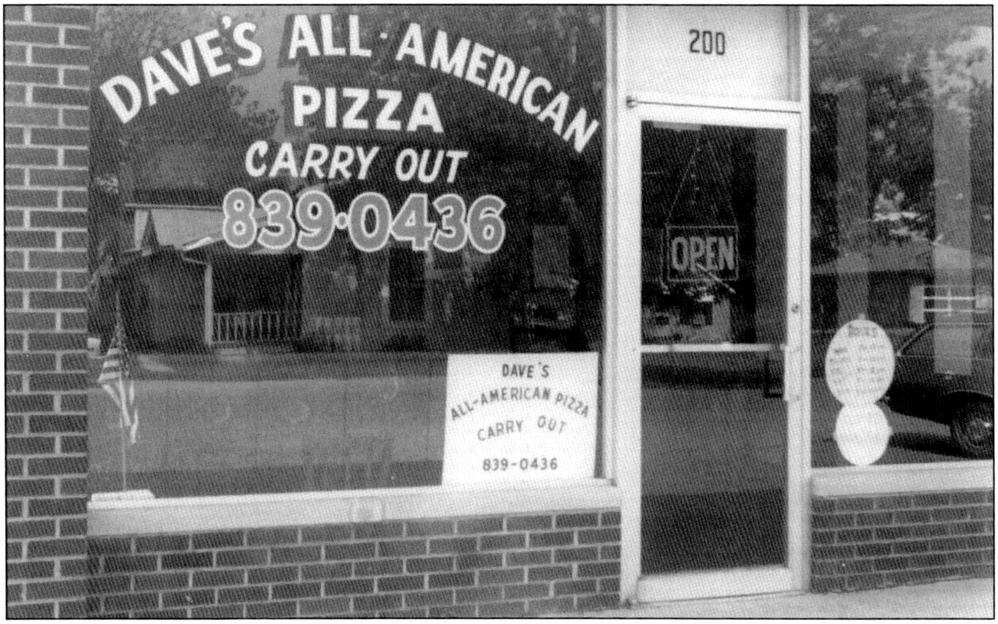

Dave's All-American Pizza actually had a location in Plainfield for a few years. Dave Byrdwell opened this pizzeria, located at 200 North Mill Street, in 1978. This shop was short lived; however, Dave's All-American Pizza is still open and thriving at the Danville, Indiana, location.

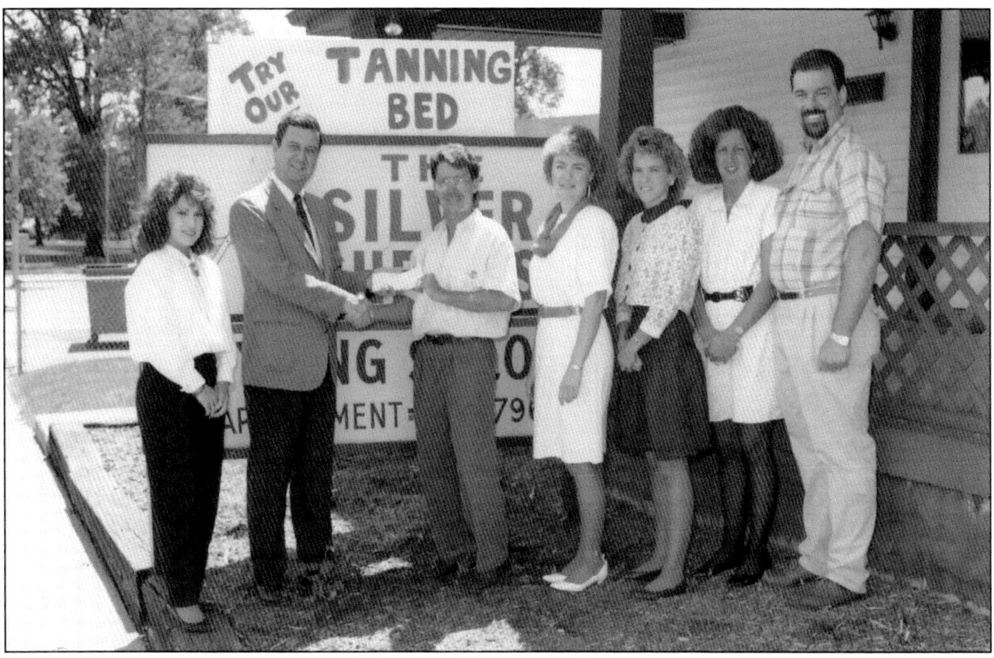

Steve Hampton and Mark Tharp have owned the Silver Shears Styling Salon for over 30 years. What started out as a small shop in the cluster of businesses at the corner of Vestal and US 40 (razed in 2011) turned into a booming business. Outgrowing their original shop, Silver Shears has been located at 116 Avon Avenue ever since. Shown here in July 1990 are, from left to right, Renee Wells, unidentified, Steve Hampton, Debbie Martin, two unidentified women, and Mark Tharp.

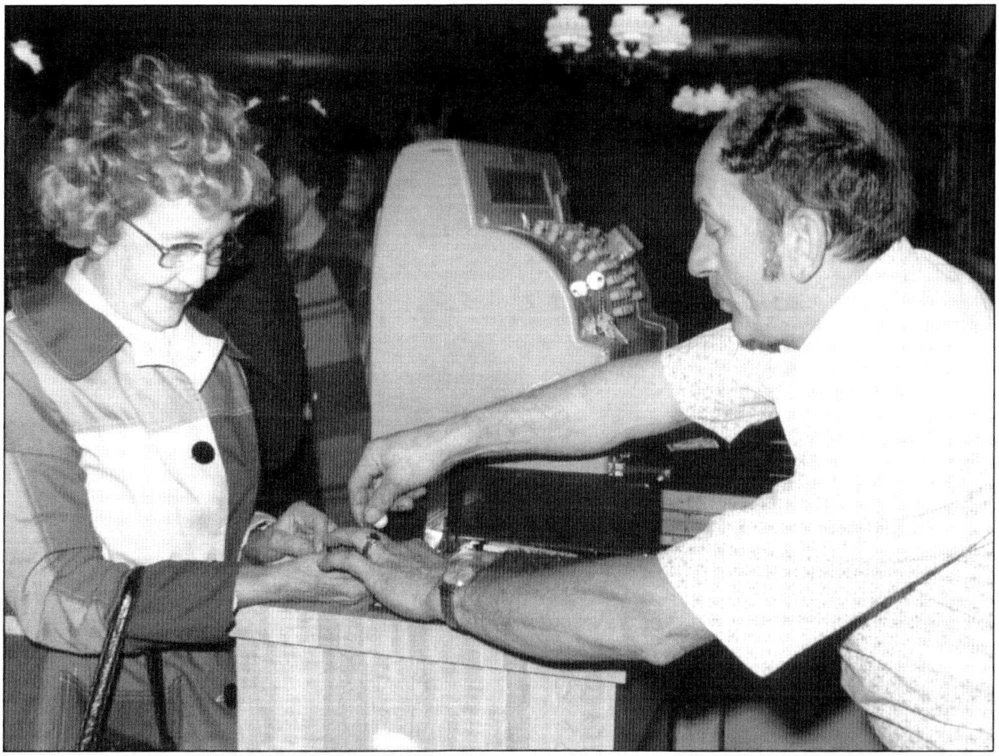

Emanuel and Stacey Apostles owned and operated Stacey's Restaurant, one of the most successful eating establishments in Plainfield. Always visible to his customers, Emanuel opened his original restaurant in 1972 at 101 East Main Street (at the corner of Main and Vine Streets). The eating establishment proved so popular that he eventually relocated to a newly erected building at 414 West Main Street near White Lick Creek. The new location provided much needed parking and a larger dining room. The new restaurant celebrated its grand opening on October 17, 1979. The cozy, family-style restaurant offered a varied menu and many homemade desserts. Stacey's Restaurant was sold to Harold and Connie Wingler in 1992 and renamed Kristy's Café. In the photograph above, Apostles is seen attending to one of his patrons as she pays for her meal.

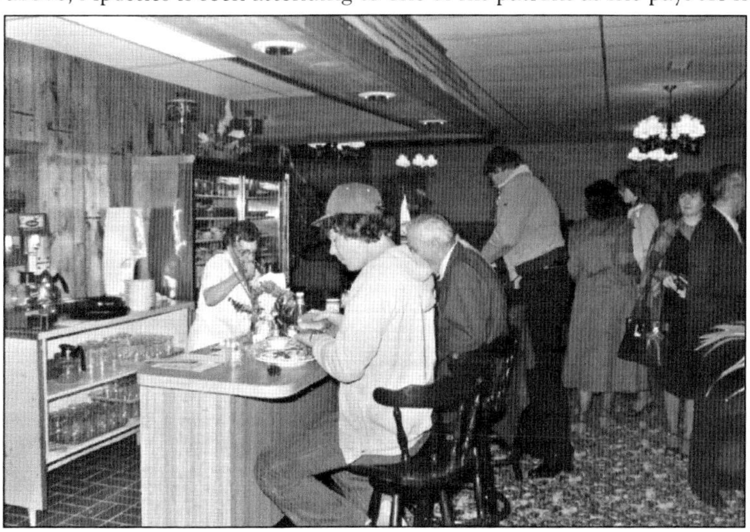

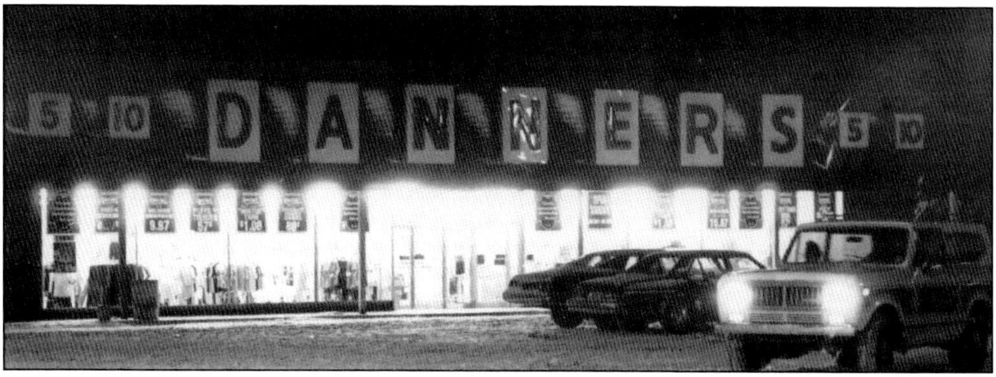

Locals knew if they needed anything, Danners 5 & 10 was the place to go. Offering a wide selection of goods, especially candy, Danner's was a modern variety store for Plainfield. Opened in 1961, Danner's was located in the Plainfield Plaza shopping center in the 1800 block of East Main Street. The store closed in January 1988.

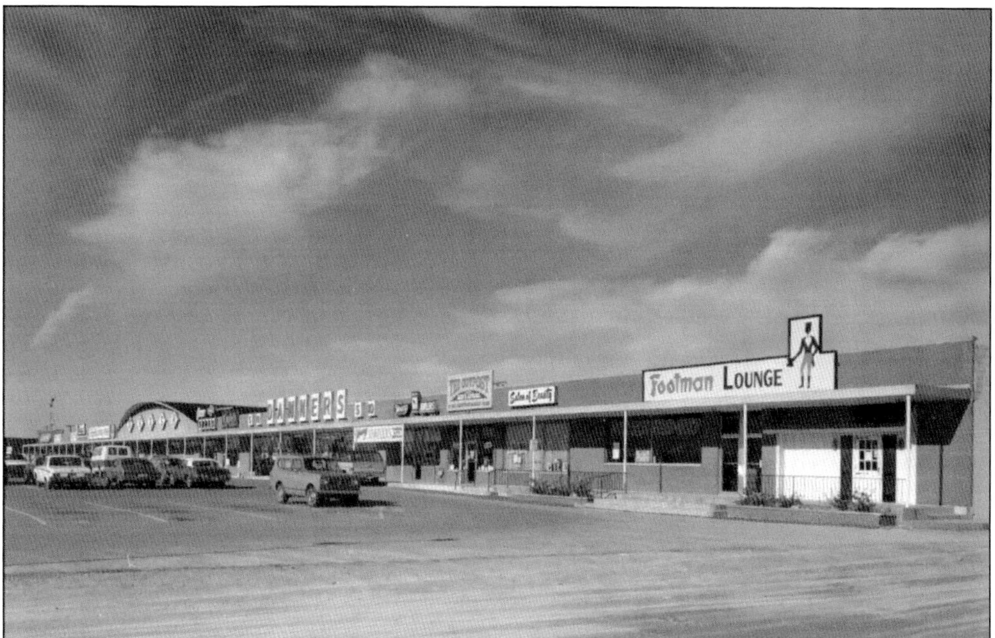

Plainfield Plaza made its debut in early 1962. One of the first shopping centers, Plainfield Plaza offered residents one location to find many goods. This photograph from the mid-1970s shows some familiar favorites: Footman Lounge, Salon of Beauty, the Outpost, Young's Jewelers, Danners 5 & 10, Campbell's, Haase Shoes, Marsh Grocery Store, Hook's Drugs, and Roselyn Bakery. Originally owned by Mel Simon and Associates, it was sold to Henry and Vivian Haase in 1977.

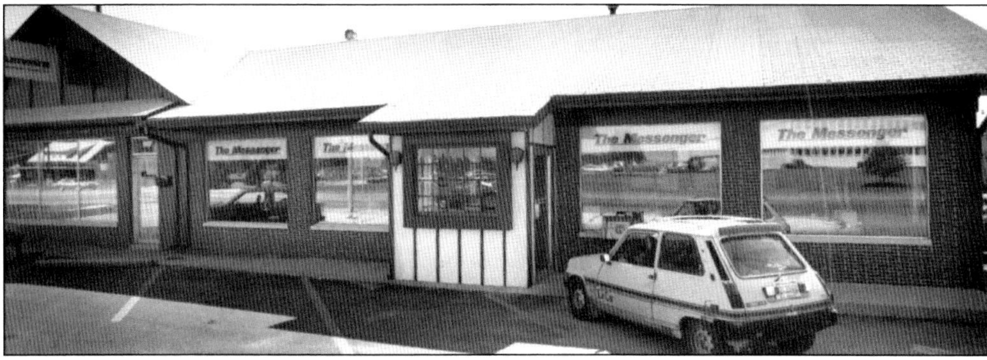

The *Plainfield Messenger* newspaper began its long publishing history in 1915, when George Lott of Vincennes, Indiana, purchased the paper. The paper outlasted many of its owners, as it was sold no less than seven times. In 1984, Tom and Judy Holzknecht purchased the paper and managed it until the last issue was published on July 21, 1994. The Plainfield-Guilford Township Public Library has archived copies of the *Plainfield Messenger* available for viewing.

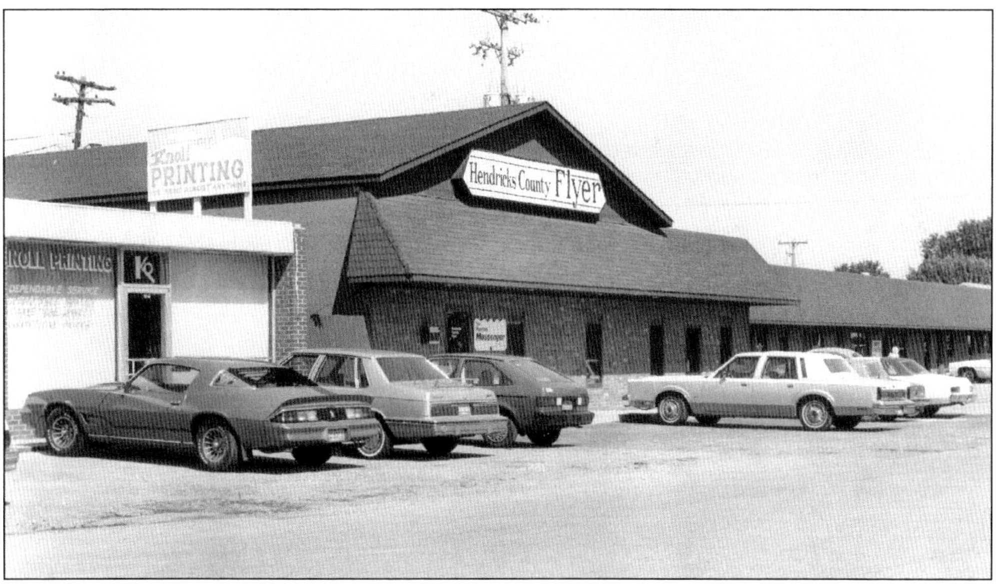

In 1965, Plainfield residents Tom and Judy Holzknecht launched a new county newspaper called the *Hendricks County Flyer*. As the newspaper gained popularity and began to grow, the Holzknechts moved their operation to 202 North Mill Street, shown in this photograph. Providing county residents with local news, the *Hendricks County Flyer* is still published twice a week out of its Avon, Indiana, office. The Plainfield-Guilford Township Public Library has archived copies of the *Hendricks County Flyer* available for viewing.

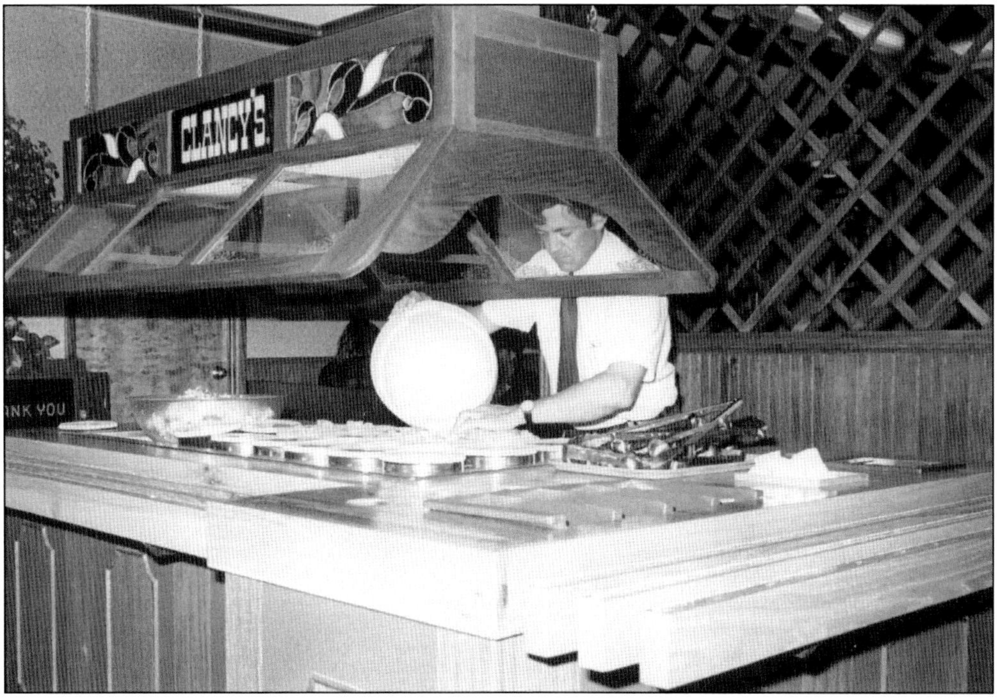

Clancy's, one of Plainfield's first fast-food restaurants, was located at 1645 East Main Street (in the spot where Donato's Pizza is today). Clancy's was one of the first fast-food restaurants to offer a salad bar. This October 1979 photograph captures the debut of the salad bar.

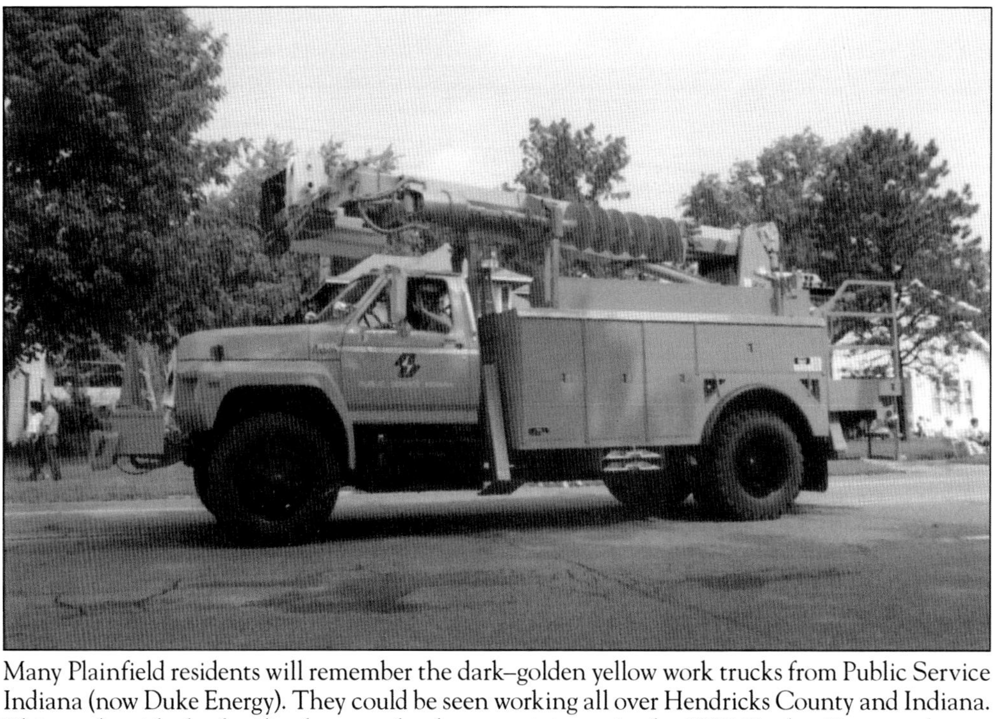

Many Plainfield residents will remember the dark–golden yellow work trucks from Public Service Indiana (now Duke Energy). They could be seen working all over Hendricks County and Indiana. This truck, with the familiar logo on the door, participates in the 1990 Quaker Day parade.

Six

Above Plainfield

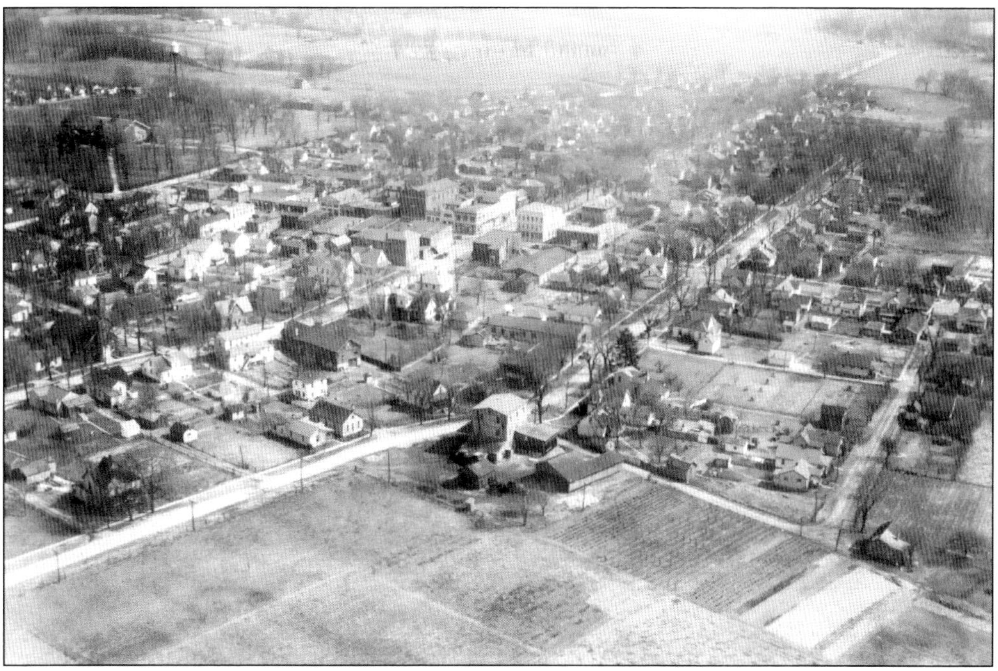

One of the most visual ways to learn about the history of an area is to view it from the air. This aerial photograph, looking southeast, shows Plainfield in the early 20th century. Front and center is the Plainfield Mill, still surrounded by farmland. The Western Yearly Meeting is at the top left, and downtown buildings are visible in the center. The image is not dated, but it's interesting to note that the photograph was taken in the winter, when the leaves were off the trees and the buildings were more visible.

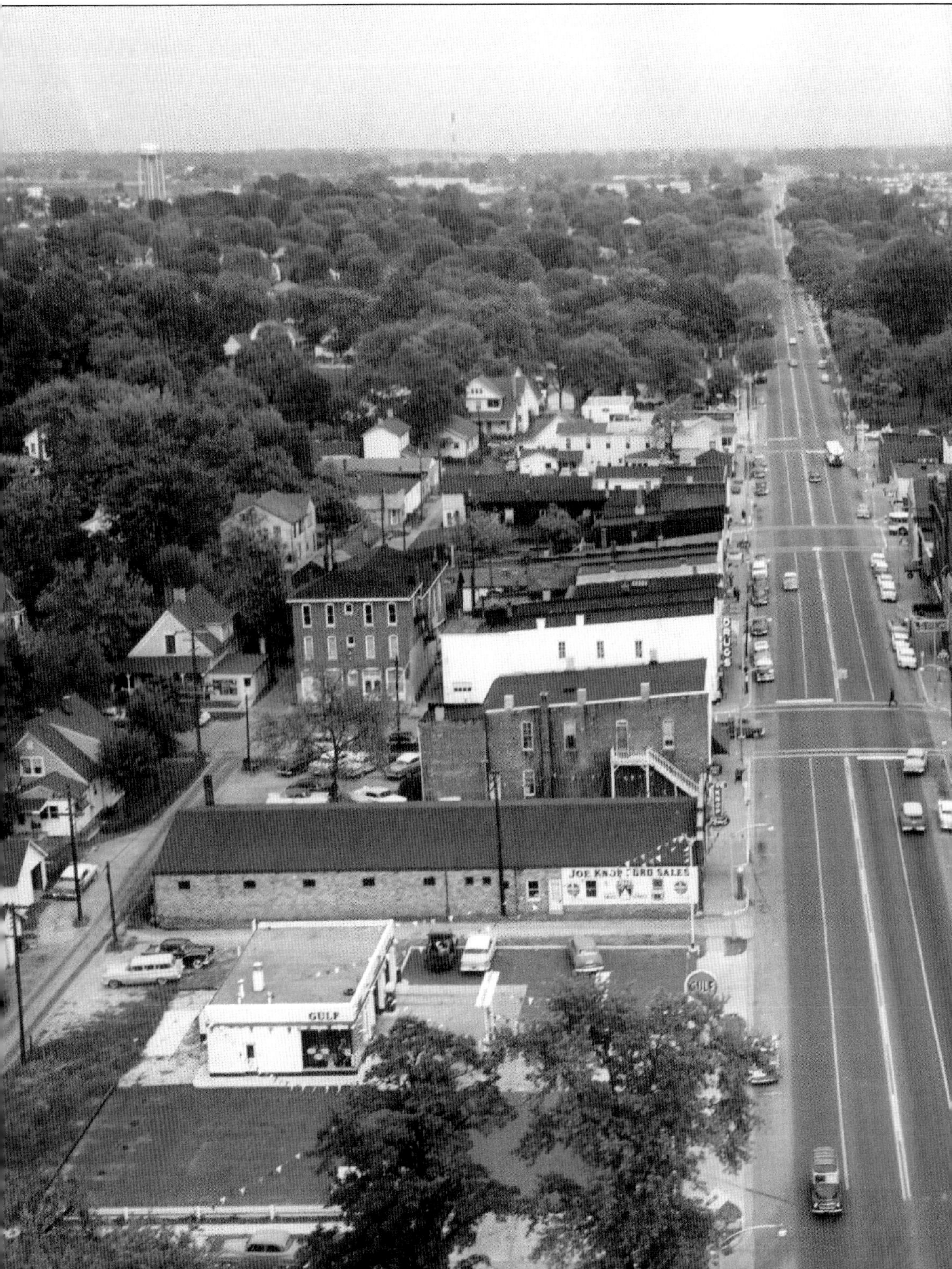
DRUGS
JOE KNOP FORD SALES
GULF
GULF

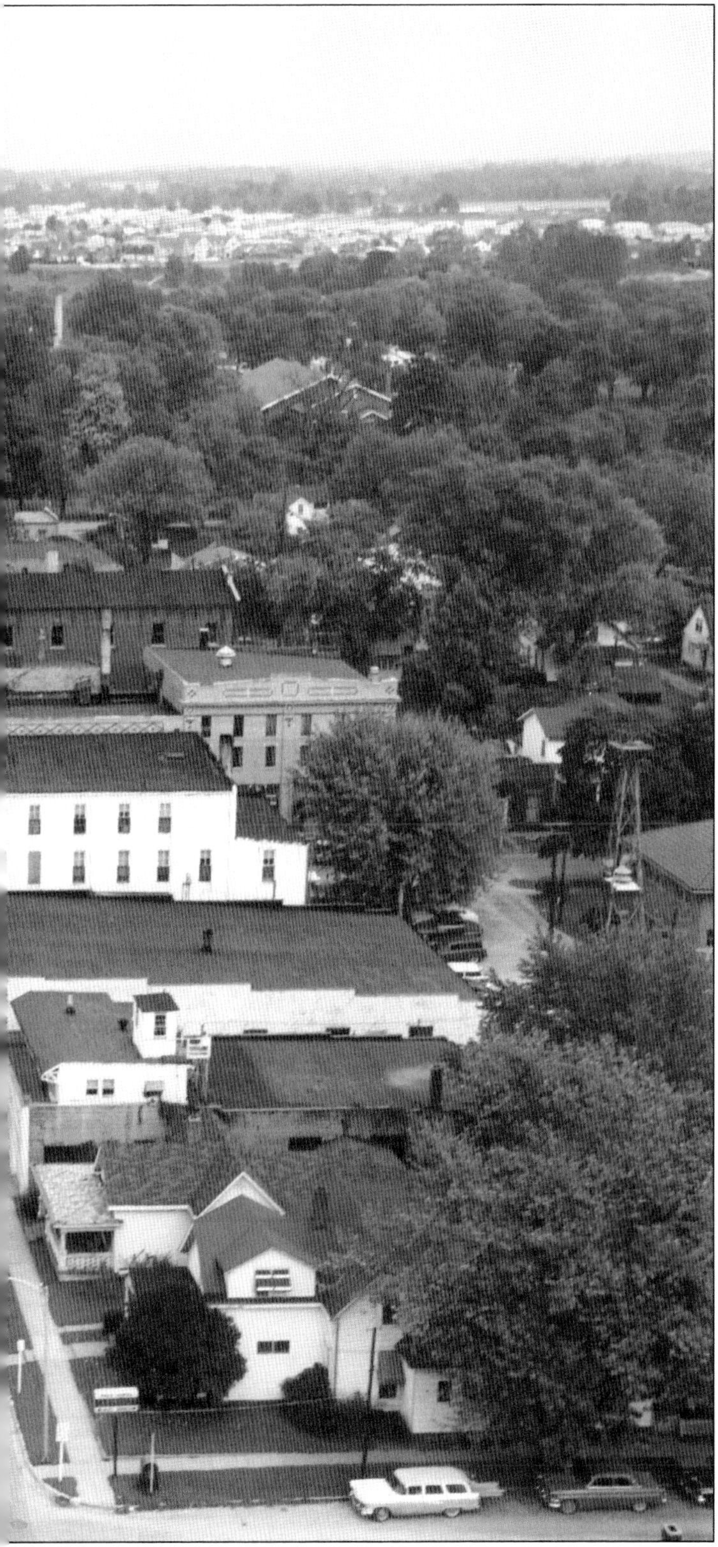

Taken in November 1958, this aerial photograph of Plainfield may seem similar to downtown Plainfield in the 21st century at first glance; however, subtle differences indicate an earlier time. The Joe Knop Ford Sales building is located at the site of the current fire station; the two-story brick Hiss building stands on the corner of Center Street where the Plainfield Town Hall is now located. The Plainfield Friends Meeting peeks out of the grove of trees in the top right corner. The water tower (top left) and the new residential homes on Simmons, Masten, Oliver, Raymond, and Hess Streets are situated "up the east hill."

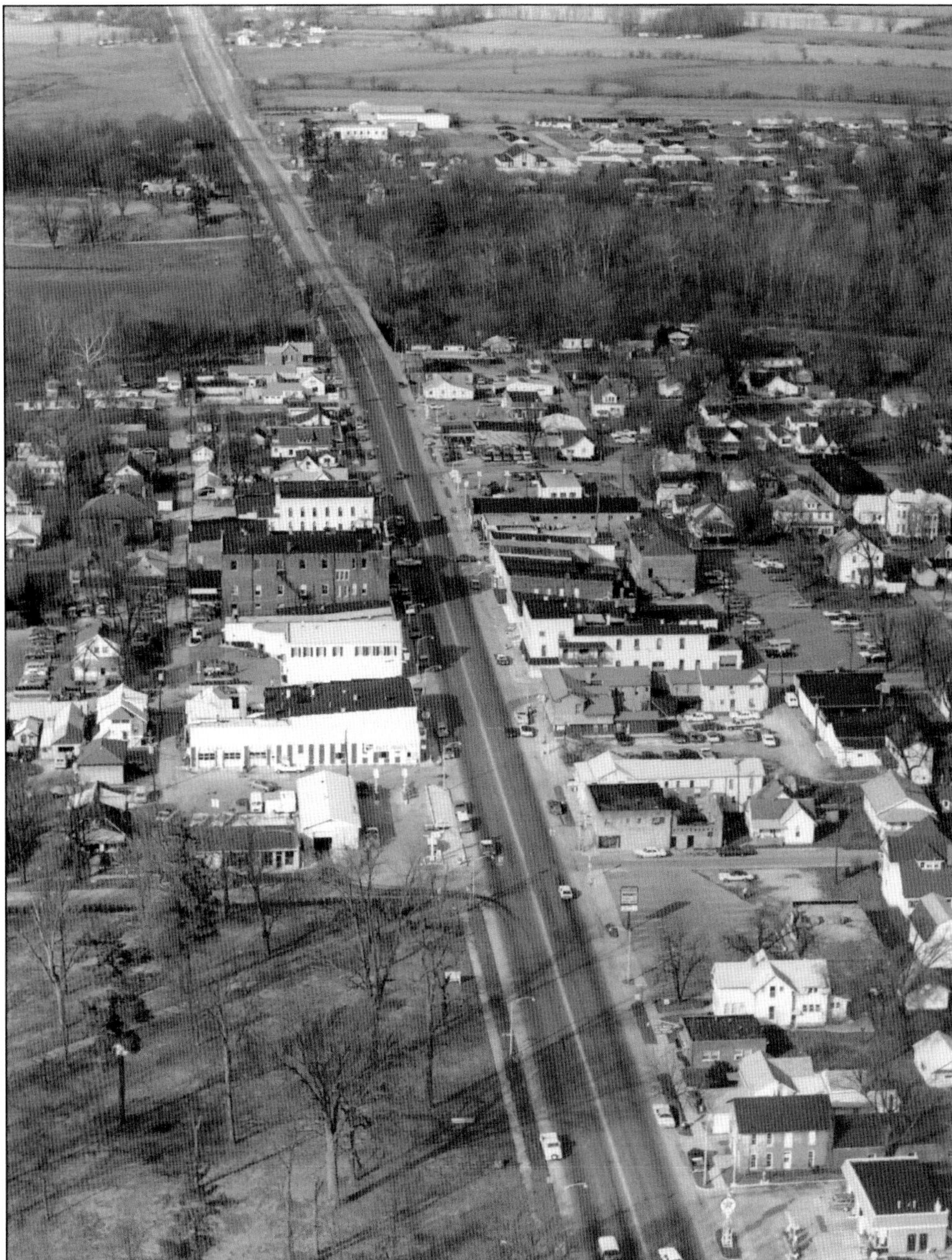

This aerial photograph from the 1970s shows Plainfield from the vantage point of facing west. Noticeable landmarks include US 40 traveling right down the center of the photograph, the white First National Bank building with its distinctive curved drive-up window lane on South Vine, the stately brick Knights of Pythias building, and in the foreground, the trees on the property of the Plainfield Friends Meeting. In the distance are the trees that line the banks of White Lick Creek, as well as the farm fields that would become the Saratoga housing development.

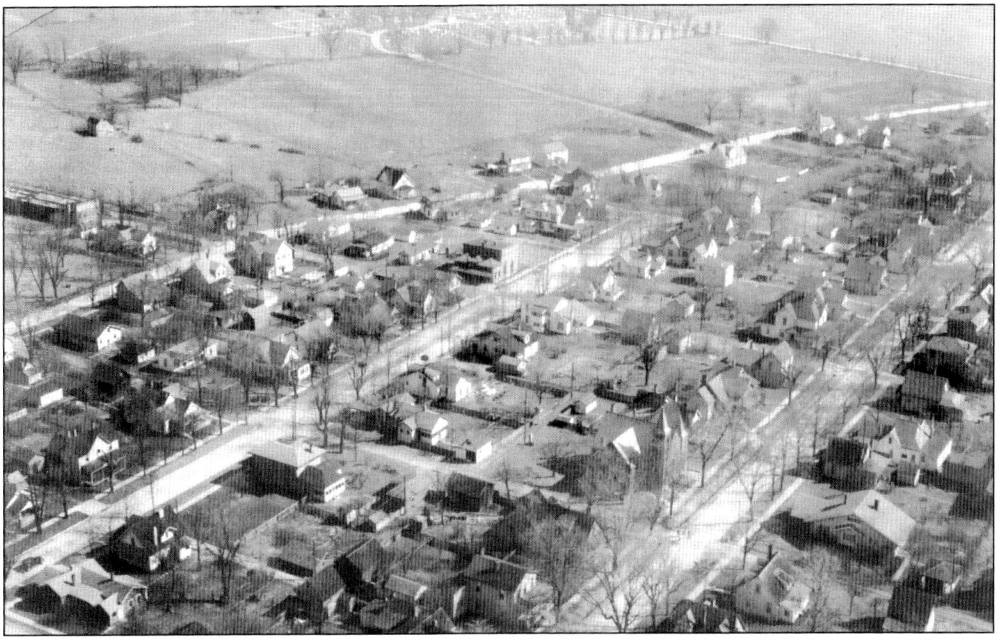

This aerial view of Plainfield shows the south side of town, including East, Vine, and Center Streets. The broad expanse of land at the top of the photograph is Maple Hill Cemetery, lined with trees around the grave markers. The interurban station is visible near the center of the photograph. The photograph is dated 1930.

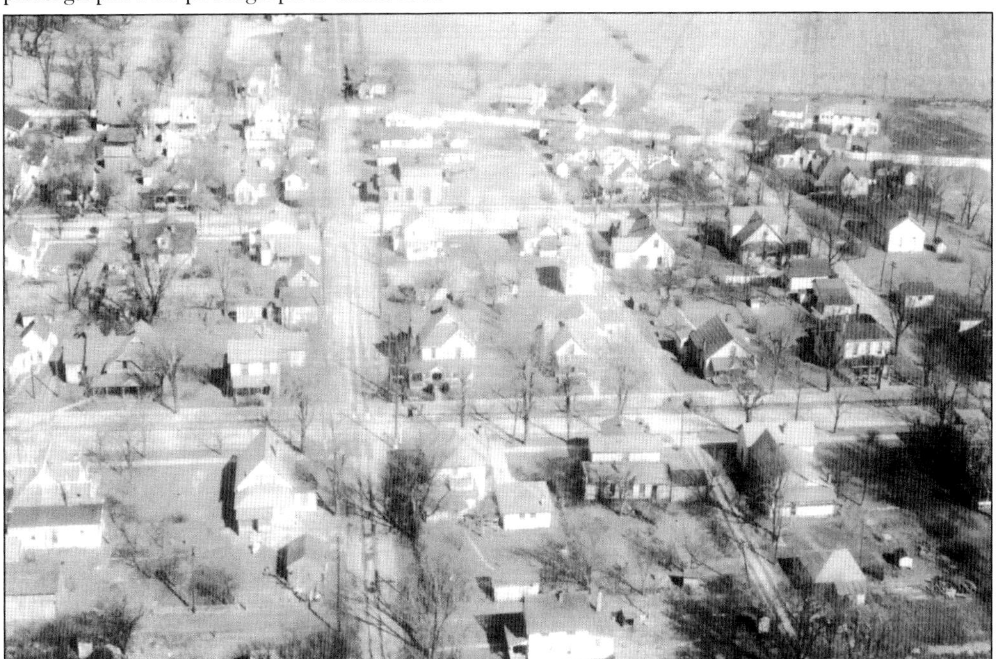

Looking directly down on the interurban tracks (now Buchanan Drive), this 1930 aerial photograph faces east from just above Mill Street. The first street at the bottom of the photograph is Center Street, followed by Vine Street, and then East Street. The interurban station is visible near the top center, right along the tracks.

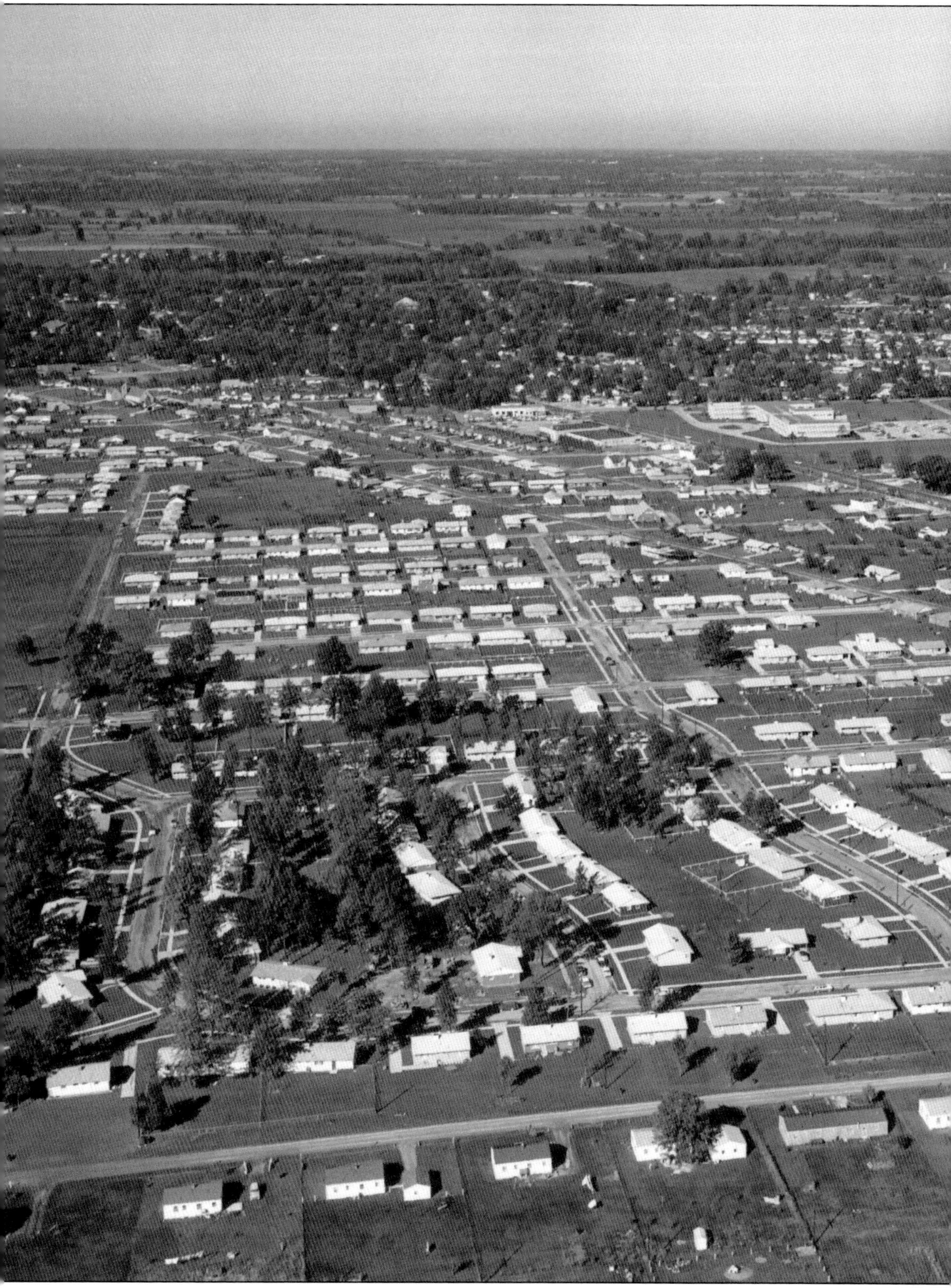

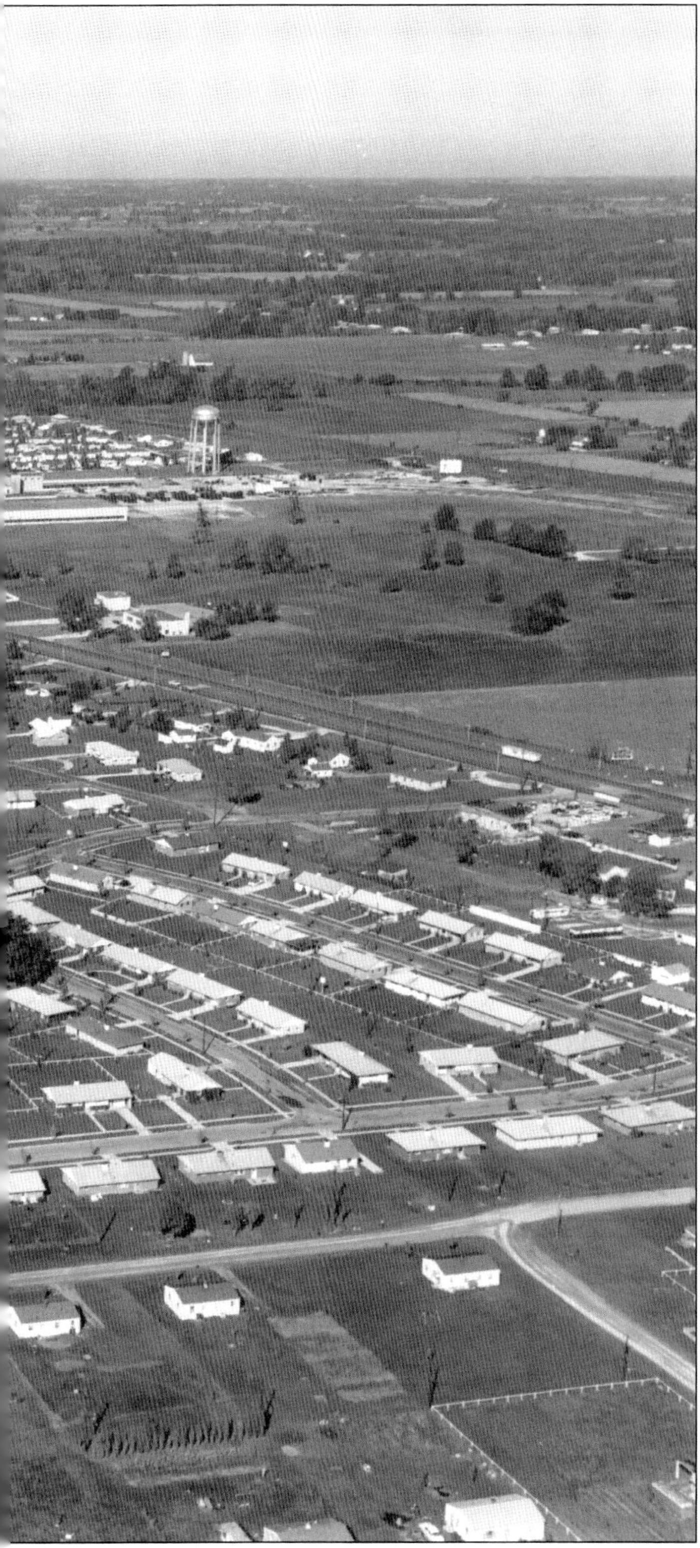

Looking west, this aerial photograph of homes in the Brentwood Heights neighborhood was taken in 1958. The streets running north to south are Elm Drive, Hancook Road, Wayside Drive, and Brookside Lane. Running east to west are Tarpon, Franklin, Aubert, Forrest, and Section Streets. The Public Service Indiana headquarters and Plainfield water tower are visible in the top of the photograph. Brentwood Heights seems much the same today but with a more established and mature look than in this early photograph of the neighborhood.

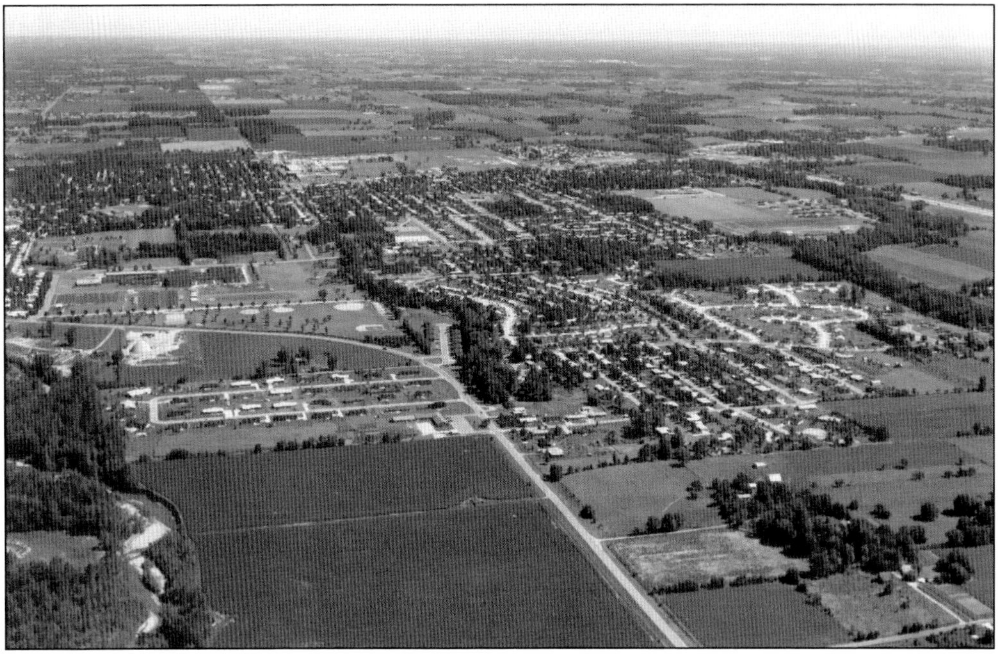

Before Hummel Park, there was a cornfield. This 1976 aerial photograph looking north shows the future site of Hummel Park (1000 S. Center Street) where the fields are seen at the bottom of the photograph. Swinford Park and Plainfield High School are visible in the middle left. The neighborhoods on the south side of town are slowly developing.

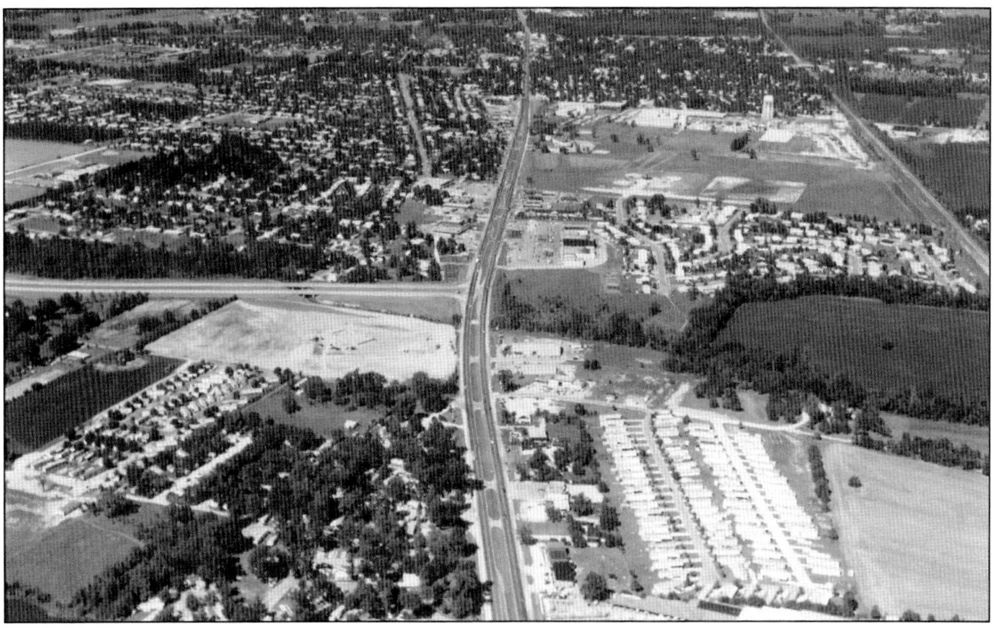

Also taken in 1976, this aerial's vantage point is from State Road 267 and US 40, facing west. Deerfield Mobile Home Park is on the right side at 2300 East Main Street. Shrum's Mobile Home Park at 3000 Clark's Creek Road is on the left side of the photograph. The popular Laughner's Cafeteria is beginning to take shape in the dirt-filled construction area (left). Plainfield's iconic white water tower stands tall in the upper right side.

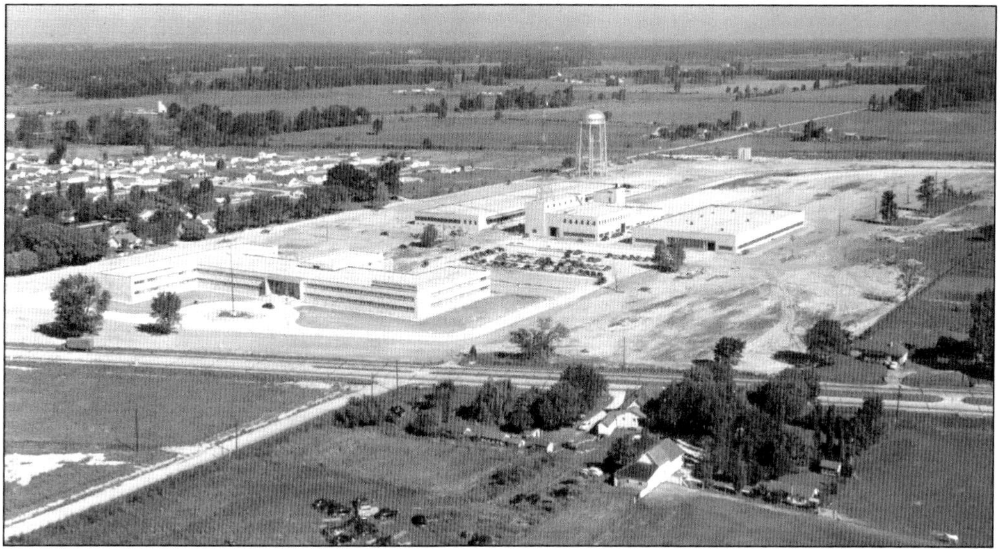

The Public Service Company, located at 1000 East Main Street, has been a stalwart business of the community since it opened its new headquarters in Plainfield in January 1951. This photograph shows not only the newly built company headquarters but also the farmland across the street, which would eventually become a residential neighborhood on Simmons, Buchanan, Hess, Kentucky, and Lawndale Streets.

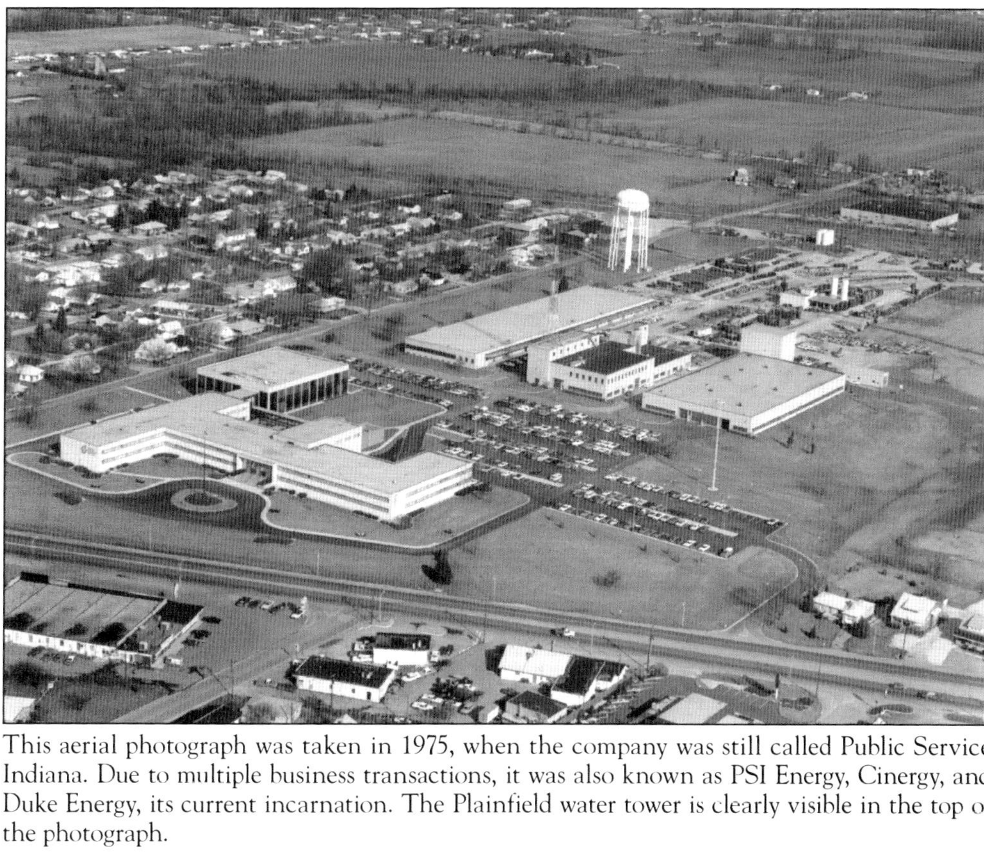

This aerial photograph was taken in 1975, when the company was still called Public Service Indiana. Due to multiple business transactions, it was also known as PSI Energy, Cinergy, and Duke Energy, its current incarnation. The Plainfield water tower is clearly visible in the top of the photograph.

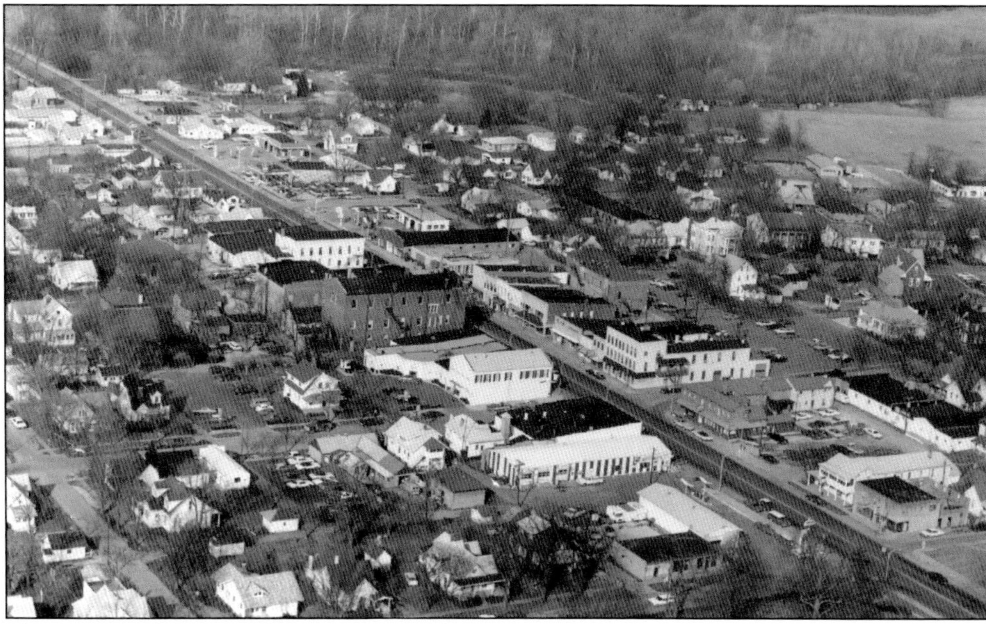

This 1975 aerial photograph's perspective of downtown Plainfield looks northwest. The photographer is situated just above the Western Yearly Meeting of Friends Church. The distinctive curved drive-up lane at the First National Bank is visible in the center of the photograph. The grove of trees in the distance lines the banks of White Lick Creek, and US 40 runs diagonally through the center of the photograph.

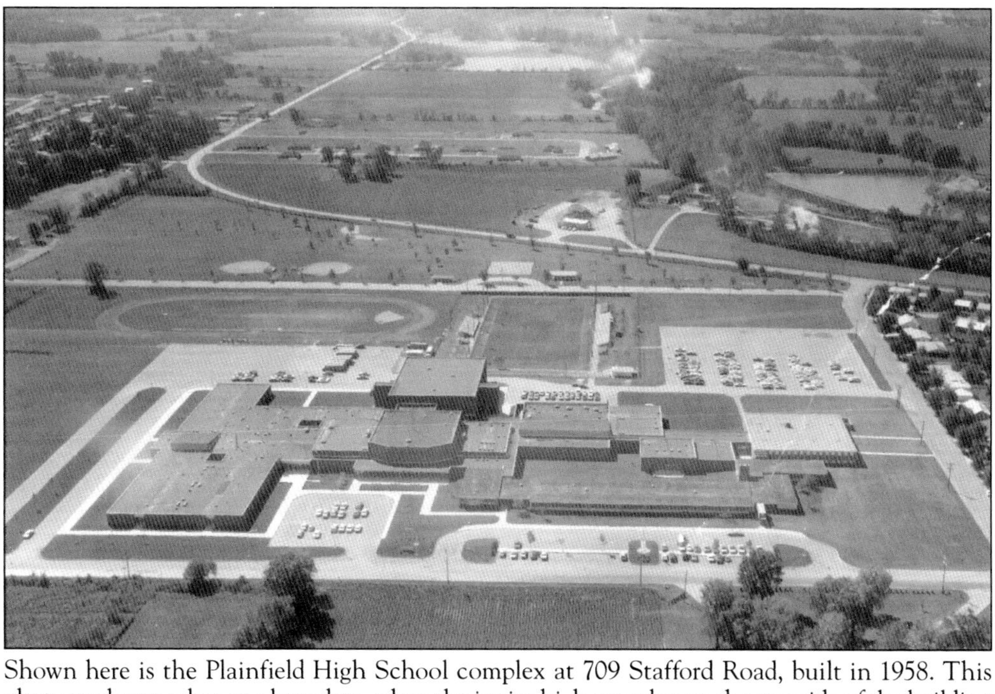

Shown here is the Plainfield High School complex at 709 Stafford Road, built in 1958. This photograph was taken at a later date, when the junior high complex on the east side of the building was completed. The small football field and track are visible on the south side of the building. In the distance is a very new Swinford Park, complete with small trees dotting the landscape.

Seven

TRANSPORTATION

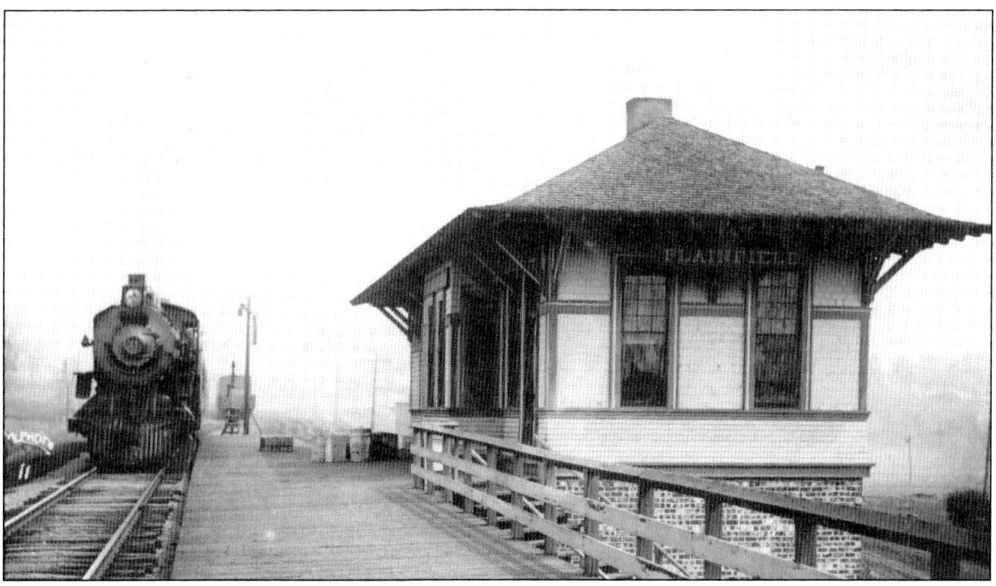

Taken around 1908, this photograph shows the Vandalia Railroad depot in Plainfield. The depot was located between North Center and North Vine Streets, parallel to the railroad tracks. Originally, the streets were called State and Depot. The railroad was the lifeblood for many towns in Indiana, including Plainfield. The first railroad through Hendricks County was completed in the 1850s.

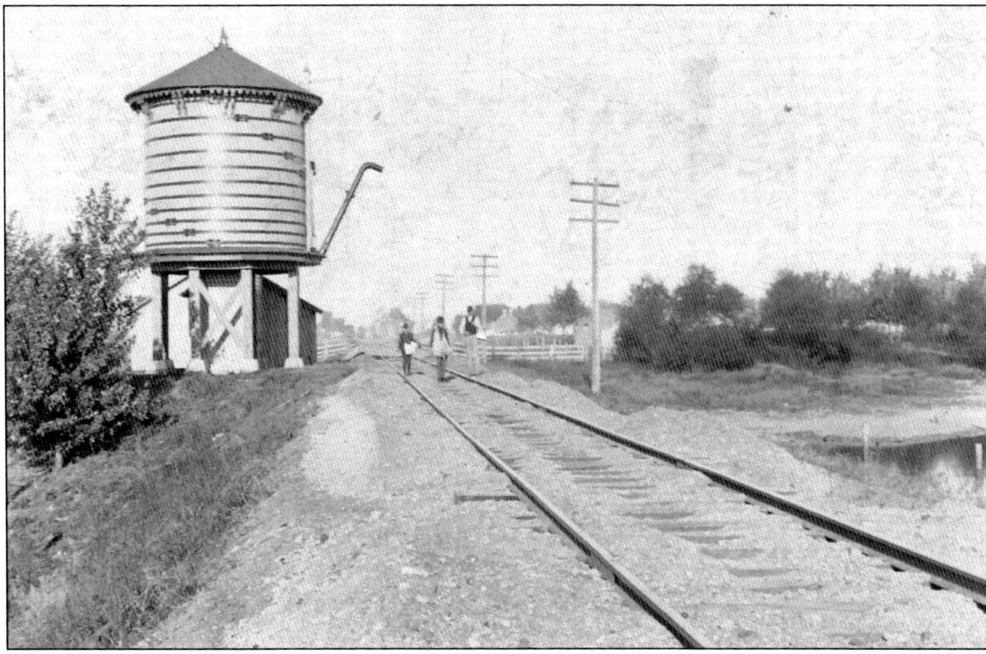

Just east of the Plainfield depot station sat the classic wooden water tank supported by horizontal steel bands, its water spout ready for the next steam engine to pass by. The tank provided water to the train's tender. Notice the three young men walking the tracks in front of the tank, carrying their satchels with them.

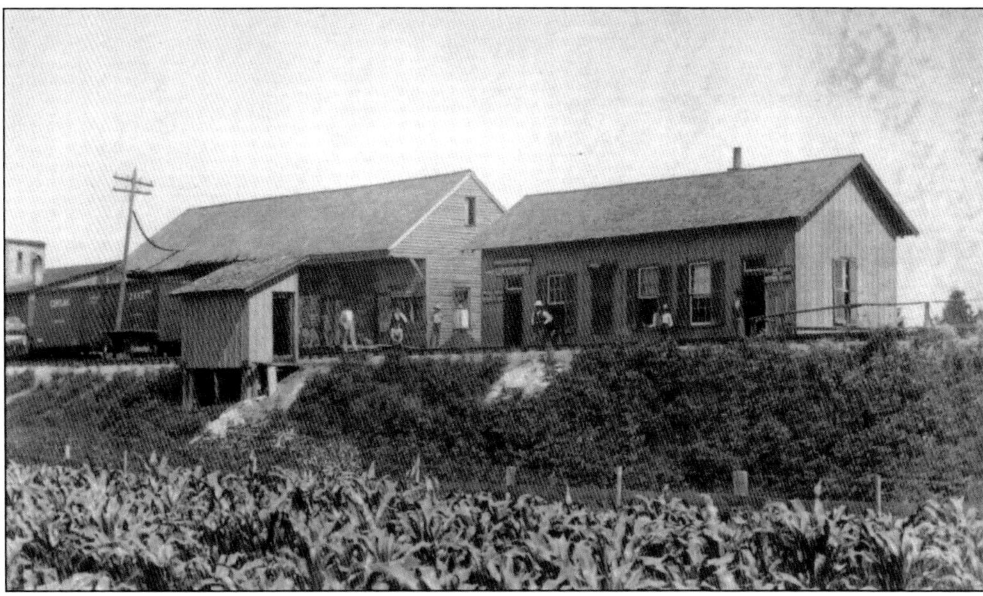

Taken by photographer J.P. Calvert, this view of the railroad in Plainfield, Indiana, shows freight buildings east of the depot, near Avon Avenue. The boxcar is CISL&C (Cincinnati, Indianapolis, St. Louis & Chicago), and the photograph was taken between 1880 and 1889. In 1889, the CISL&C merged with the Cleveland, Columbus, Cincinnati & Indianapolis Railway to form the Cleveland, Cincinnati, Chicago & St. Louis Railway. The sign by the door reads "Purchase tickets before entering the cars."

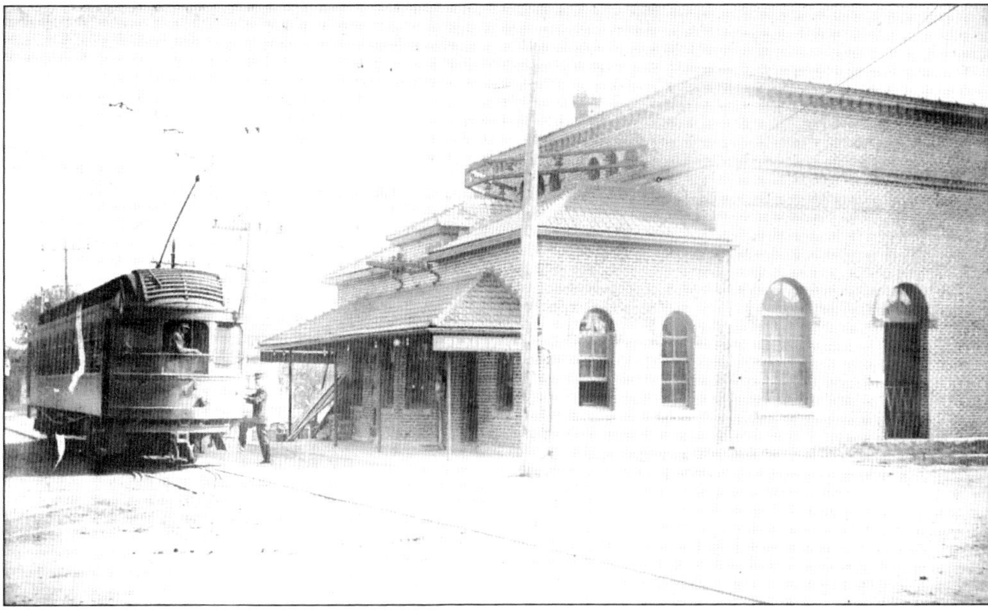

The Terre Haute, Indianapolis & Eastern Company's Plainfield interurban station was located at the corner of Buchanan and S. Vine Streets. Interurban rail service to Plainfield began in 1902 and lasted until 1940, when the last electric rail car came through town. Caleb Carter, who lived diagonally across the street, served as the ticket agent for many years. He worked seven days a week, 12 hours per day and earned $80 each month. The historic building, which was restored in 2003, is owned by the Town of Plainfield and used as a rental facility.

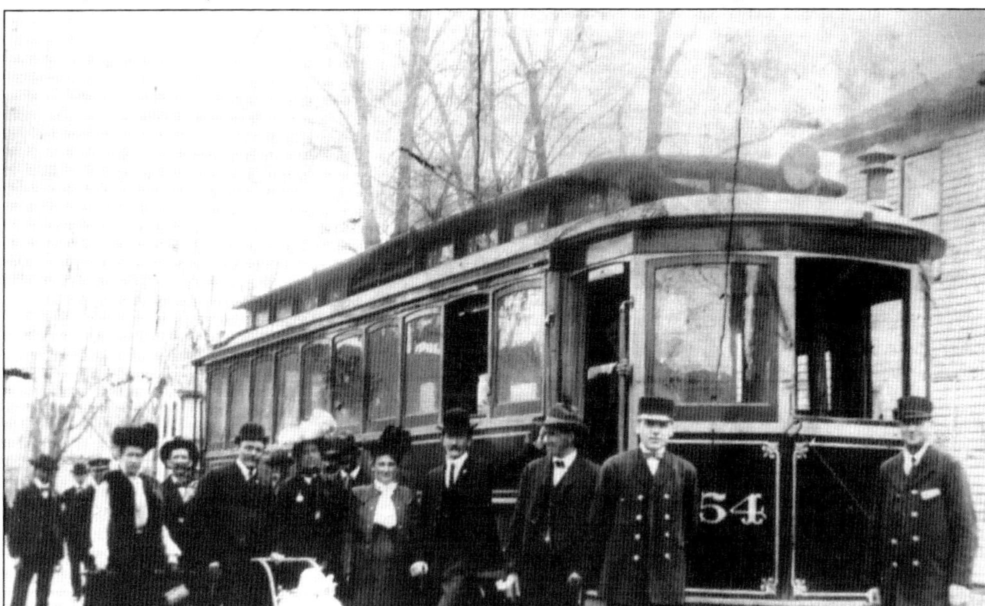

During a brief stop in 1904, passengers took a moment to pose for a photograph while waiting to board interurban car no. 54 in Plainfield. The unidentified conductor and trainman are standing in front of the car. The interurban lines split at the station on Buchanan Street. One line continued west, and the other turned north toward US 40.

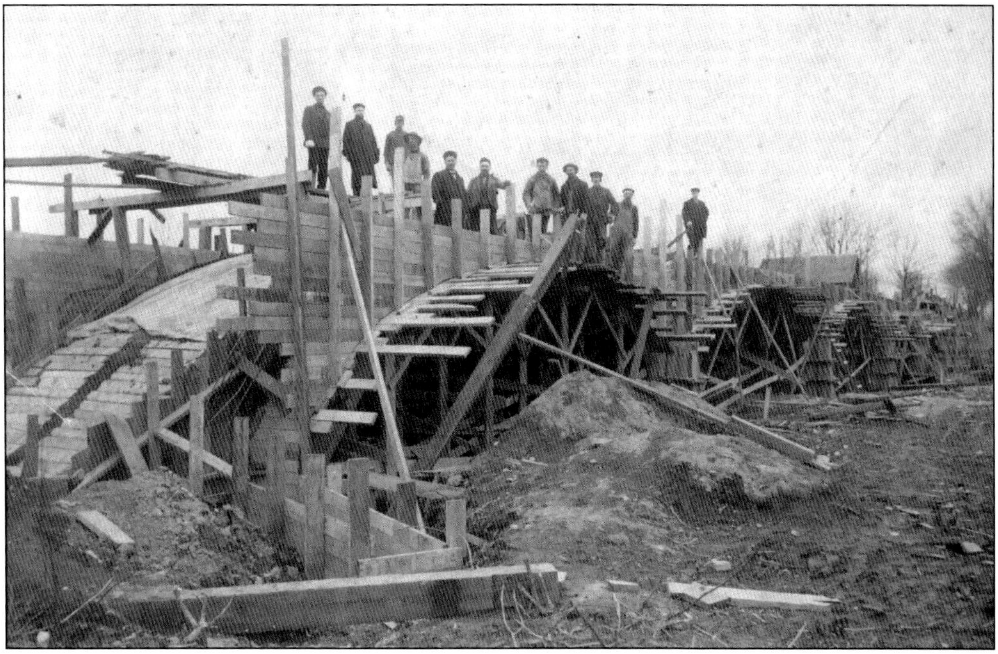

This 1907 photograph shows a crew of men constructing the interurban bridge over White Lick Creek, just west of Plainfield. The tracks ran west out of town, through the Indiana Boys' School property, and continued through Hendricks County and on to Putnam County. The distinctive arches have been framed and are awaiting a permanent foundation.

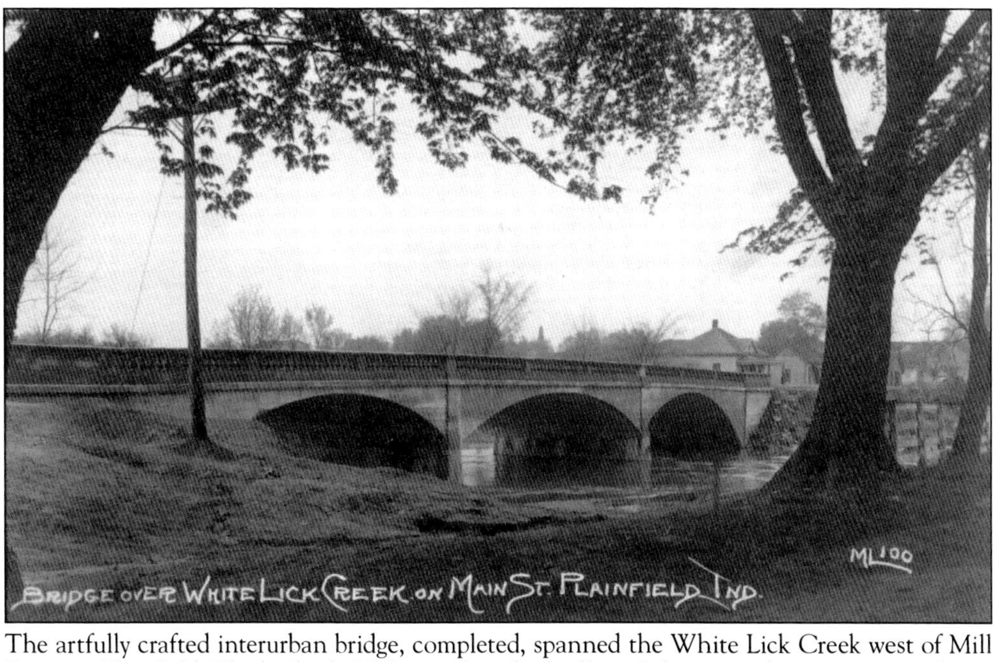

The artfully crafted interurban bridge, completed, spanned the White Lick Creek west of Mill Street in Plainfield. The bridge held the tracks, which allowed the interurban cars to travel east and west through Hendricks County. According to newspaper accounts, local sentiment doubted that the bridge would ever be completed, so it was big news when it was ready for interurban cars to travel over it.

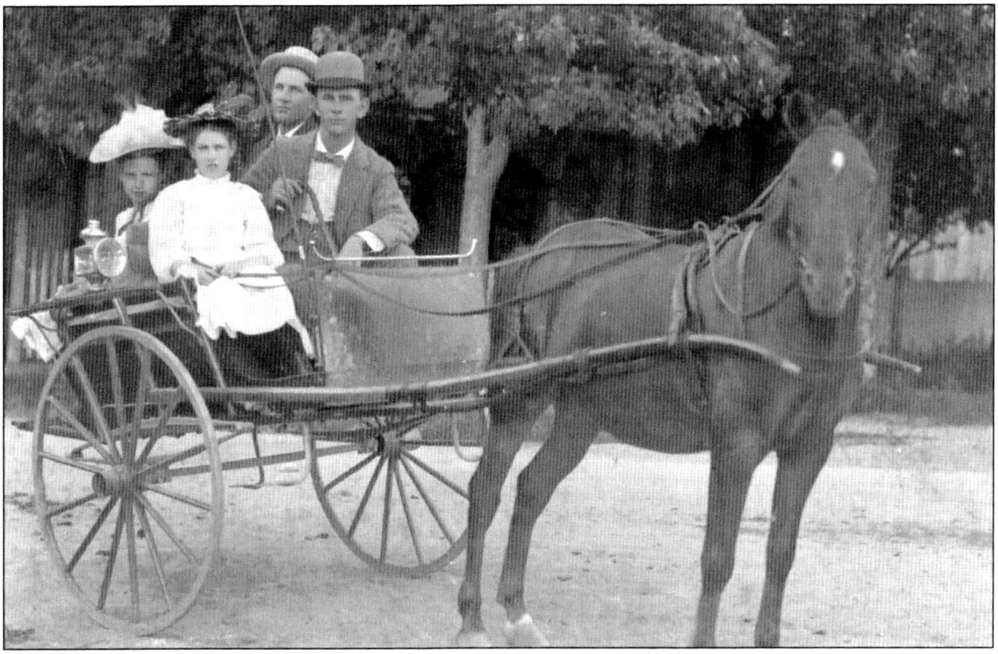

Plainfield residents enjoying a horse-drawn buggy ride are, from left to right, Edith Ellis, Hortense Moore, Charles Vestal, and Ralph Swearingen. This photograph was taken in the early 1900s. Although it appears as if the two young men could be courting their belles, marriage records show that all four of them married other people.

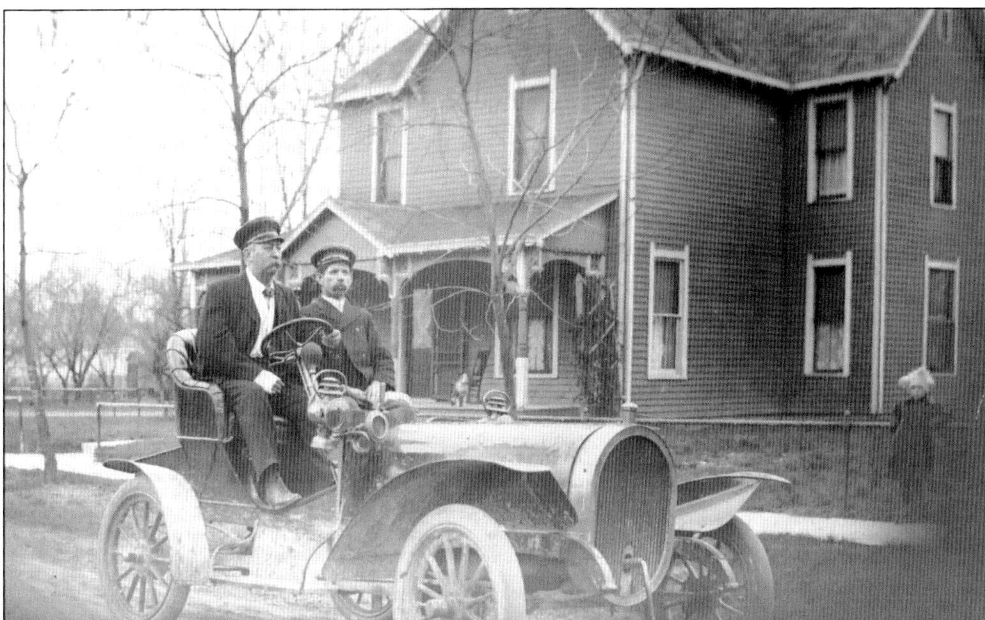

W.L. DeWeese and a Mr. Vaughn sit proudly in their Maxwell automobile in 1902. The car is in front of the George Black house at the corner of Buchanan and South East Streets. Oftentimes, cars were designed with oversized fenders, as seen here, to protect riders from the muddy conditions of the streets.

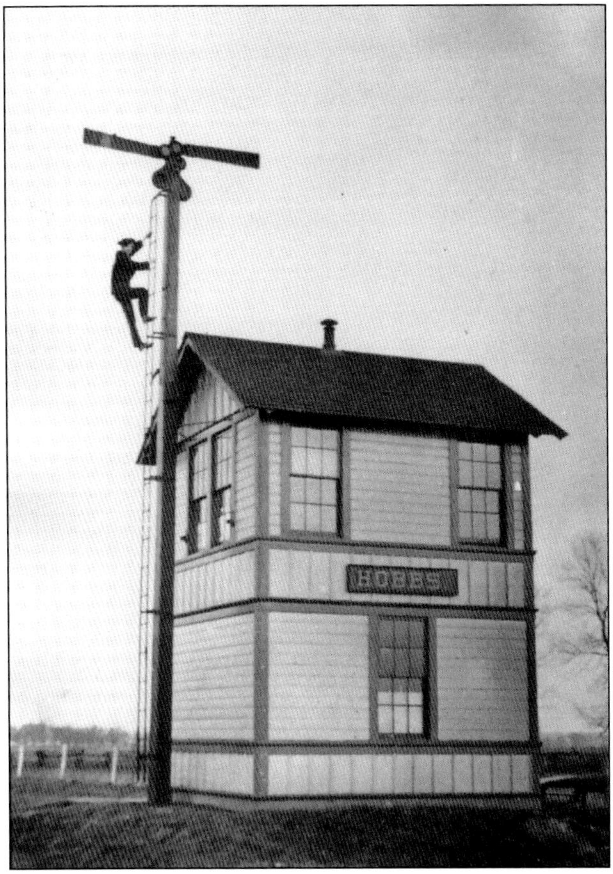

Hobbs Tower, designed to signal railroad cars as they pass the Hobbs spur line, was located on the east side of Plainfield. This c. 1906 photograph shows a Hobbs Nursery Company employee scaling the tower to put up the semaphore lamp, which was used at night. The tower was one mile west of Six Points Road.

Patrons disembark from the interurban cars after arriving in Plainfield. The cars are on the north track, heading toward US 40 on Vine Street. In the distance, the buildings at the corner are slightly visible, including the Cope Building at 104 West Main Street. The clock reads 2:48 p.m.

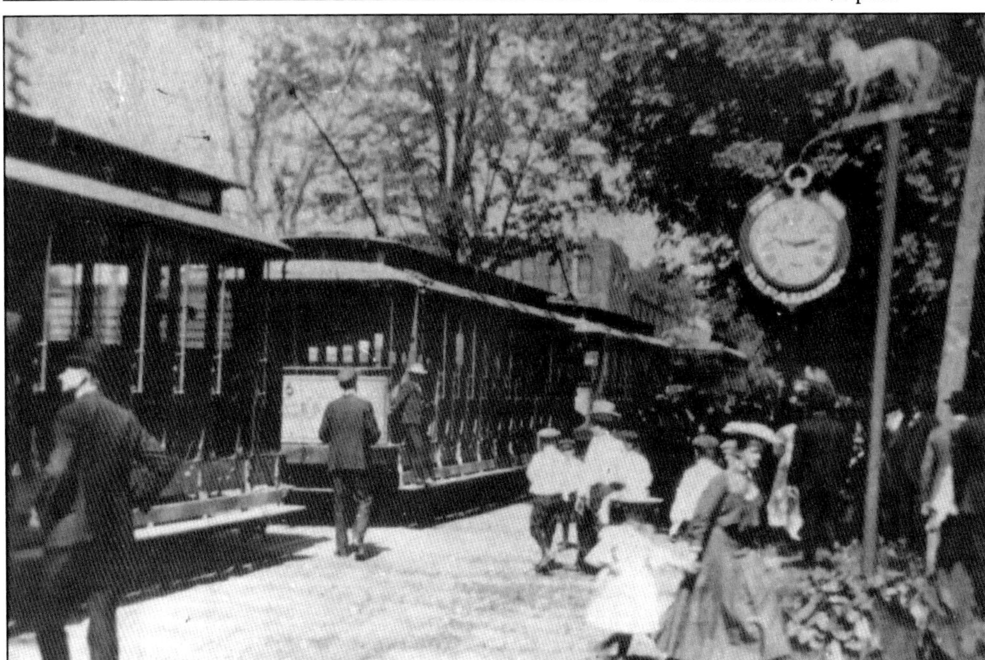

Eight

FUN TIMES

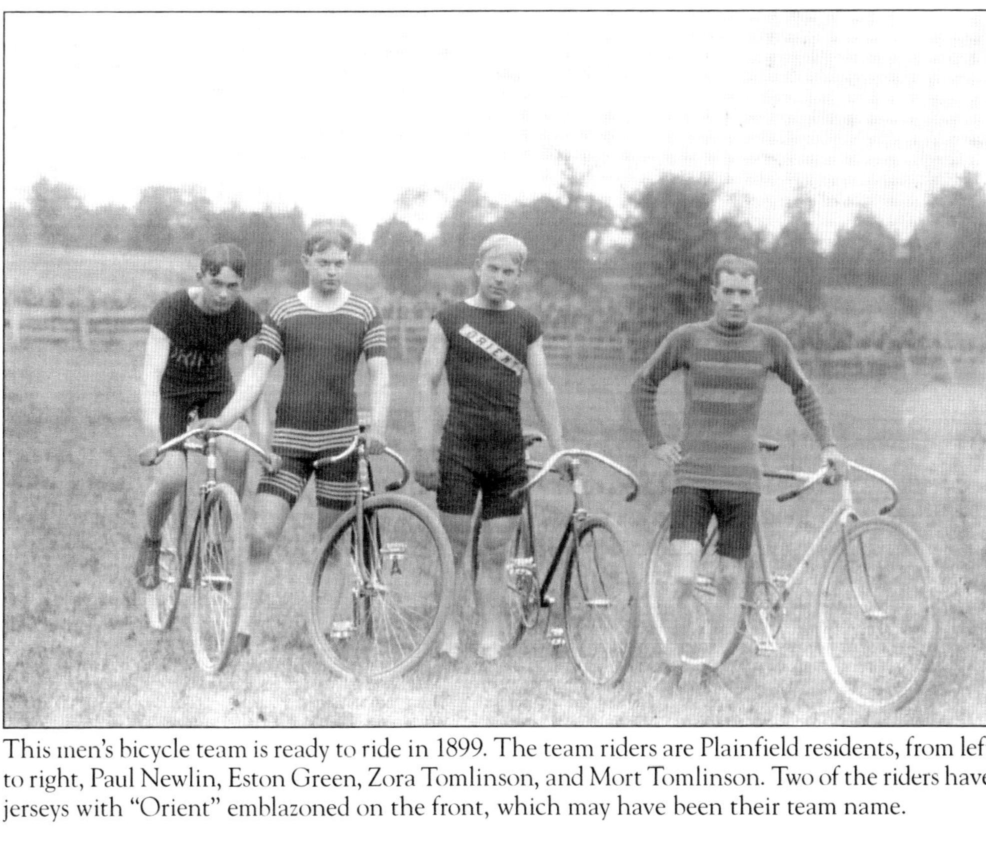

This men's bicycle team is ready to ride in 1899. The team riders are Plainfield residents, from left to right, Paul Newlin, Eston Green, Zora Tomlinson, and Mort Tomlinson. Two of the riders have jerseys with "Orient" emblazoned on the front, which may have been their team name.

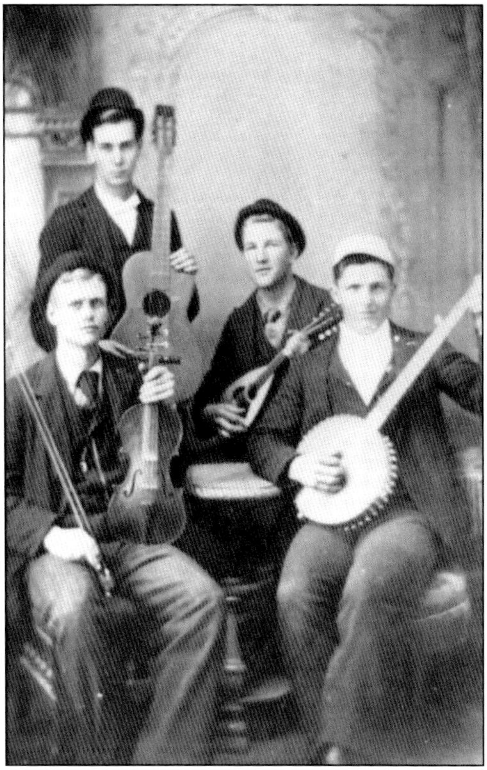

Possibly Plainfield's first bluegrass musical combo, this quartet from Central Academy posed for a portrait in 1898. The musicians are Orzo Hadley (violin), Pleasant Morgan (guitar), Ralph Swearingen (mandolin), and Guy Seaton (banjo). Musical groups were popular at this time as the Chautauqua movement made its way across the county, encouraging residents to invest their time in matters of cultural interest.

This group of dapper-looking rabbit hunters has just returned from a very cold day of hunting. It appears that only Ernest Cooper and Dot Bly were successful on the venture, as they hold their bounty. The men are, from left to right, Cooper, Emmett Bly, Dot Bly, and two unidentified men. The specific Plainfield street location is not known.

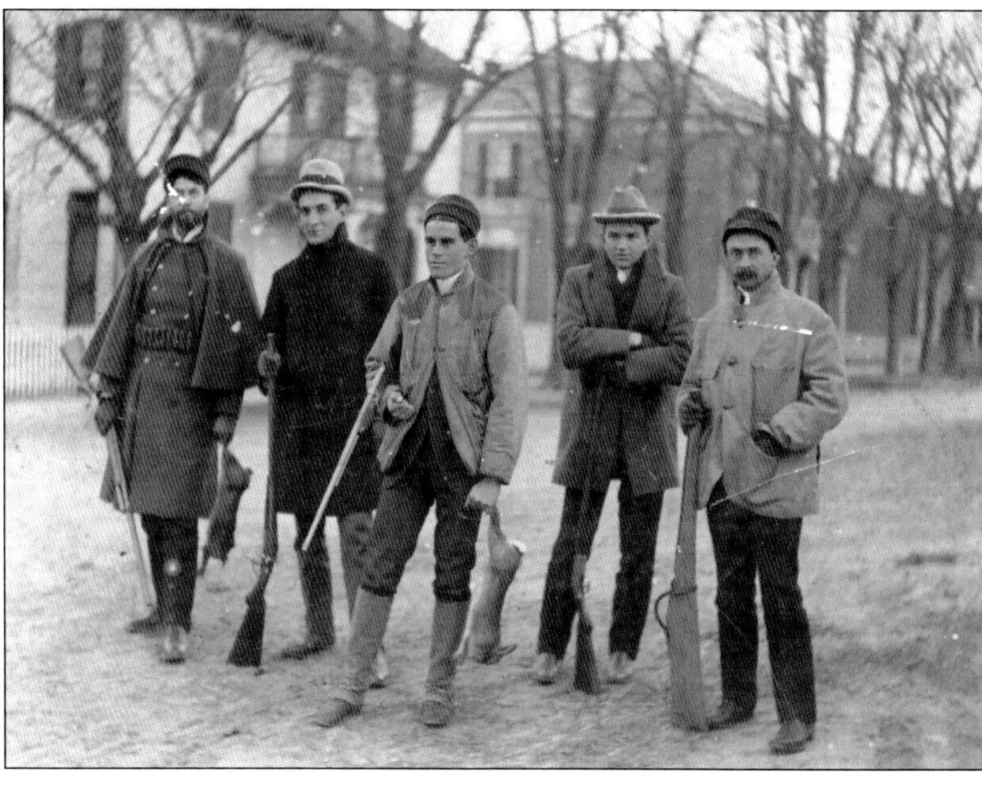

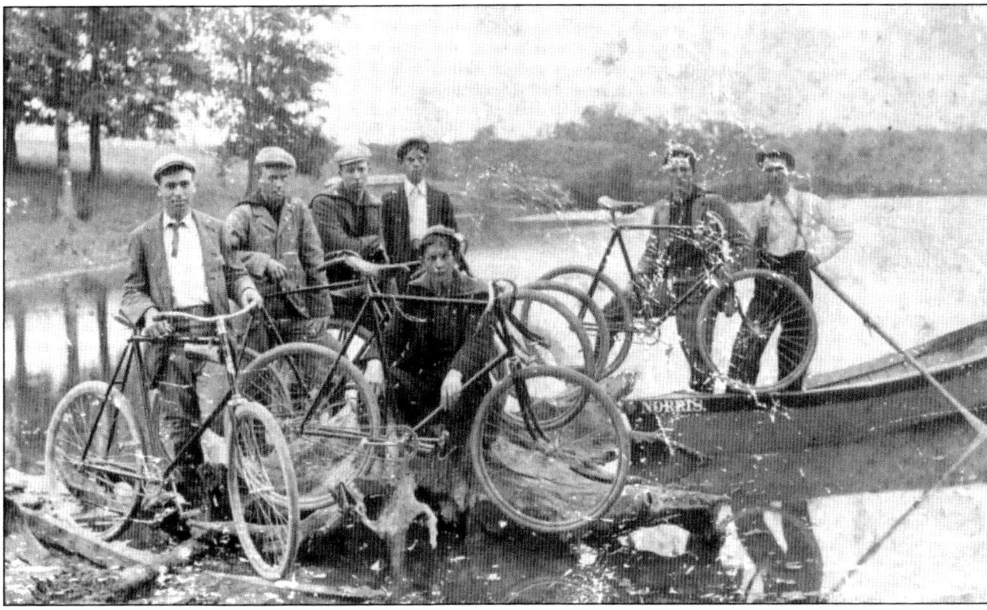

This 1897 photograph of the Plainfield Bicycle Club shows the members posed with their bicycles at Hadley's Pond, north of Plainfield. The bicycle club members from left to right are Arvid Stanley, Joe Hiss, Everett Townsend, Ralph Reagan, Earl Stout (seated), Verl Osborn, and Hubert Douglas.

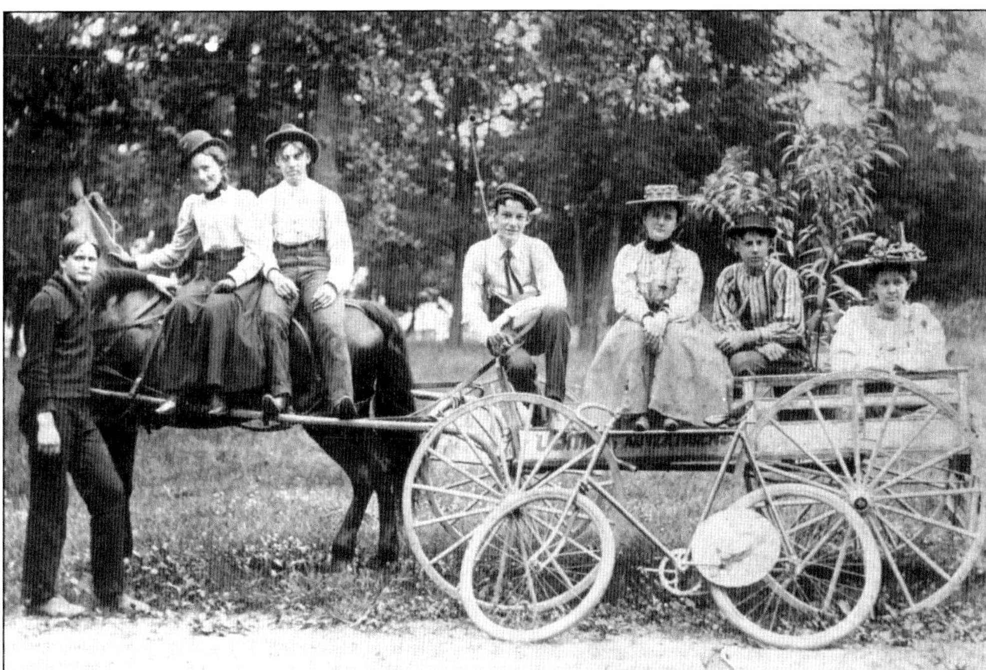

Posed for a good time, this group of Plainfield High School students looks to be enjoying an afternoon outing. Identified here in this 1898 photograph are Frank Frazier (standing) and Lizzie Evans and Chester Miller (seated on the horse). The names of the students on the wagon are illegible on the original photograph.

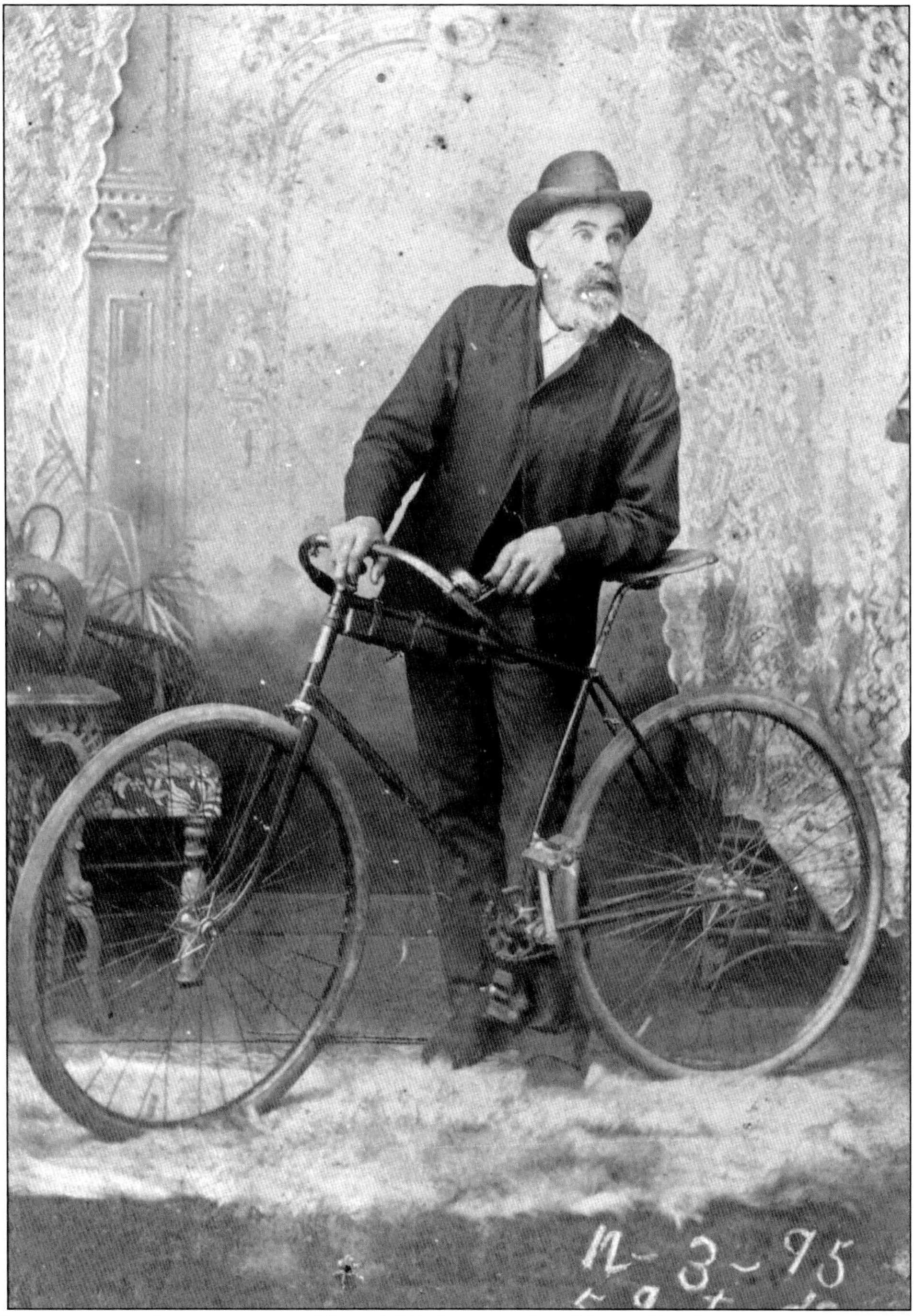

Not one to stand on ceremony, Plainfield photographer Moses Tomlinson commonly took photographs of himself using his own modern equipment. In fact, he was known to snap a shot each year on his birthday. This photograph is from December 3, 1895, when he was 59 years old. He owned a photograph studio in Plainfield, and throughout his lifetime, he earned the title of "master" photographer. Moses lived until he was 90 years old, passing away on January 30, 1927. He is buried in Maple Hill Cemetery.

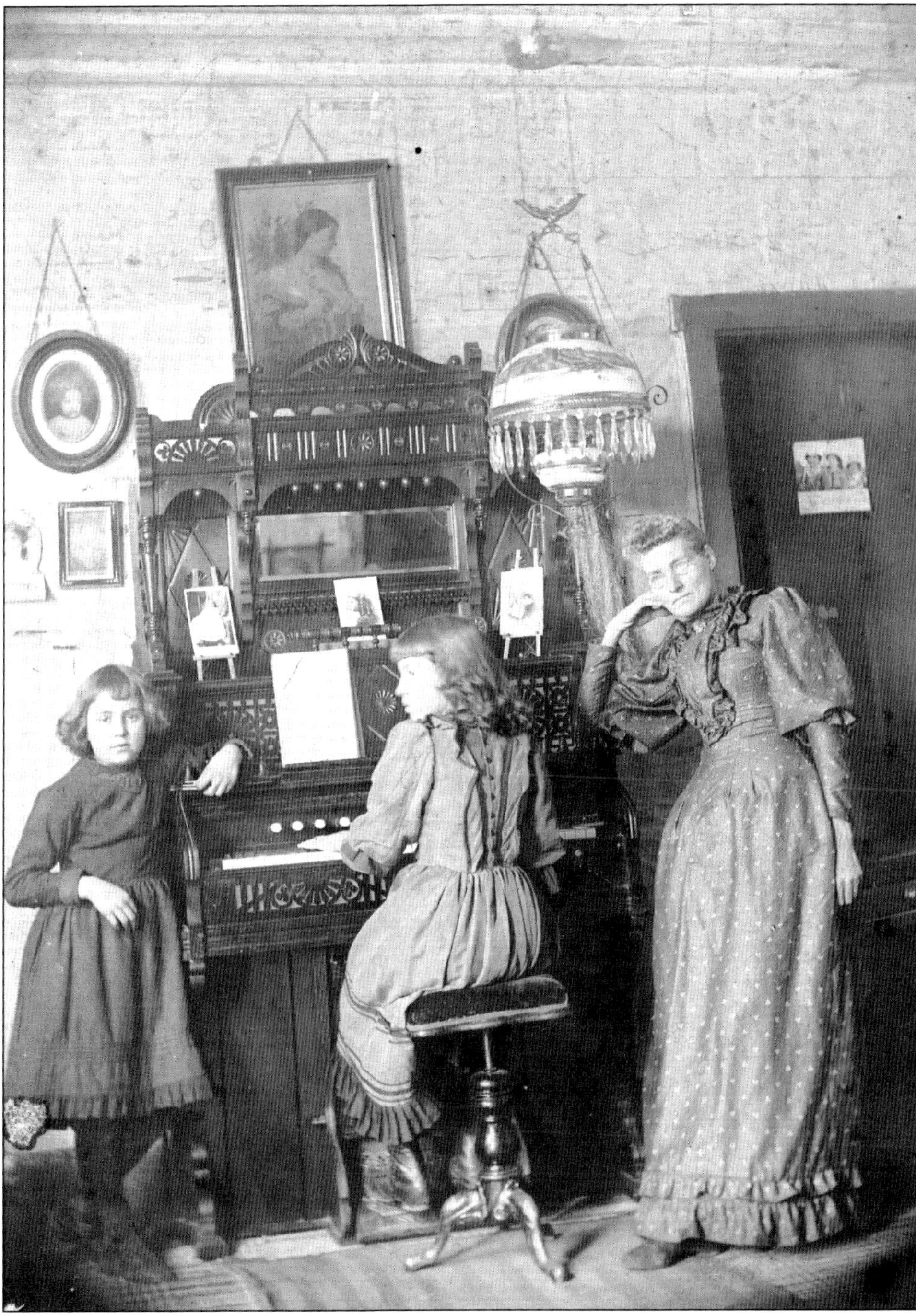

Seen here in a photograph from 1898 is Martha Jane Jackson Tomlinson and daughters Artelia and Eunice (playing), as they enjoy the music from the organ in their parlor. Moses Tomlinson, a prominent Plainfield photographer, was the husband of Martha and father of Artelia and Eunice. There are several portrait photographs on the organ and the wall, most likely taken by Moses. Martha and Moses Tomlinson had five other children: Generva, Ray, Worth, Gurney, and Frank.

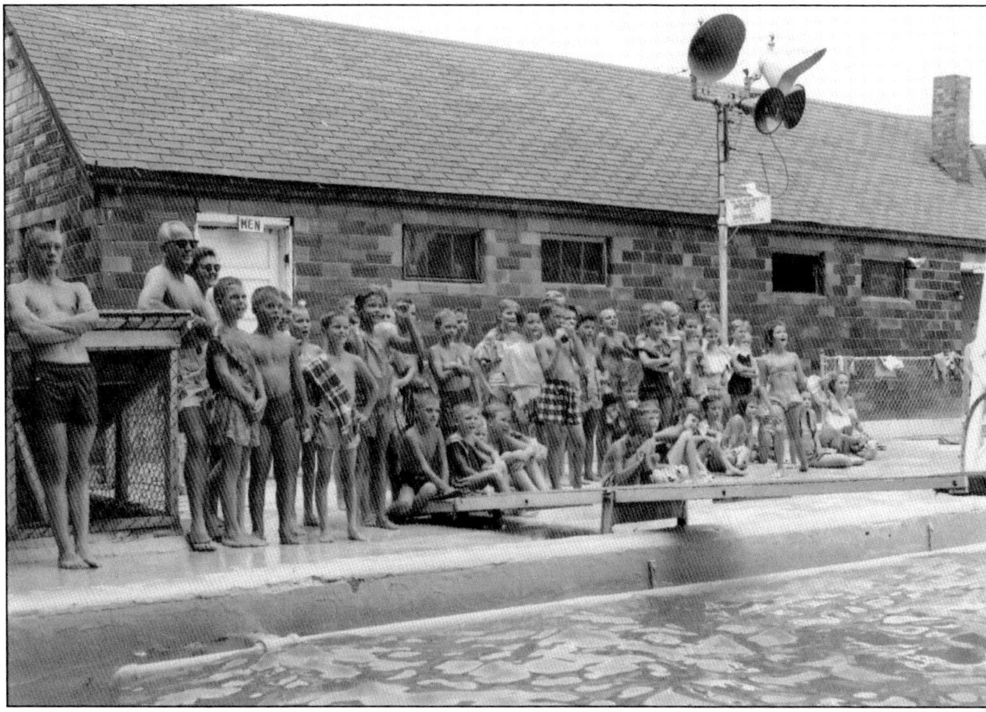

One of the favorite summertime locations in Plainfield was the Sunshine Swimming Pool. Gen. Forest Calbert opened his Sunshine Swimming Pool and Tourist Camp on the south side of US 40, west of downtown. The swimming pool opened on May 31, 1930. These two photographs are from the summer of 1958. When longtime Plainfield residents reminisce about their childhood, they fondly remember the Sunshine Swimming Pool. They recall taking swimming lessons here, obtaining summer family season passes for $10, and purchasing food from the snack shop. In addition to the pool, the complex also included very popular tourist cabins and a service station. The pool was closed during the years of World War II. After Calbert's death, the pool was operated by his son Fred. The property was sold in 1942 to the Pure Oil Company and then again to the Gordon/Postlewaite family before being acquired by the Plainfield Optimist Club in 1958. The Sunshine Swimming Pool closed in 1964.

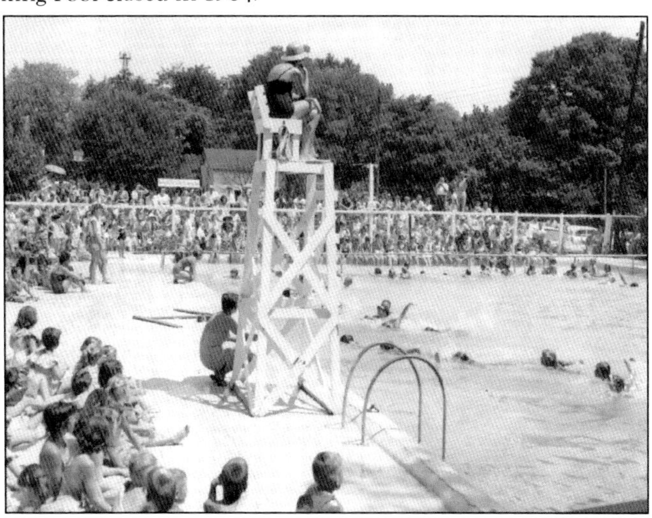

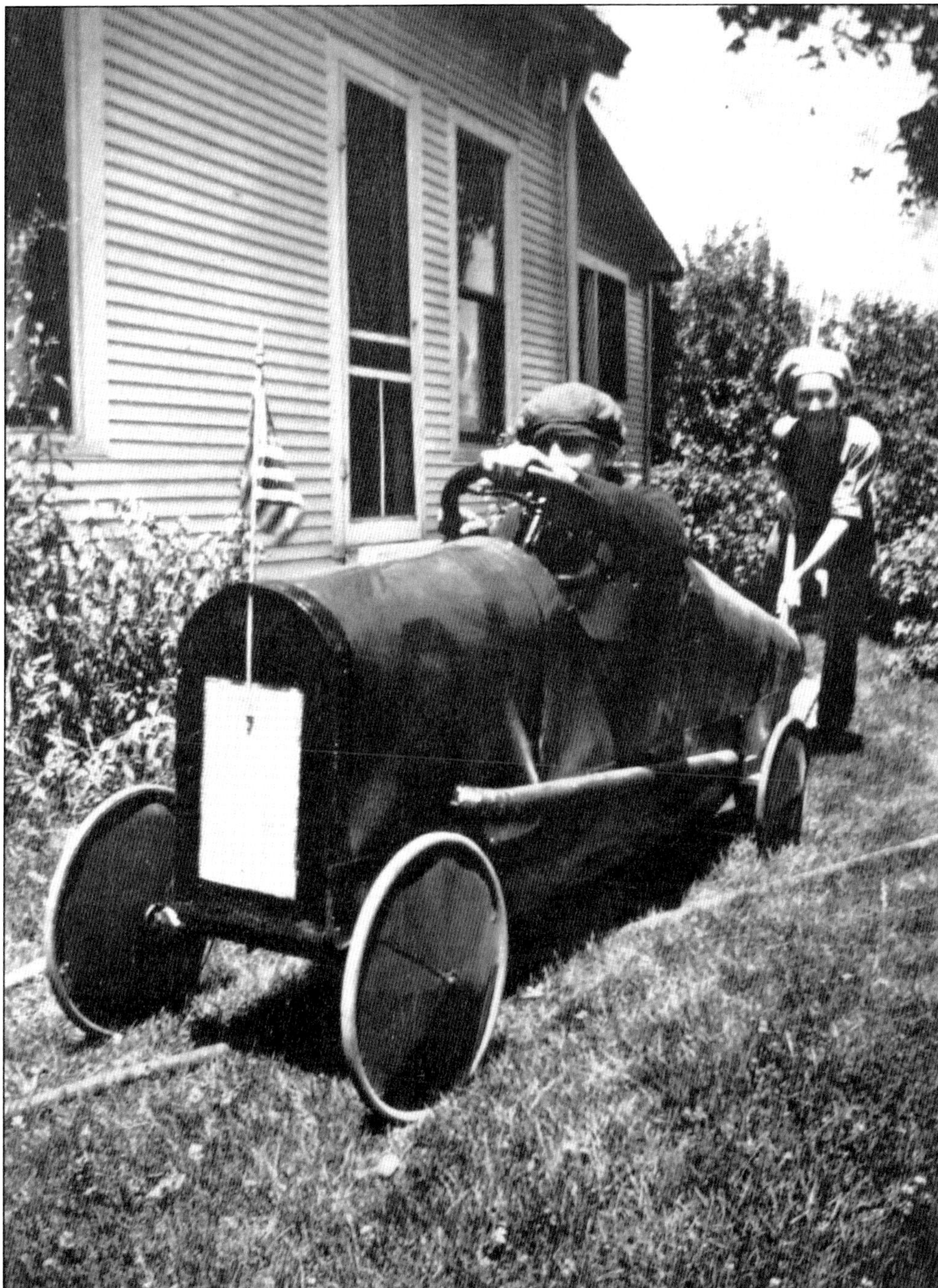

Unfortunately, this photograph has no identification, but the joyous expression of these young soapbox car enthusiasts is hard to resist. The term *soap box derby* was christened in 1933 when a Dayton, Ohio, reporter encountered three boys racing homemade, engine-less cars down an inclined street. Probably taken in the summer, this photograph shows foliage in full bloom in the distance. The hood of the car proudly sports an American flag front and center.

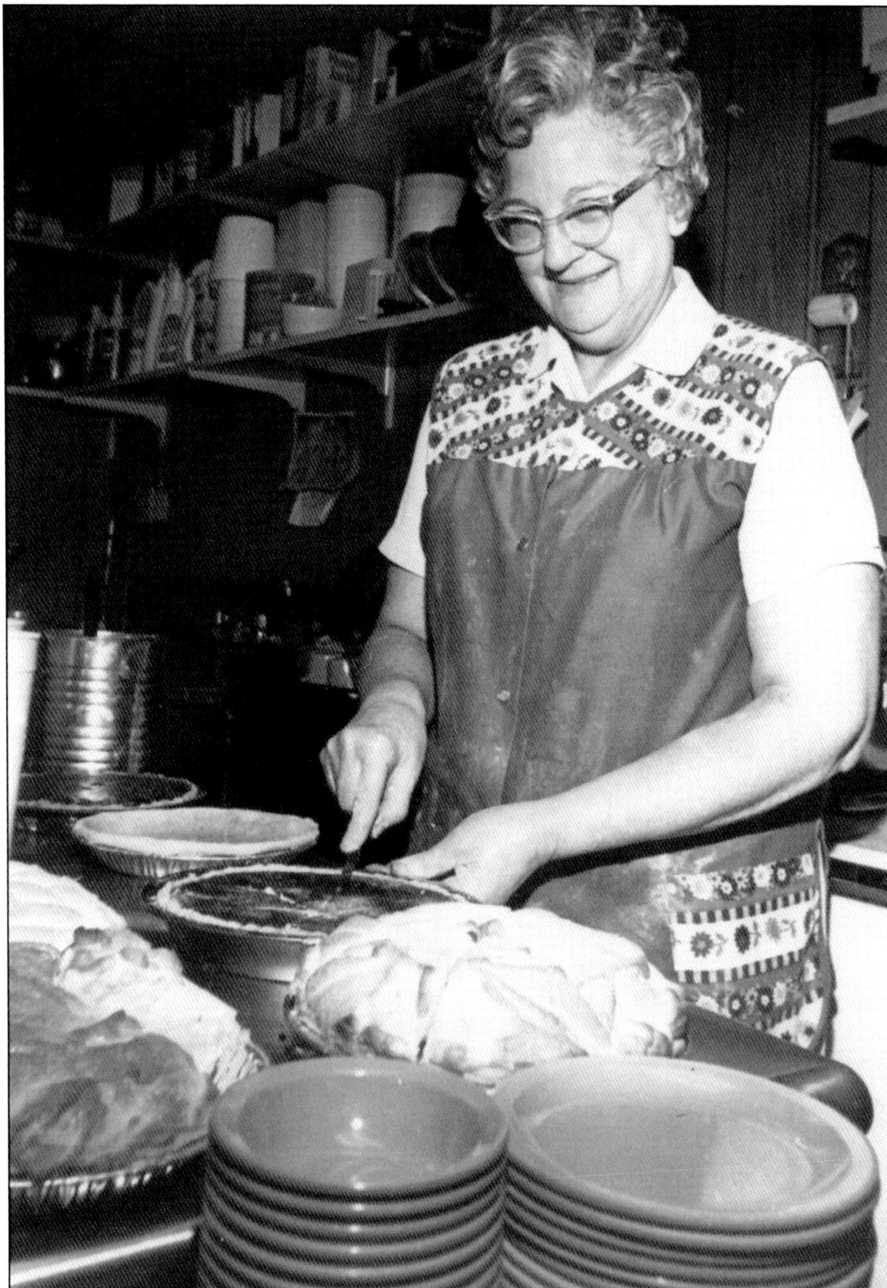

Edna Blanton's homemade pies were very well known in Plainfield. This photograph shows her, on November 11, 1976, preparing to cut a piece from the last homemade pie in her shop, Edna's Pie Shop. Blanton moved to Plainfield in 1941 and went to work for Evelyn Patrick, who owned the Circle Inn, which was located at 110 East Main. In 1949, Blanton purchased the Circle Inn, moved it to 101 East Main in 1954, and changed the name to Blanton's Restaurant. She sold the restaurant in the summer of 1971 and opened her pie shop four months later on November 17. Blanton made pies for several local restaurants, including the Country Kitchen and Kristy's Restaurant. She died on October 14, 1993.

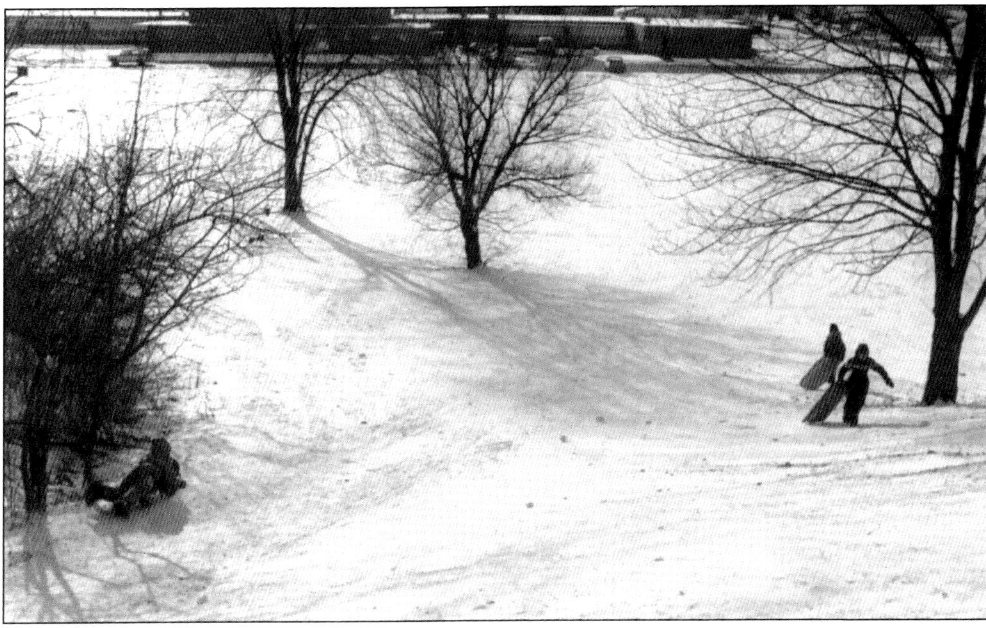

Two very popular Plainfield sledding locations are Hobbs Hill and Maple Hill. Hobbs Hill, as seen in the above photograph in 1980, provides town children a place to have some winter fun. Located just west of Hobbs Street, the hill sends the brave ones hurling down toward the back of Van Buren Elementary School. Just a little south of Hobbs Hill is Maple Hill Cemetery, which has also offered children of all ages a snowy place to spend some time outdoors. Pictured from left to right below, trudging back to the top of the hill for another downhill run in February 1978, are Dean Campbell, Vince Smith, and Calvin Arnold.

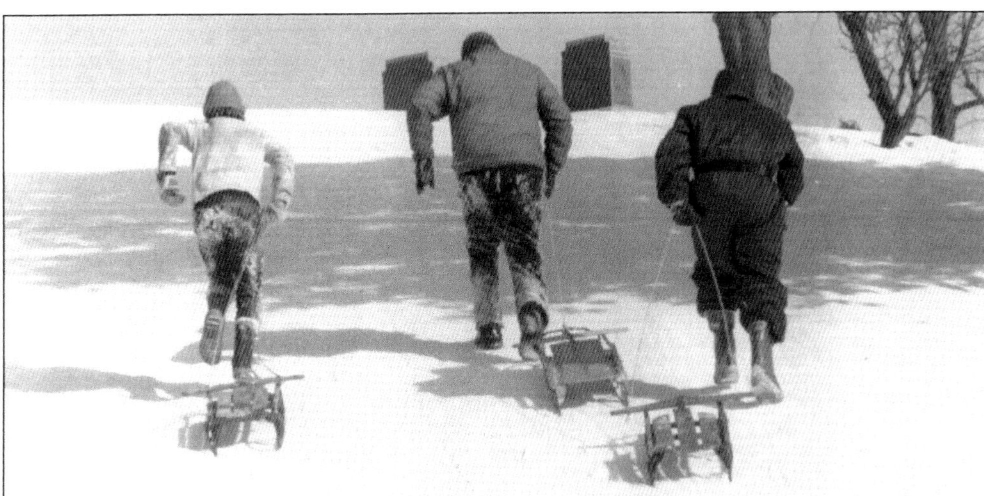

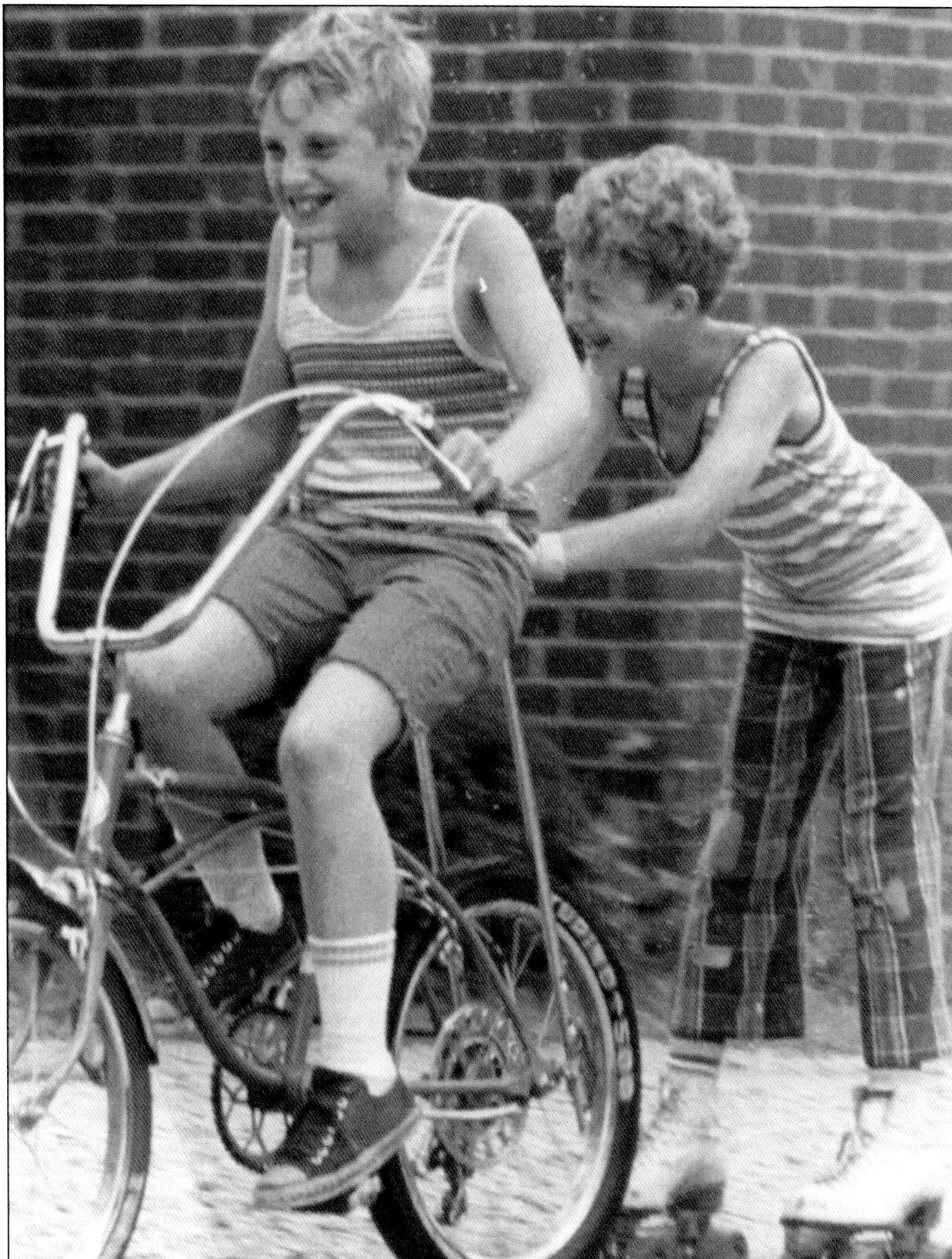

Having fun are young Plainfield residents Richard Smith (left) and Jeff Wiggins. This July 1979 photograph is a blast from the nostalgic past, complete with a Schwinn Stingray bicycle, roller skates, Chuck Taylor shoes, tube socks, plaid pants, and striped shirts. Unbridled enthusiasm is clearly evident on the faces of the boys. The photograph was originally published in the *Plainfield Messenger* and accompanied by an article that told of several days of rain that had kept residents cooped up inside. As the inclement weather subsided, these two youngsters took full advantage of a dry, sunny day.

Nine

INDIANA BOYS' SCHOOL

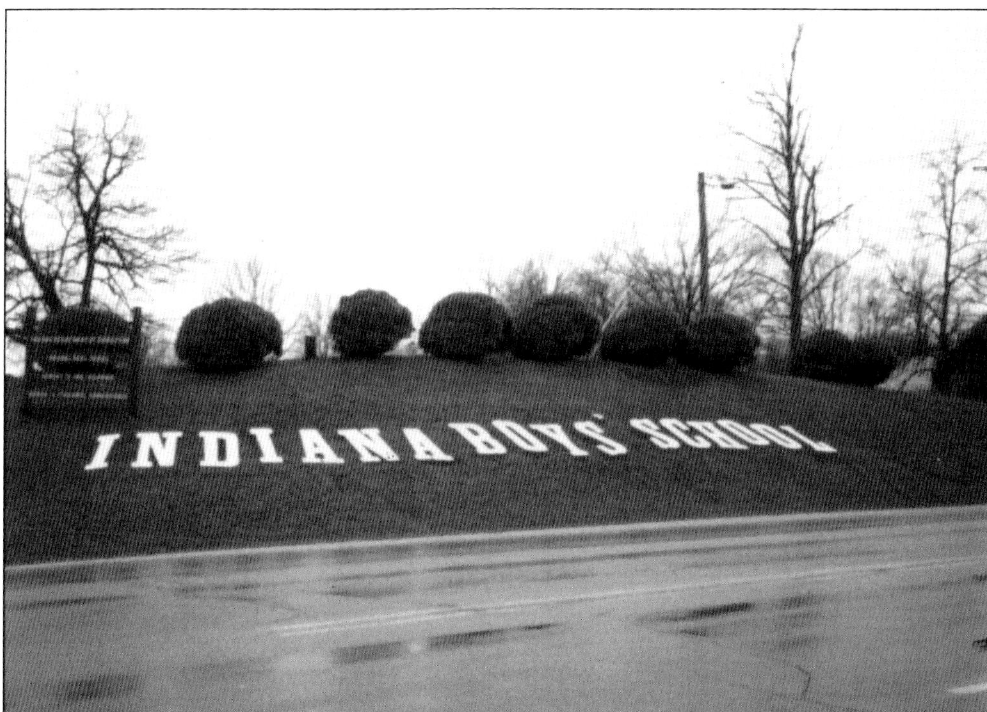

In 1867, Indiana governor Conrad Baker purchased 225 acres of land near Plainfield to form a House of Refuge for delinquent boys. Several buildings were constructed, and on January 26, 1868, the first boy (from Hendricks County) was registered at the school. By year's end, there were 112 registered. Throughout its history as a reform school, the institution taught various vocations and provided training and education for the boys. Pictured here are the very familiar white concrete letters on the hill at the entrance to the campus. The five-foot-high letters, which were installed in 1927, were removed when the grounds was renovated in the mid-2000s.

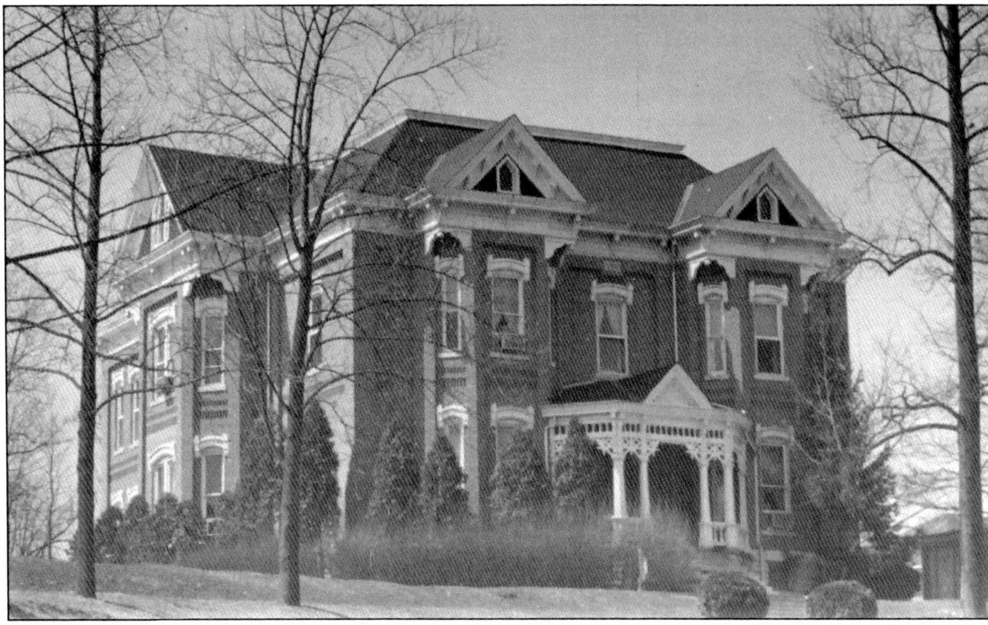

Taken in 1974, this photograph shows the impressive Administration Building of the Indiana Boys' School. This gracious building was constructed in 1893 as the superintendent's residence. The 8,512-square-foot space was converted for administrative use in 1925. The renovation involved remodeling the lower floor into office space. The upper floor was converted to living space for the assistant superintendent.

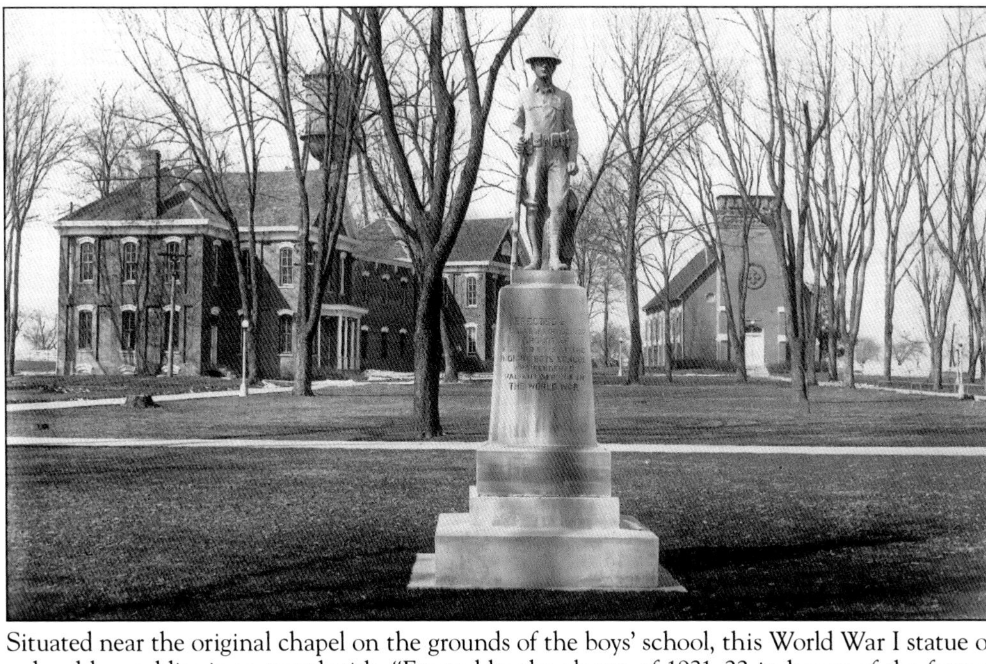

Situated near the original chapel on the grounds of the boys' school, this World War I statue of a doughboy soldier is engraved with, "Erected by the classes of 1921–22 in honor of the former boys of the Indiana Boys' School who rendered valiant service in the World War." According to the groundskeeping staff, the statue was destroyed when a tree fell during a storm and broke it into pieces. It was never replaced.

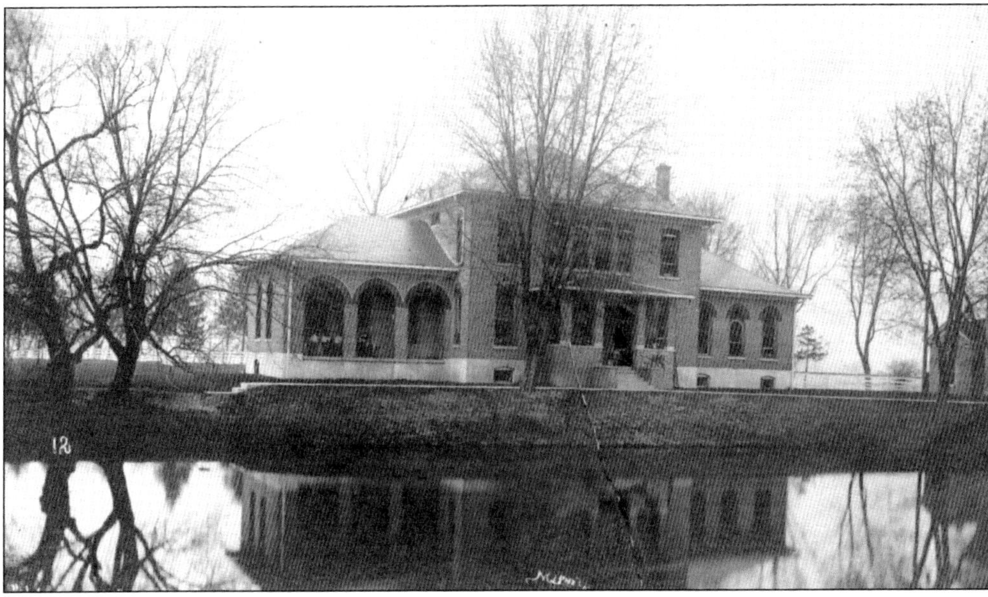

The Indiana Boys' School offered full health care for the young residents of the institution. On staff was a full-time physician who looked after the boys and made sure they had proper medical care. The above photograph shows the second hospital that was built on the property. This location provided a serene lakeside setting, which surely provided a calm atmosphere for the sick. The image below shows Dr. Larkin attending to a patient. Sadly, the fate of the hospital did not fare well, and it was razed in 1973 and 1974.

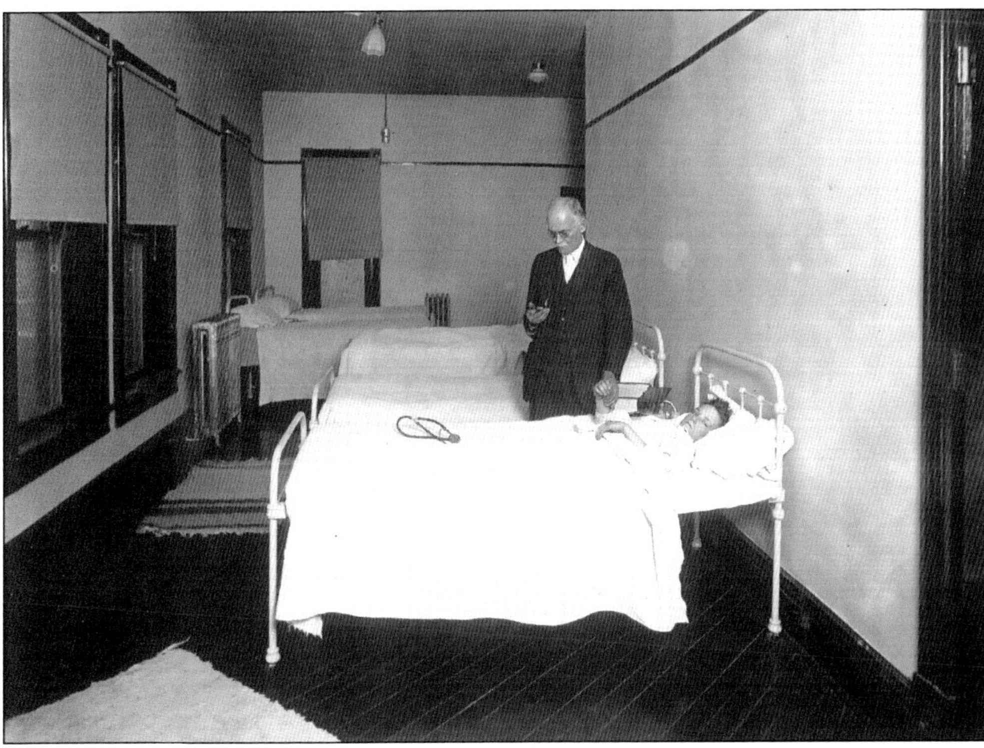

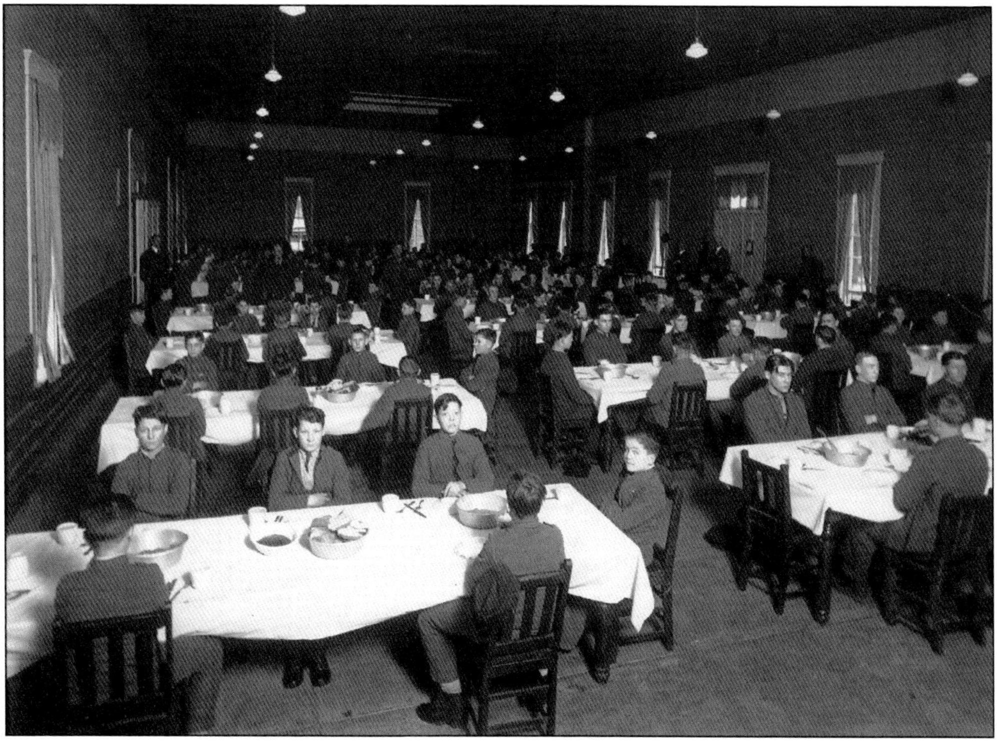

Discipline and order were part of the structure provided for the residents at the Indiana Boys' School. Even though there was a family environment at the school, it was necessary to maintain a steady, consistent lifestyle that offered the boys the structure some were lacking. These two photographs illustrate the military-like order that was maintained at the school. The dining hall, built in 1893, housed over 100 boys for three meals each day. In the above photograph, taken about 1917, the tables are covered with white tablecloths, and the boys are properly seated at their places. There were several dormitories, or cottages, where the boys lived. In the below photograph, from 1918, the boys of Washington barracks stand by their beds in one of the dorms.

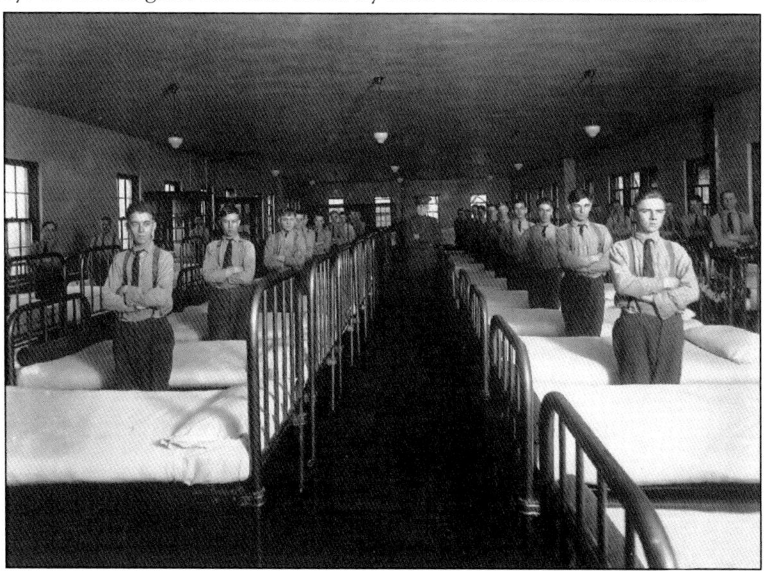

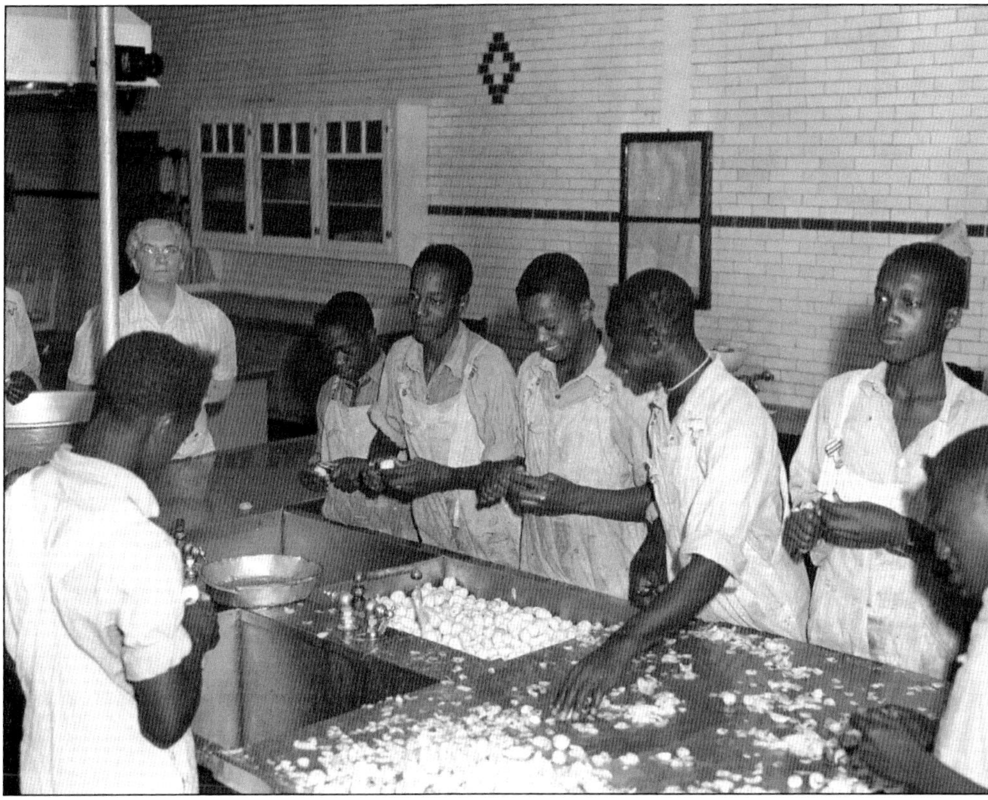

Part of the school's mission was not only to reform the boys, but also teach them trades that they could use later in life. The variety of trades also benefited the school. Under the watchful eye of cook Retta Atwood, this group of young men spends time peeling potatoes for the evening dinner.

Providing three meals a day for the residents of the Indiana Boys' School meant spending a great deal of time in the kitchen preparing meals. Here, the boys bake multiple pans of bread, five loaves at a time. Stacks of empty bread pans below the oven indicate that the baking process was nonstop.

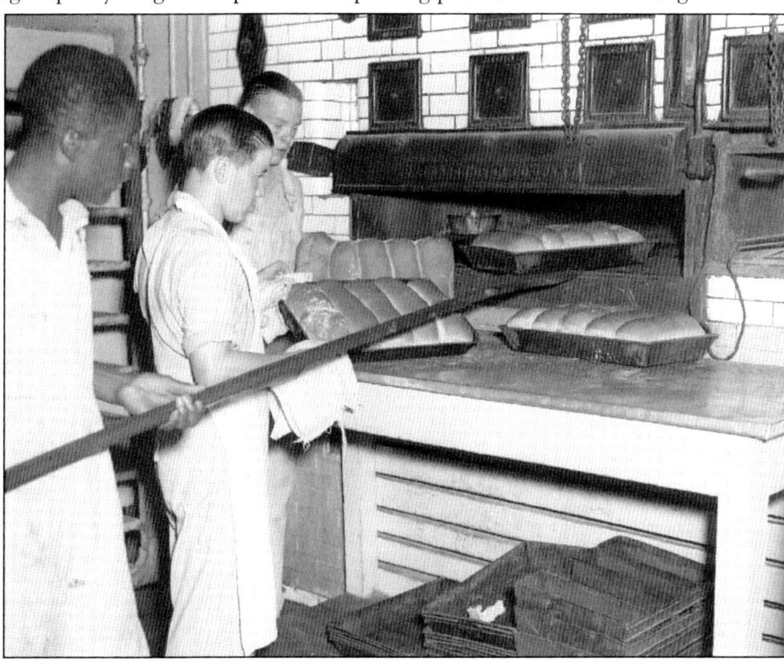

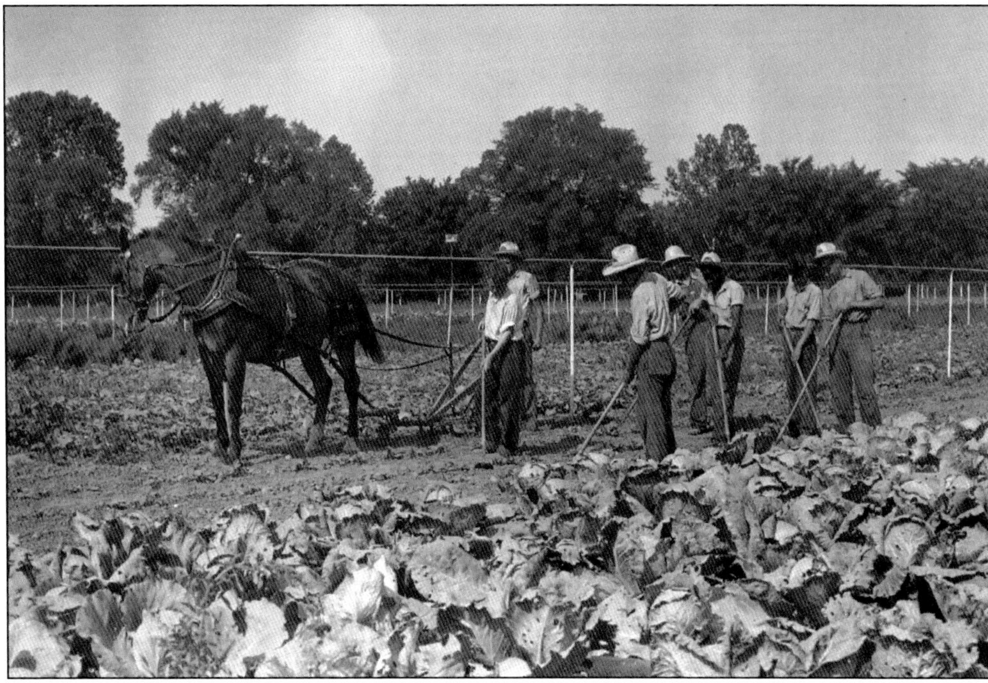

Learning how to grow vegetables and tend a garden were some of the skills the boys learned at the school. Although it was hard work, the end product was rewarding, as the crops were used by the cooks in the kitchen to feed the boys. Extra produce was provided for sale to local residents. In the above photograph, planting the seedlings one at a time, these boys care for the lettuce crop. Non-mechanized equipment (horse and hoe) also meant keeping particular care while in the fields. Below, under the instruction of farm manager Frank Bauer, these boys plant additional crops among the mature cabbage plants ready for harvest. Bauer was employed at the school from 1934 to 1971, at which time he retired.

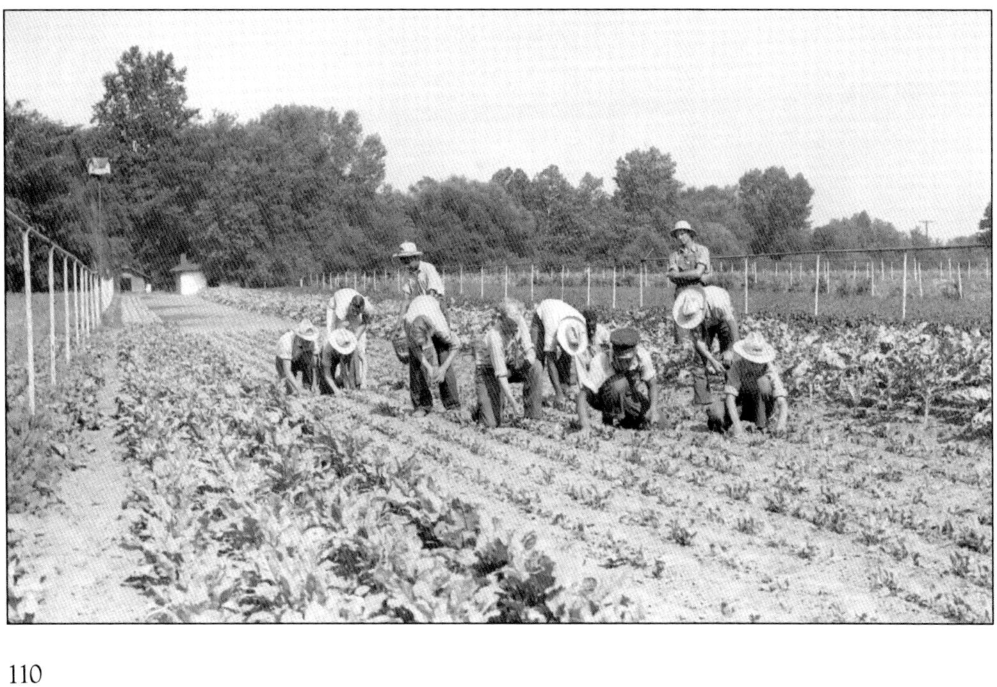

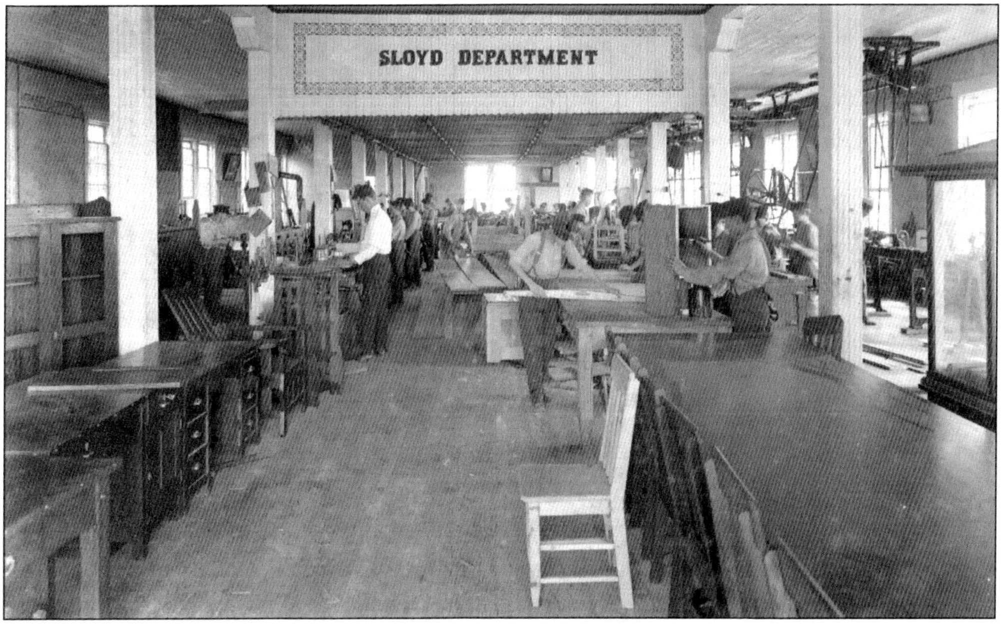

In this photograph, boys learn the craft of furniture making under a method known as Sloyd learning, as depicted by the sign in the room. Originating in Finland in 1865, Sloyd was an educational system of handicraft-based learning programs. The Sloyd concept reached the United States during the 1880s. The Indiana Boys' School practiced the system to train the boys in useful trades.

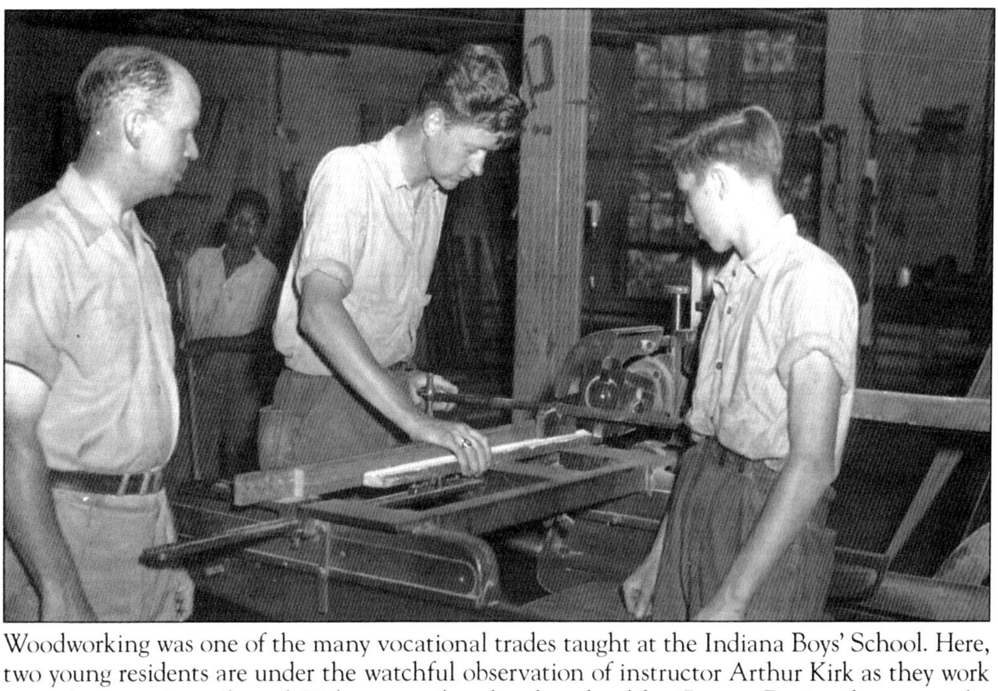

Woodworking was one of the many vocational trades taught at the Indiana Boys' School. Here, two young residents are under the watchful observation of instructor Arthur Kirk as they work on sculpting a piece of wood. Kirk was employed at the school for 47 years. During those years, he assumed many positions at the school. Not only was he the industrial teacher of woodworking, he also was the supervisor of details and cottages, director of maintenance, and deputy superintendent.

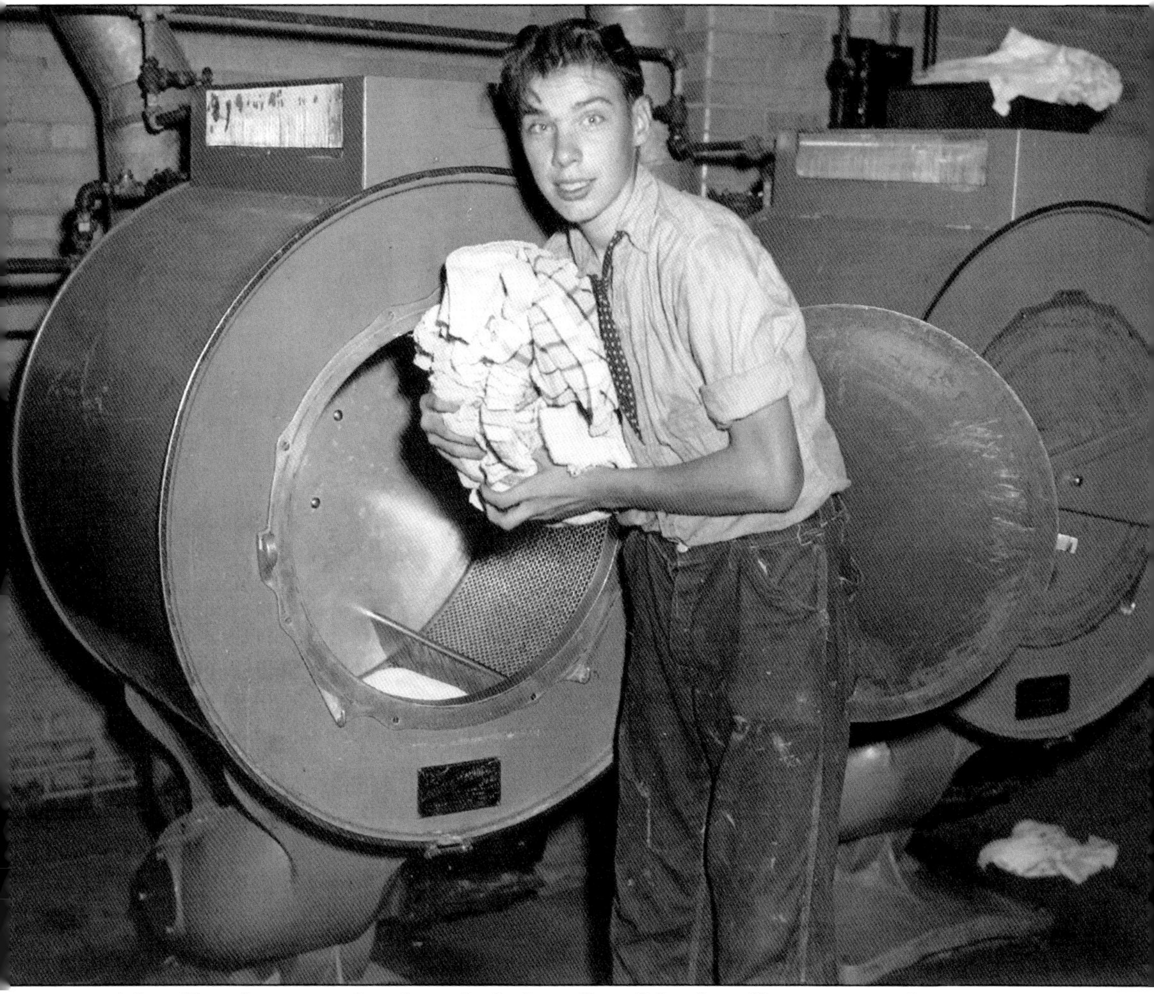

A lot of laundry was produced at a the Indiana Boys School, and keeping up with it was a constant task performed by the boys who lived there. This unidentified young man tends to one of the many industrial dryers used to manage the large amounts of laundry.

Ten

AROUND TOWN

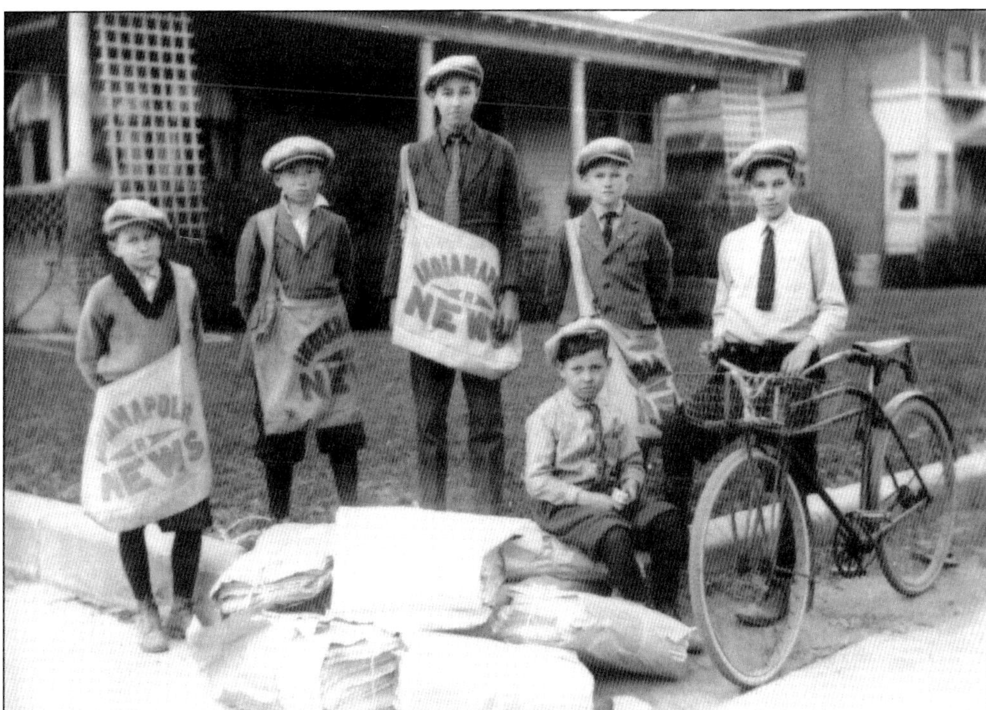

With their canvas bags ready to go, these newspaper delivery boys pose at the northeast corner of East and Main Streets in Plainfield. The newspaper was the *Indianapolis News*, and the carriers from left to right are (seated) John C. Miller; (standing) Harold Bly, Robert Bly, Harold Stanley, Wendell Bly, and John Praay.

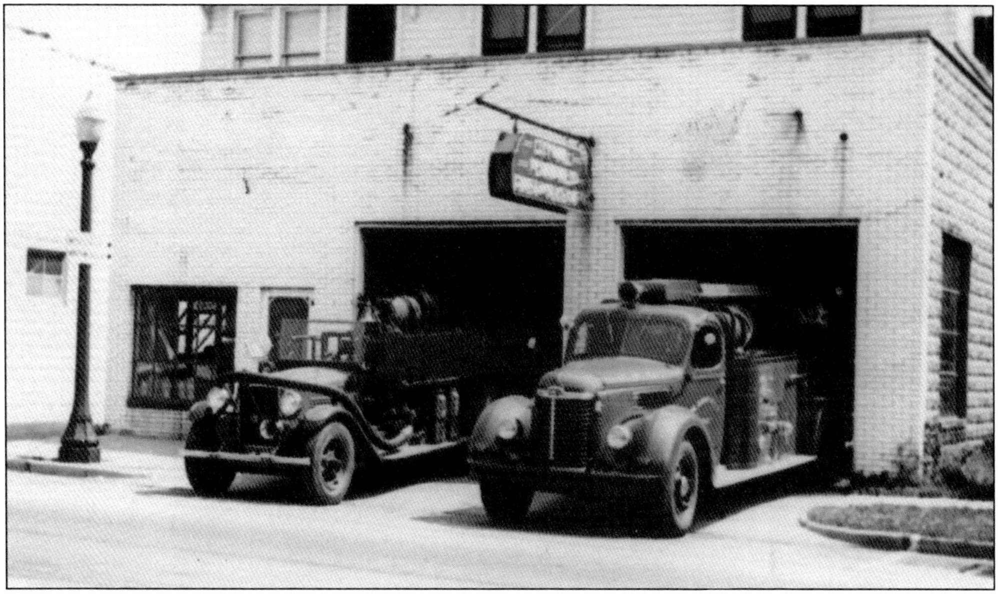

The Plainfield Fire Department was once located on the south side of West Main Street, between Center and Mill Streets. The building, erected in 1936 by Carlos Swinford, originally housed a mechanic's garage. In 1948, Swinford, who was Plainfield's first fire chief, moved the department to this location. Before then, the town hall and fire department had been located on South Vine Street. Swinford organized the fire department and was responsible for acquiring the first fire truck (a Model T). Through his efforts, fire hydrants were installed in Plainfield.

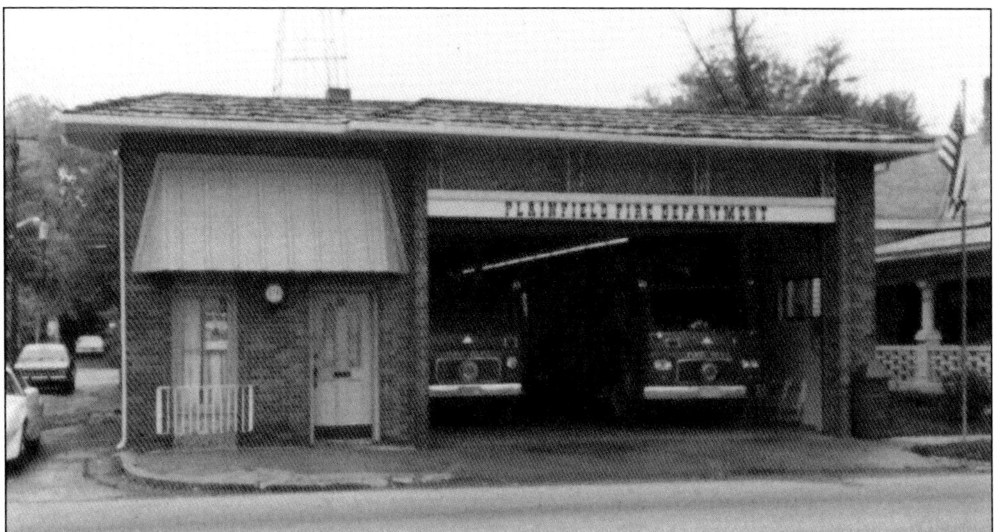

The fire department building was remodeled in the fall of 1969, as shown in this photograph, but was still located on the south side of West Main Street. The new look of the building was designed to resemble the gaslight architecture common in New Orleans. The remodeling involved removing the upstairs meeting room. All town departments remained at this location until 1968, when the new municipal building was constructed across the street at the corner of North Center Road and Main Street. At that time, as the others moved across the street, the fire department remained in this building.

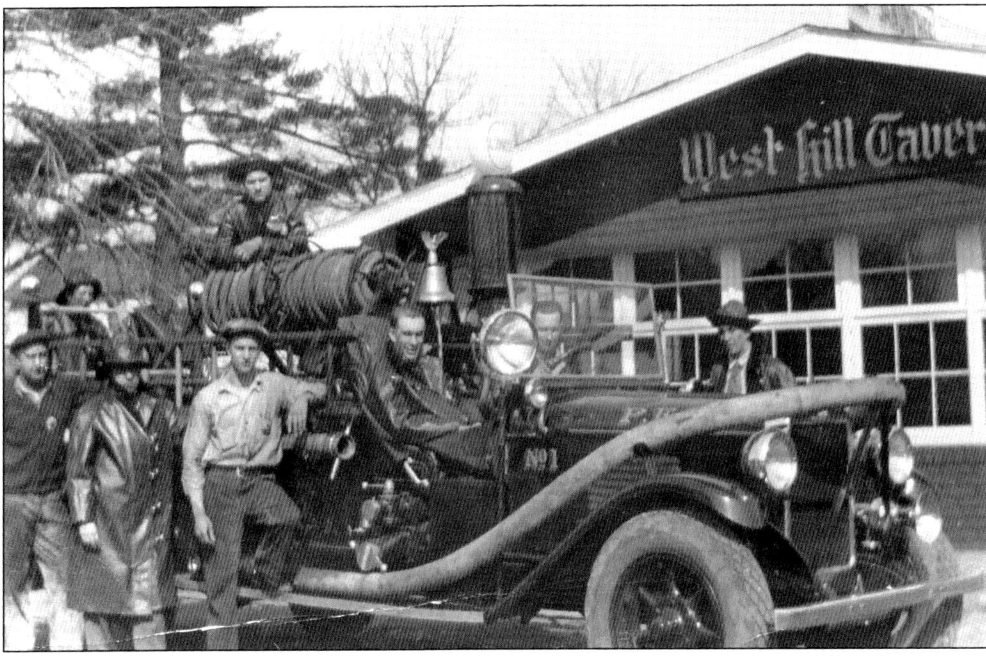

Surrounding their fire truck, the Plainfield Fire Department pose in front of the West Hill Tavern. This photograph from the 1930s includes Frank Calbert, Walter McKnight, James Moore, Jude Hancook, Tom Ruebeck (on top of the truck), Carlos "Red" Swinford (Far right behind the truck), and Jude Schwier, and Mink Calbert (seated from left to right in the truck). The West Hill Tavern was located west of Plainfield on the north side of US 40 near Vestal Road.

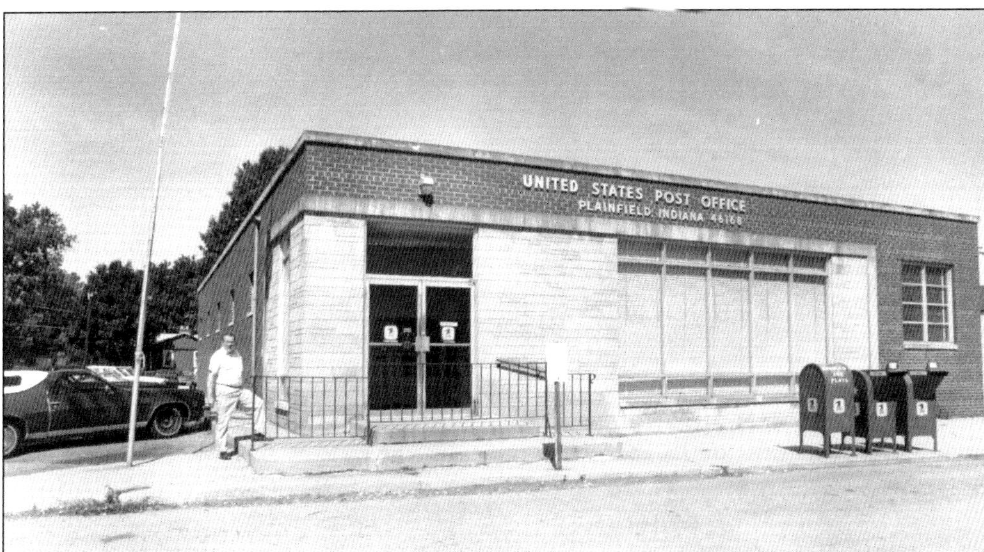

It was a big day in Plainfield on September 13, 1958, when the new post office at 164 North Mill Street was dedicated. The post office had previously been located in two downtown buildings, most notably at the northeast corner of Vine and Main Streets. The dedication of the new building was organized by the Plainfield Jaycees. Assistant postmaster general Bert Barnes was the featured speaker, along with Indiana congresswoman Cecil M. Harden, who had been instrumental in helping Plainfield obtain the new facility.

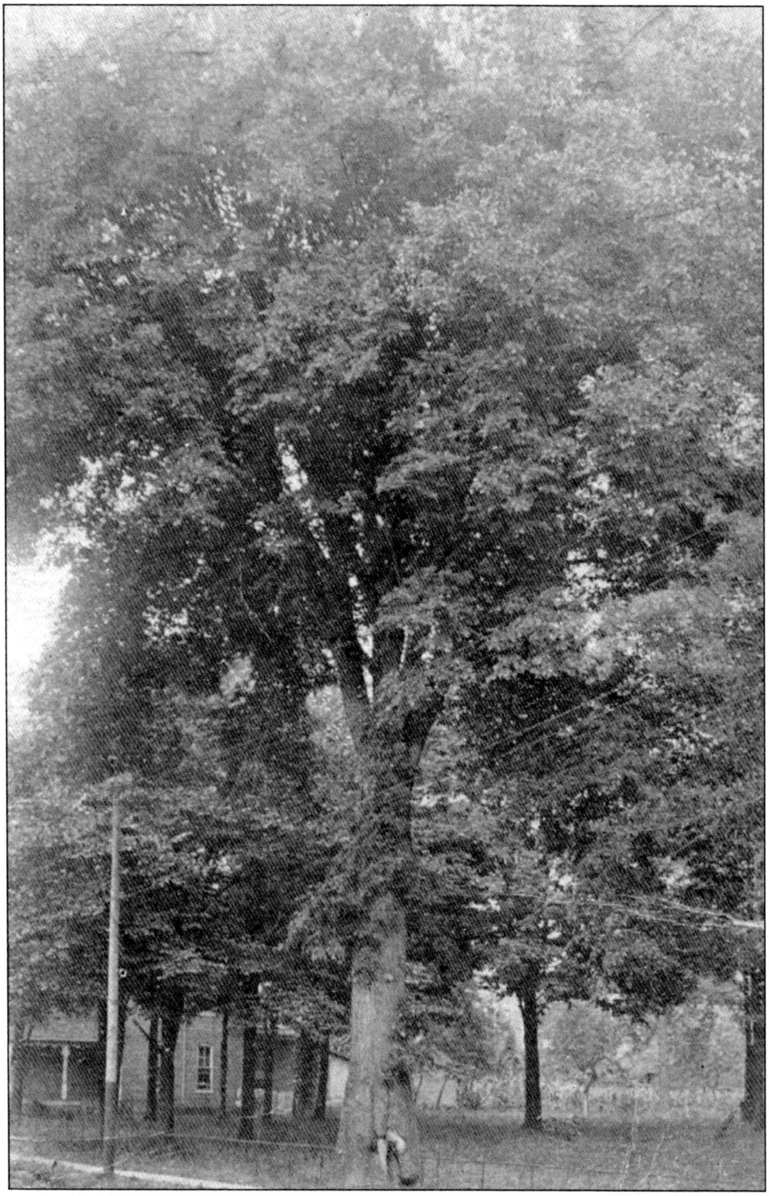

As far as legends go, the one involving Pres. Martin Van Buren and an elm tree in Plainfield is a big one that happens to be true. This photograph shows the original elm tree marking the spot where, on June 3, 1843, Van Buren was ceremoniously tossed from his stagecoach into the muddy National Road. This served as a reminder to the president that the National Road was in horrible shape and needed to be improved. The incident came about because, when he was president, Van Buren vetoed a bill passed by Congress appropriating funds to make the road more passable. After his presidency, Congress named Van Buren a commissioner to inspect the road and report his findings. In 1843, he started on his road tour, and by June 3, he was scheduled to travel from Indianapolis to Terre Haute. A deal was made with stagecoach driver Asa Wright to provide Van Buren a rough ride along the route. Wright did a good job whipping up his team of horses so that when they got near the intersection of Avon Avenue and Main Street, the horses went one way, the stage went the other way, and Van Buren was tossed into the mud.

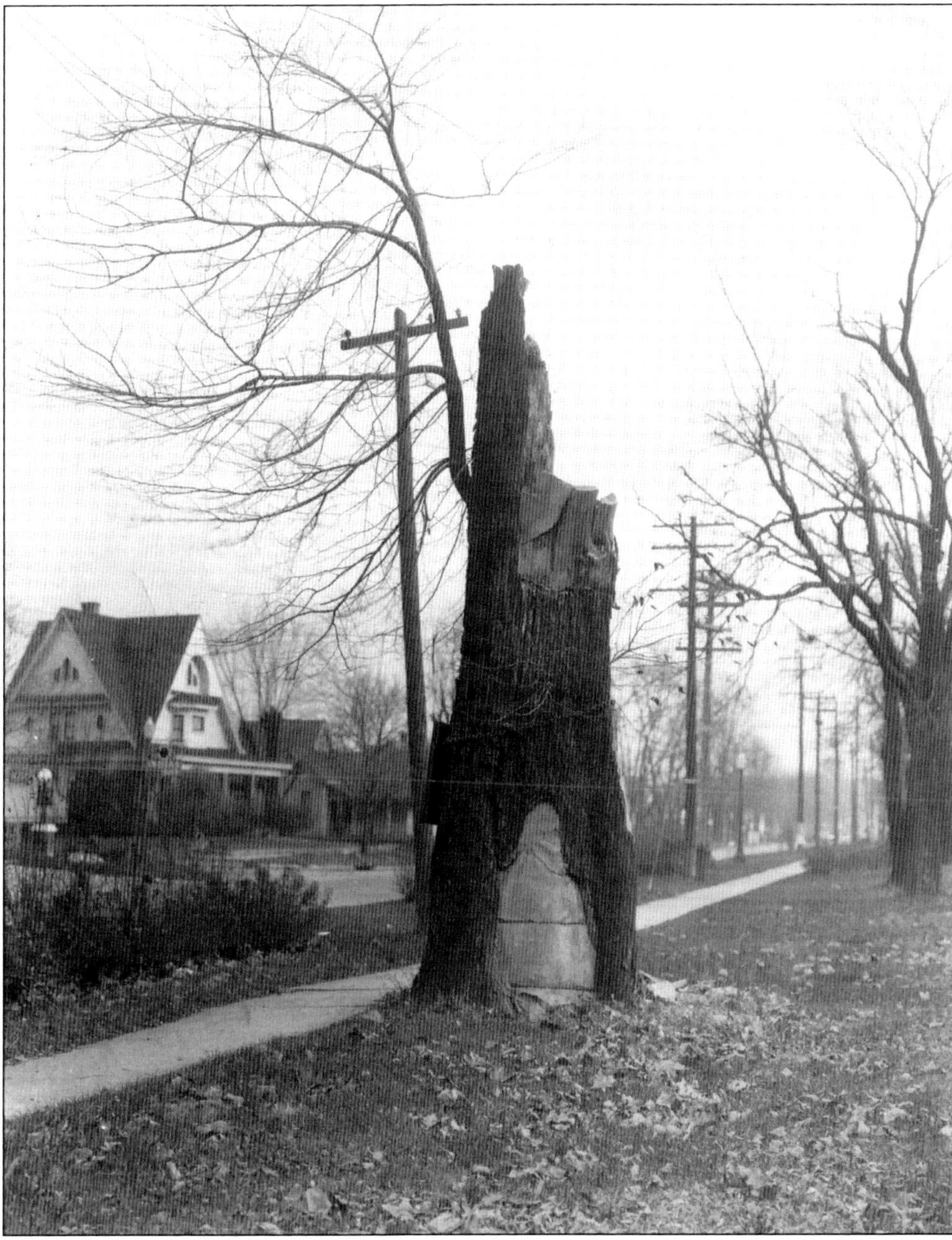

The elm tree lasted many years, marking the spot of the incident involving Pres. Martin Van Buren. But nature has a way of changing things, and during a violent storm in 1928, the tree was struck by lightning and almost totally destroyed. The remains of the famous elm tree, seen here, were eventually removed. The Lions Club erected a large boulder on the spot and installed a commemorative plaque donated by the Caroline Scott Harrison Chapter of the D.A.R. on it. Interestingly, through the efforts of the industrial arts department at Plainfield High School, pieces of the famed elm tree didn't go to waste. W.J. Schaffer's classes made souvenirs from the wood, including ashtrays, gavels, clock cases, small lamps, and candleholders. The souvenirs were sold in the Spot Cash Store and Nutter's Variety Store.

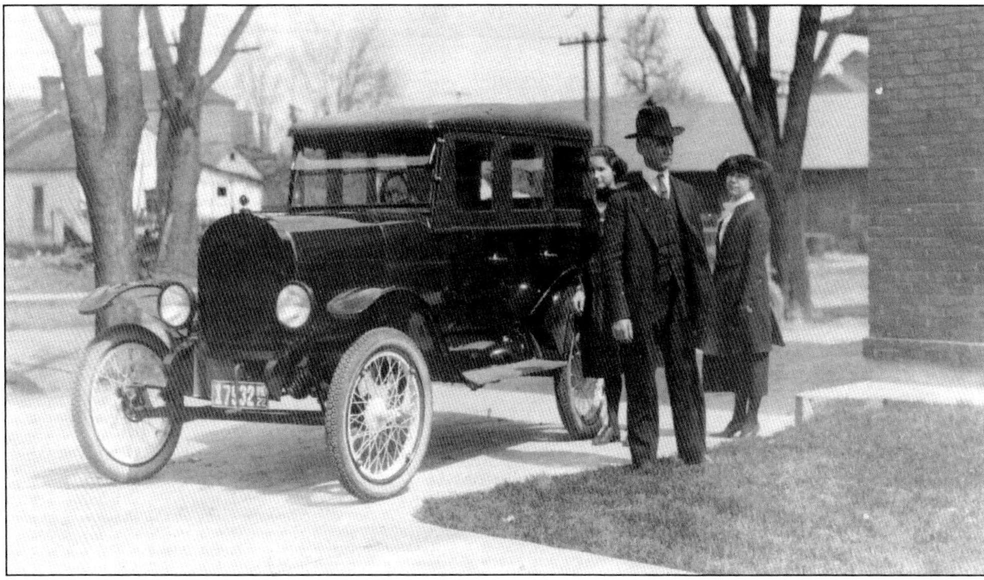

In this 1922 photograph, a family prepares to go on a Sunday drive. Dr. Ernest Cooper and daughters Portia (right) and Lucia await their journey. The license plate on the automobile reads "17932 IND 22." The car is not identified but is likely a 1921 or 1922 Cadillac.

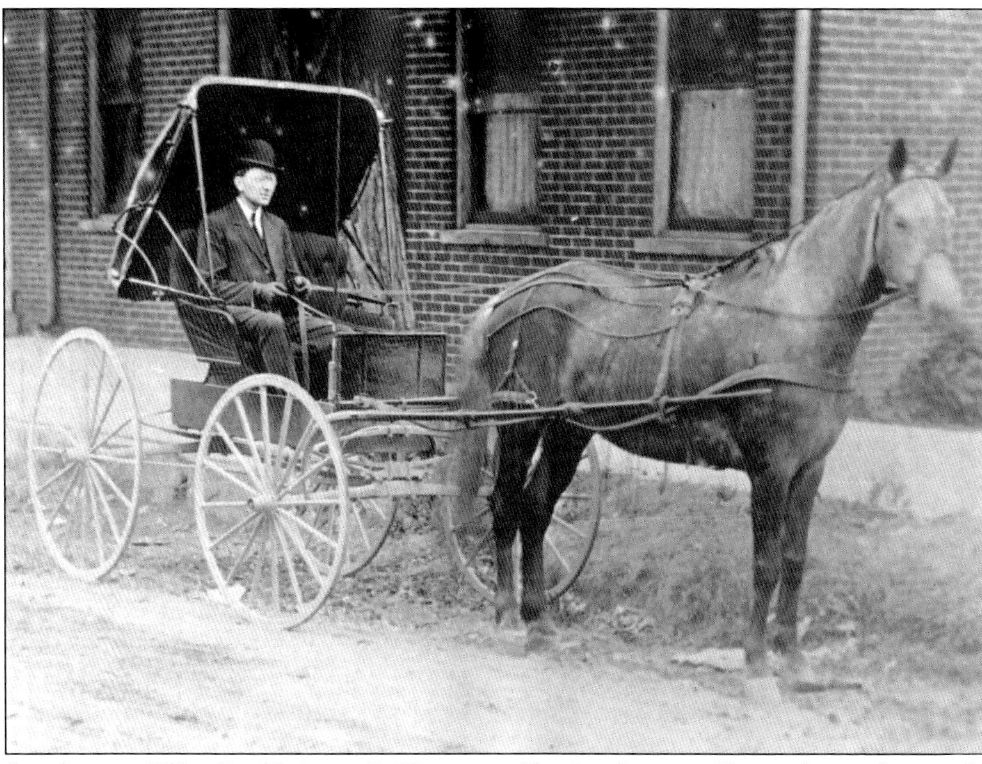

Seen here in 1902 is Dr. Clarkston B. Thomas and his first horse-and-buggy during the time he started practicing medicine in Plainfield. Dr. Thomas was the successor of local physician Jesse Reagan. Dr. Thomas's office was first located in Dr. Regan's office on East Main Street. He then relocated to the Commercial Hotel building (104 East Main Street).

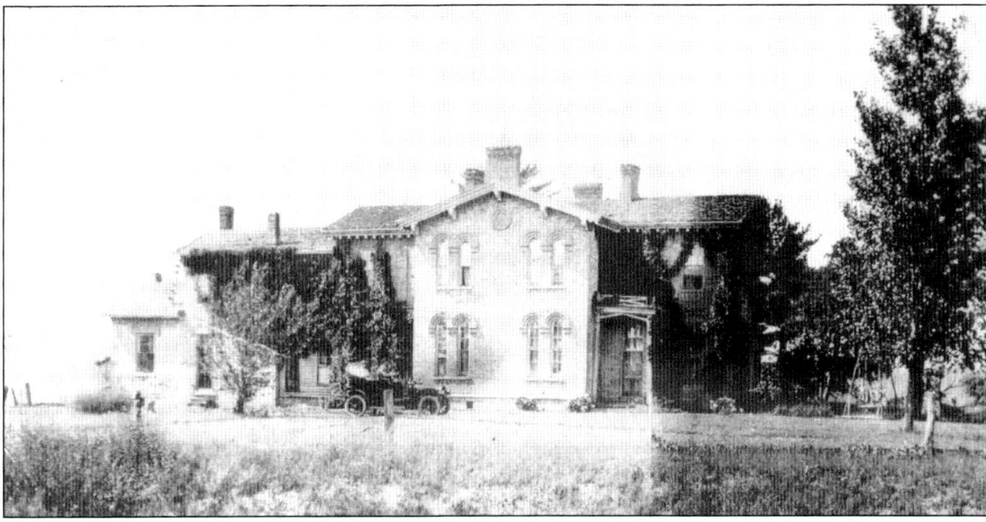

What was a magnificent mansion of the time, Crescent Hill came to a sad end on March 26, 1930, when it was destroyed by fire. The home was built in the 1860s by Charles Lowder, who sold it to John Hanna in 1882. Hanna and his family moved into the home on September 6, 1882. Hanna died unexpectedly on October 24, having lived there for just over six weeks. The home was located on the west side of Vestal Road near the railroad tracks.

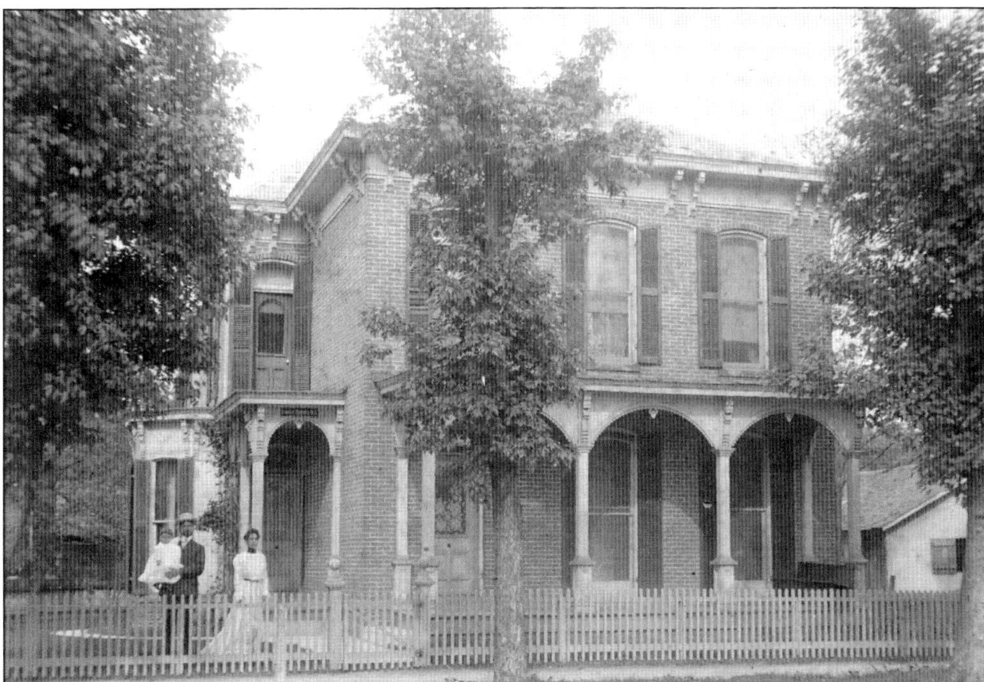

Built about 1870 by the John Strong family, Dr. Ernest Cooper's residence at 125 South Center Street in Plainfield was a stately, well-manicured home. This photograph from 1904 shows Dr. Cooper holding daughter Portia and standing next to his wife, Eleanor Hanna Cooper. The Cooper home was next to Dr. Cooper's office, which made it a convenient place to live. Local legend tells that there was a tunnel from the home to the office so that Dr. Cooper could easily get to work, no matter the weather.

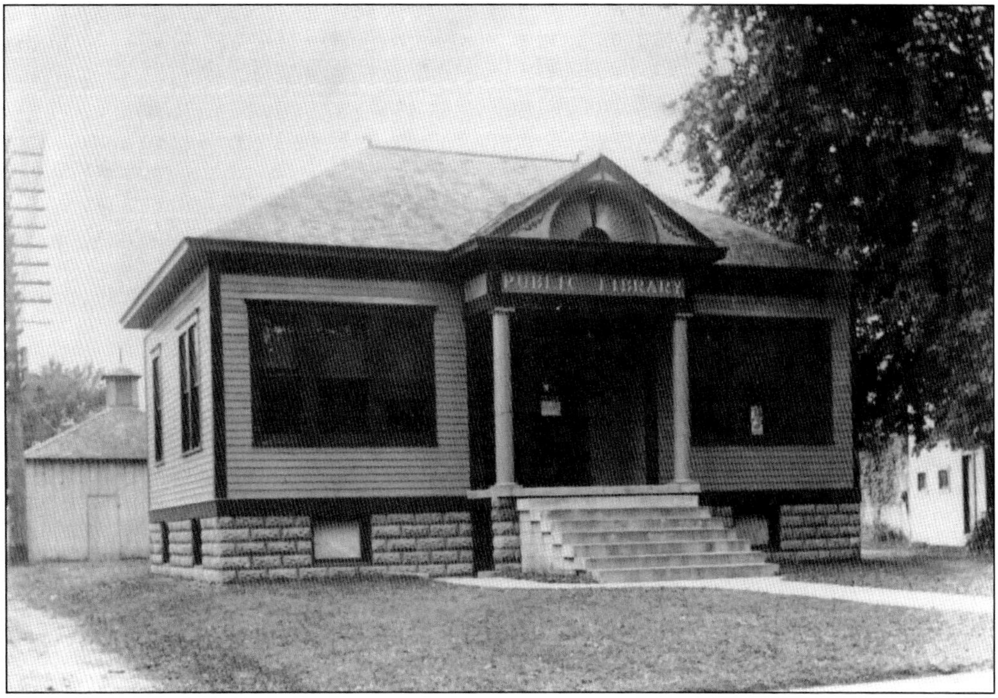

The Plainfield Library Association was formed by three women's organizations on March 21, 1901. The new library's first home was on the northwest corner of East and US 40 (current location of Hill's Cobbler Shop), where it remained until 1905. This 1911 photograph shows the library when it was located at 130 North Vine Street. This second library building was dedicated on January 2, 1905. The library was tendered to the town on May 12, 1905.

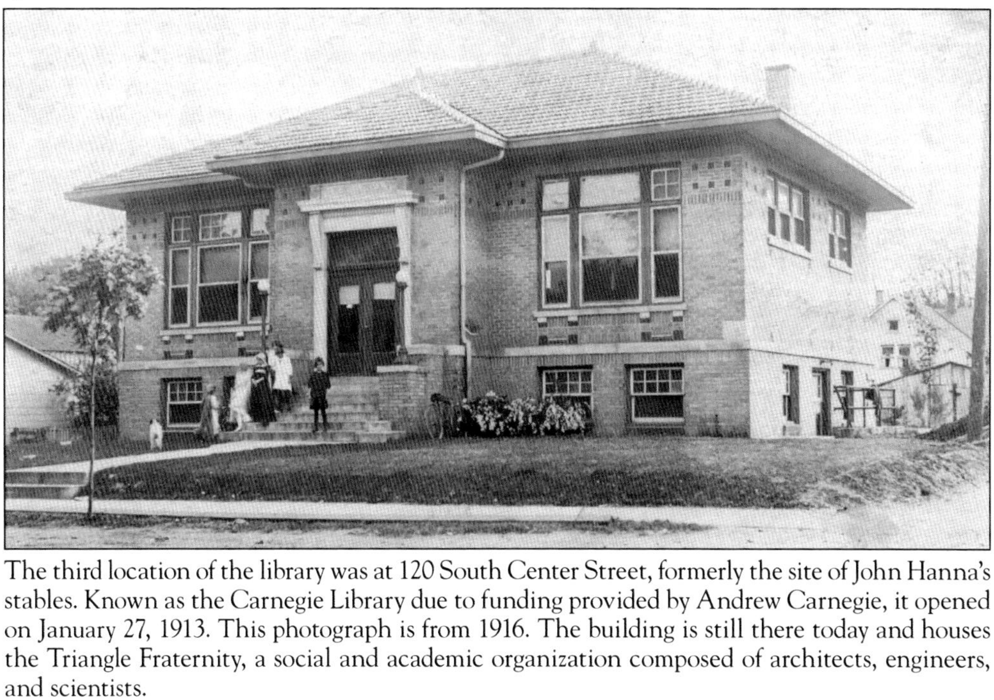

The third location of the library was at 120 South Center Street, formerly the site of John Hanna's stables. Known as the Carnegie Library due to funding provided by Andrew Carnegie, it opened on January 27, 1913. This photograph is from 1916. The building is still there today and houses the Triangle Fraternity, a social and academic organization composed of architects, engineers, and scientists.

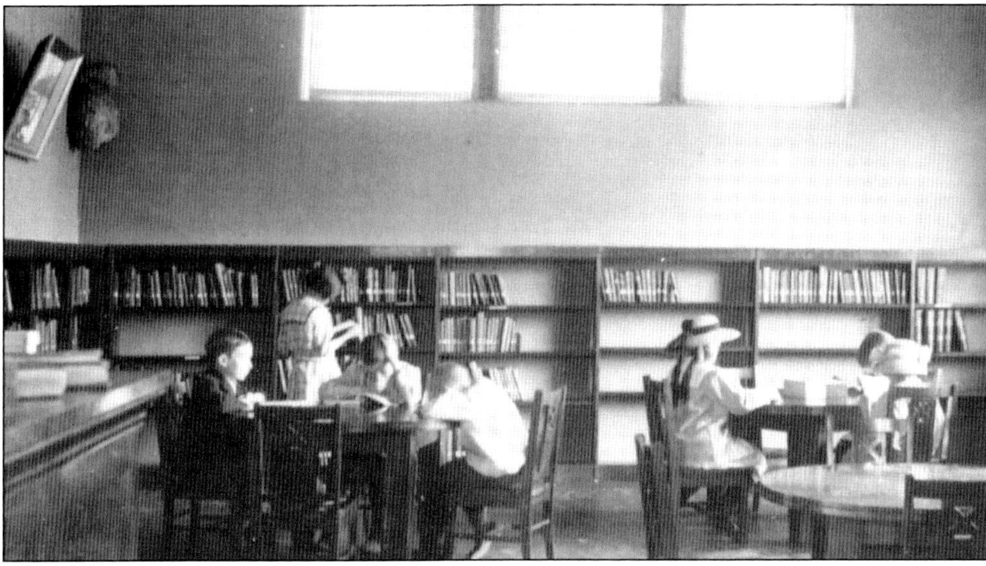

When the library first opened in 1913, there was plenty of space for books and patrons. This interior photograph shows the Children's Room around 1916. Several young patrons enjoy reading their book selections, which had to please the Woman's Reading Club, the Friday Club, and the Women's Christian's Temperance Union. These three organizations were primarily responsible for raising awareness and funds to build the new Carnegie Library building.

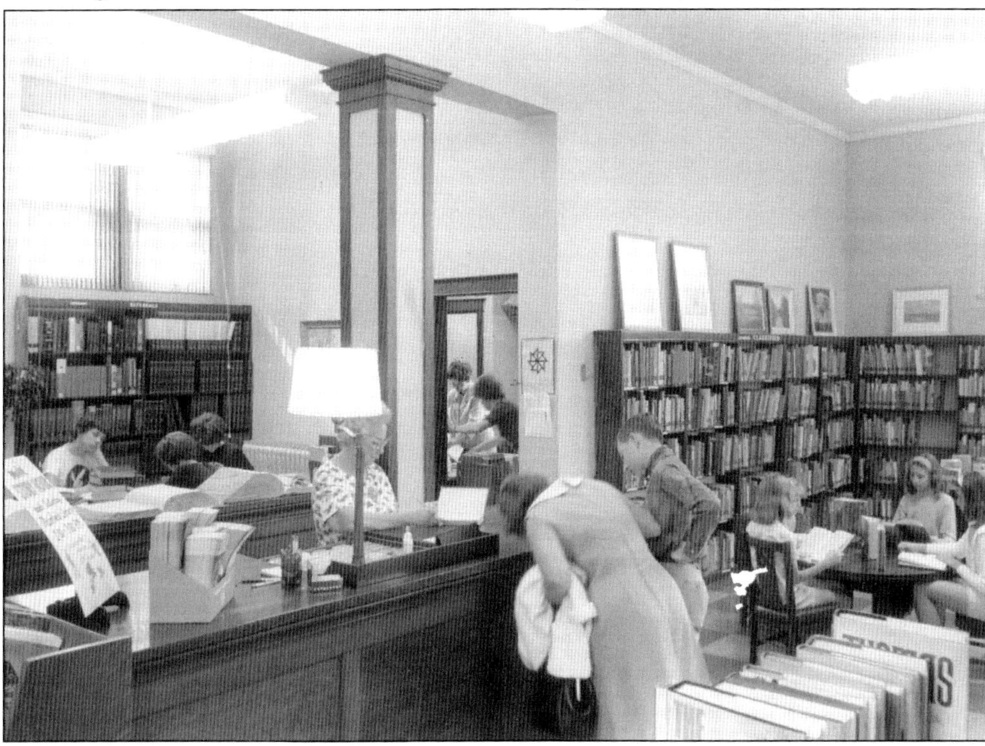

This photograph of the Carnegie Library at 120 South Center Street was taken in 1964. Still busy with patrons and packed with books, the library was as well used then as the present library is today.

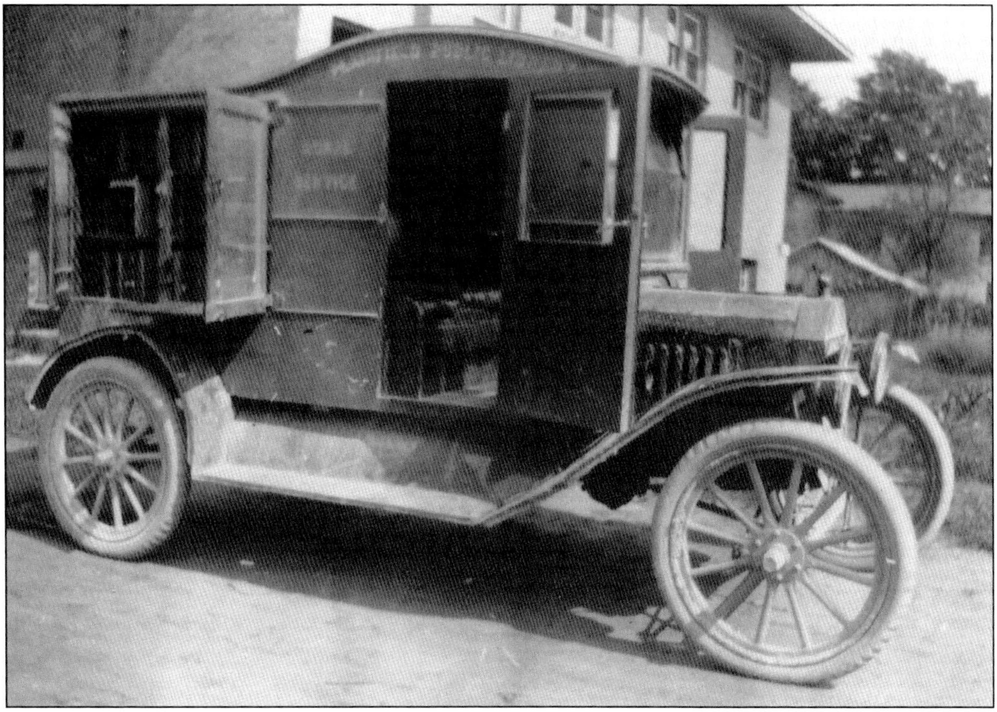

Reported to be Indiana's first bookmobile, this custom auto bookwagon provided library service to rural residents of Plainfield and Guilford Township. The body of the vehicle was designed by local physician Dr. Ernest Cooper (who was on the library board) and made by wagon maker Elwood Wasson. It was mounted on a 1916 Ford chassis.

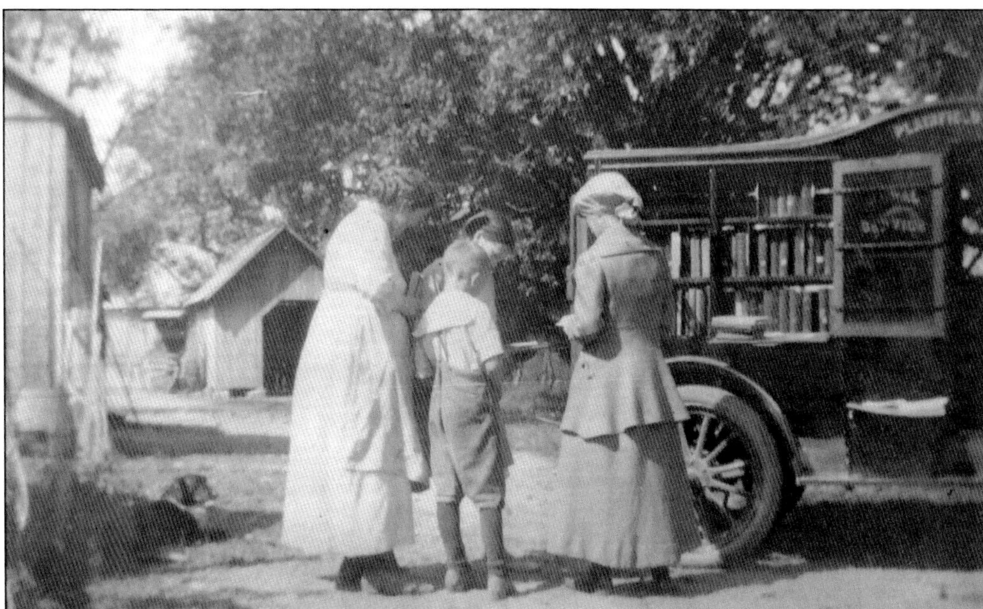

Librarian Mayme Snipes drove the bookmobile around Guilford Township, bringing books to the people when they were unable to make it into town to the library. This photograph, taken around 1918, shows Snipes assisting a young farm family with their selections.

By the 1970s, the library was using a food service box truck from the Plainfield Community School Corporation as its bookmobile during the summers. This photograph from August 1977 shows librarian Dinah Farrington at one of the stops along the route. Her young patrons from left to right are (first row, sitting) Johnny Buschee (on Farrington's lap), Joey Merriman, Debbie Sutton, and Laurel Thomas; (second row, standing) Terrie and Kim Sutton.

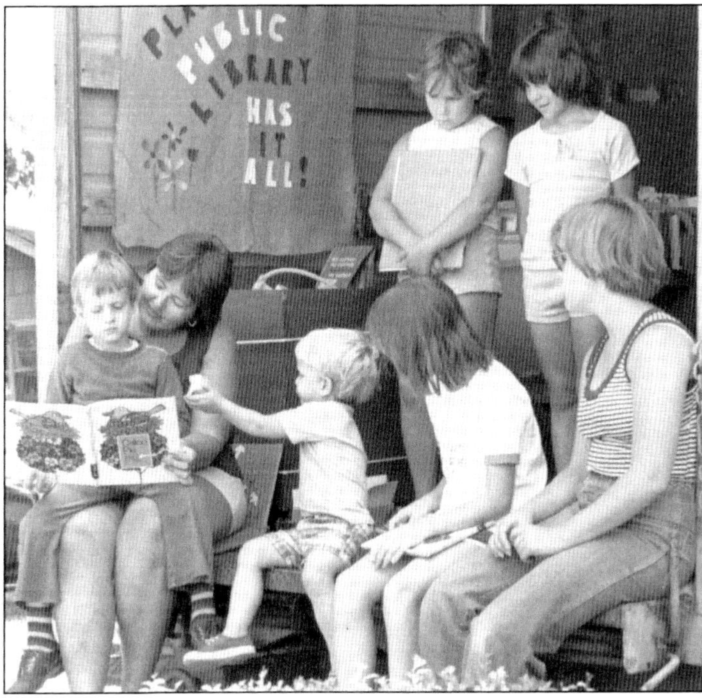

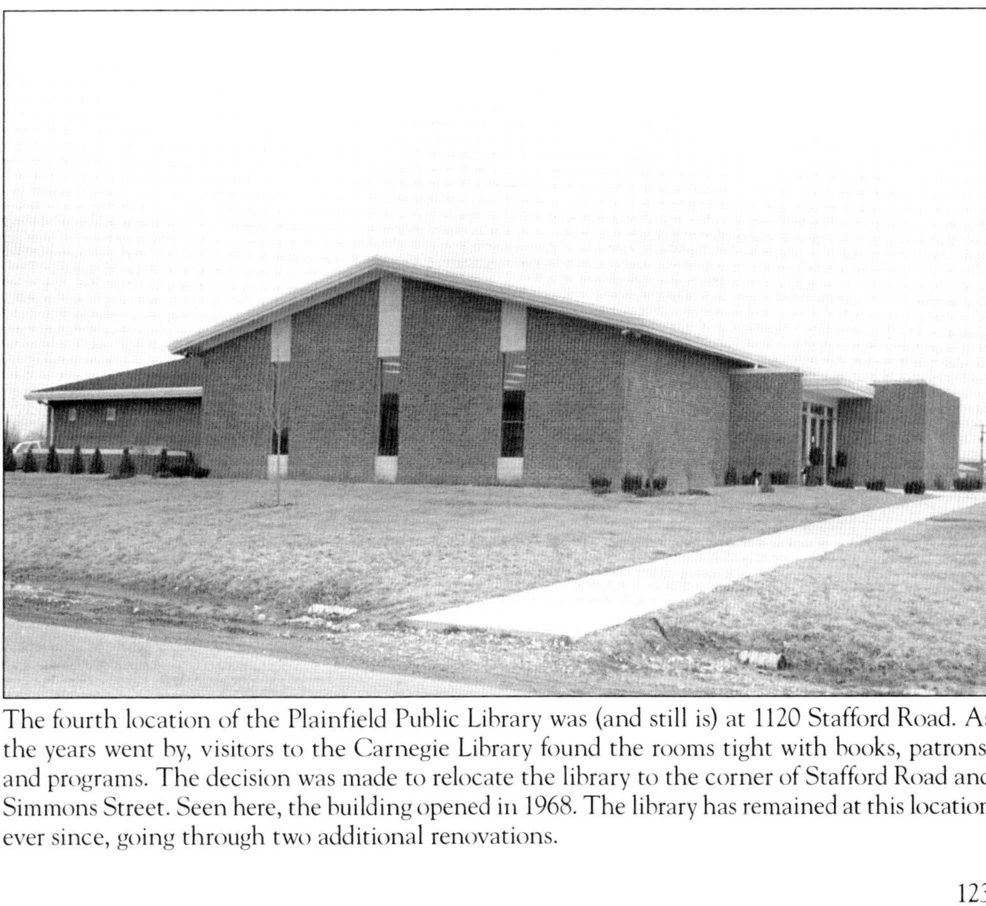

The fourth location of the Plainfield Public Library was (and still is) at 1120 Stafford Road. As the years went by, visitors to the Carnegie Library found the rooms tight with books, patrons, and programs. The decision was made to relocate the library to the corner of Stafford Road and Simmons Street. Seen here, the building opened in 1968. The library has remained at this location ever since, going through two additional renovations.

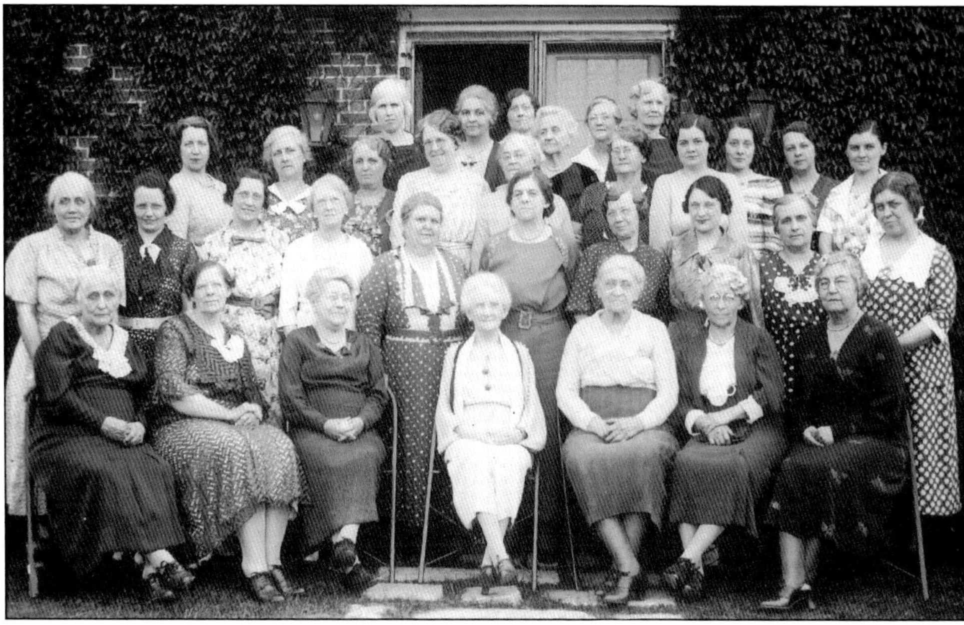

The Plainfield Friday Club, one of the town's earliest social organizations for women, is still active today. The club held a picnic on May 15, 1936, on the grounds of the Indiana Boys' School. Members of the club shown here are (first row, from left to right) Julia York, Fannie Cox Farrell, Mary Gossett, Belle Havens, Mary Douglas, Viola Prewitt, and Anna Jamison; (second row, from left to right) Net Jessup, Adah Johnson, Mary Havens Fletcher, Bess Harvey, Cora Vestal, Sallie Vestal, Flora Coble, Maude Hall, Nina Duke, and Hortense Hanna; (third row, no particular order) Helen Hobbs, Maeda Miller, Betty Pike, Mayme White, Roberta Brown, Myrtle Loy, Hilda Jessup, Alice Hampton, Amy Hadley, Catherine Cox, and unidentified; (fourth row, from left to right) Helen Bridges, Hazel Jessup, Gertrude Dill, Willie A. Moore, and an unidentified housekeeper at the boys' school.

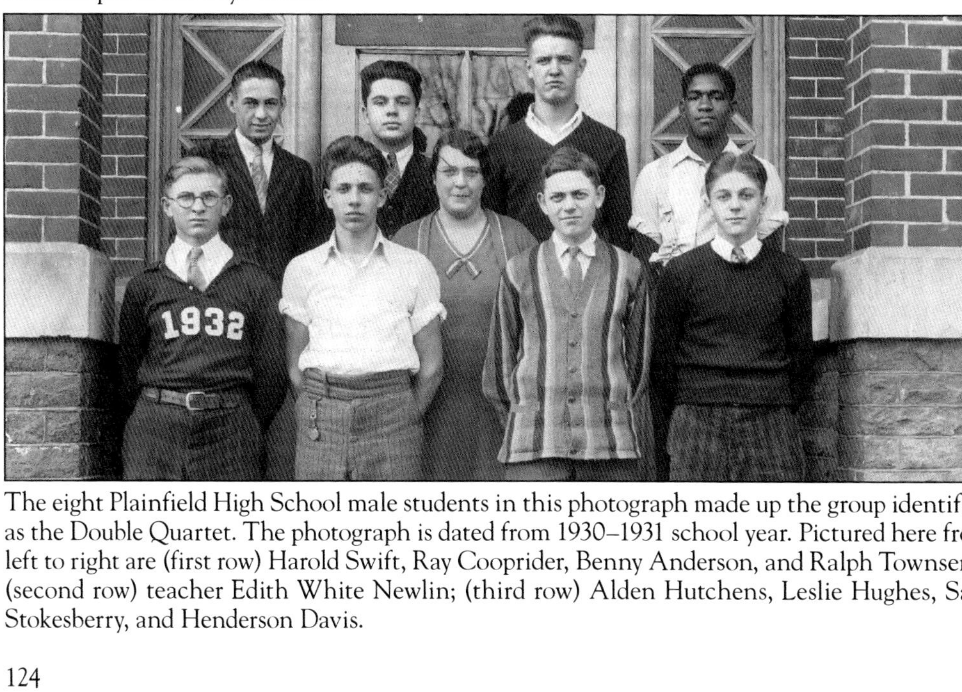

The eight Plainfield High School male students in this photograph made up the group identified as the Double Quartet. The photograph is dated from 1930–1931 school year. Pictured here from left to right are (first row) Harold Swift, Ray Cooprider, Benny Anderson, and Ralph Townsend; (second row) teacher Edith White Newlin; (third row) Alden Hutchens, Leslie Hughes, Sam Stokesberry, and Henderson Davis.

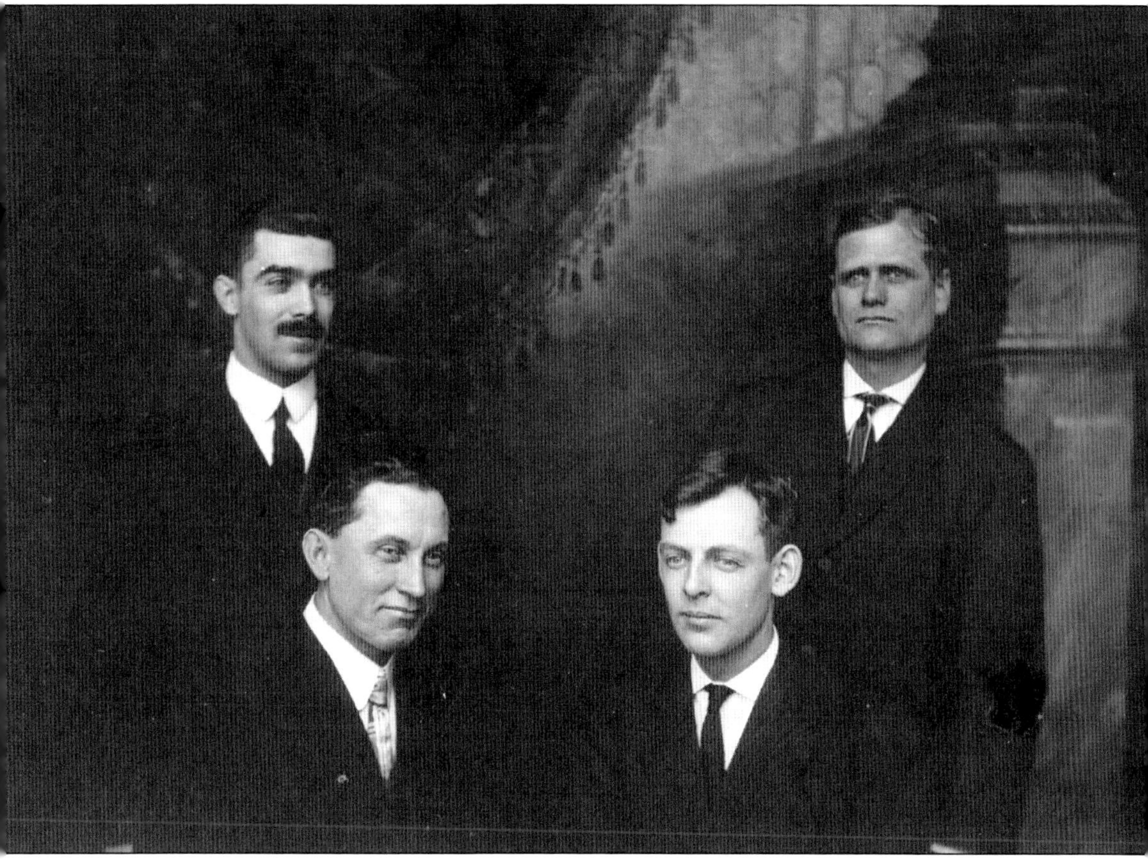

Among the various musical entertainment groups in Plainfield was a local quartet, pictured here in this 1905. The members of the group from left to right are (first row) Griffith W. Milhous and Orla Jordan; (second row) Emil Mills and Orzo Hadley.

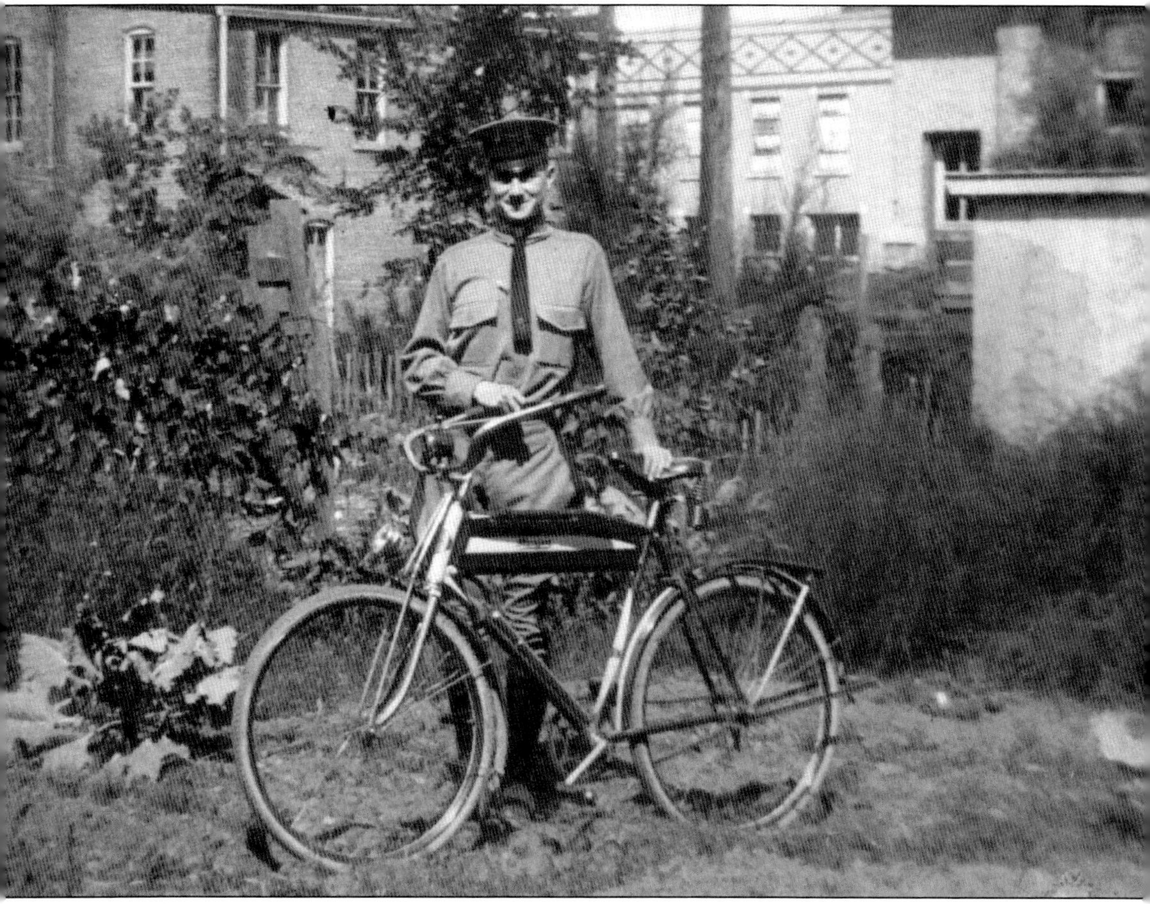

This fun photograph, taken sometime after 1913, shows a young man, proud of both his bicycle and his uniform. The setting is behind the Plainfield Carnegie Library, located at 120 South Center Street. Visible in the background is the Knights of Pythias building, which was just across the street. Unfortunately, the man is not identified, but it's safe to say he was pleased to pose for this photograph.